BUILDING JERUSALEM

Jewish Architecture in Britain

Interior of St Petersburgh Place, London. *Beverley-Jane Stewart*

BUILDING JERUSALEM
Jewish Architecture in Britain

Edited and introduced by
SHARMAN KADISH

VALLENTINE MITCHELL
LONDON • PORTLAND, OR.

First published in 1996 in Great Britain by
VALLENTINE MITCHELL & CO. LTD.
Newbury House, 900 Eastern Avenue,
London IG2 7HH

and in the United States of America by
VALLENTINE MITCHELL
c/o ISBS, 5804 N.E. Hassalo Street, Portland,
Oregon 97213-3644

British Library Cataloguing in Publication Data
Building Jerusalem: Jewish Architecture in
Britain
  I. Kadish, Sharman
  726.30941
  ISBN 0-85303-283-1 (hardback)
  ISBN 0-85303-309-9 (paperback)

Library of Congress Cataloging-in-Publication Data
Building Jerusalem: Jewish architecture in Britain / edited and
  introduced by Sharman Kadish
    p.   cm.
    Includes index.
    ISBN 0-85303-283-1. — ISBN 0-85303-309-9 (pbk.)
    1. Architecture, Jewish—England. 2. Synagogue architecture—
England. 3. Architecture—England—Conservation and restoration.
4. Synagogue architecture—England—Conservation and restoration.
I. Kadish, Sharman, 1959–
NA5461.B89   1996
720'.89'924042 — —dc20   95-3374
                                                              CIP

Typeset in Berling
by Vitaset, Paddock Wood, Kent
Printed in Great Britain by
Bookcraft (Bath) Ltd., Midsomer Norton

FOR SYD

CONTENTS

List of Illustrations ix

List of Tables xi

List of Appendices xi

Acknowledgments xii

Glossary xiii

Notes on Contributors xv

1 Introduction SHARMAN KADISH 1

2 Between Europe and the New World: Britain's Place in Synagogue Architecture CAROL HERSELLE KRINSKY 18

3 Building Jerusalem in the 'Islands of the Sea': The Archaeology of Medieval Anglo-Jewry RAPHAEL M. J. ISSERLIN 34

4 Compromising Traditions in Eighteenth-Century London: The Architecture of the Great Synagogue, Duke's Place CLARENCE EPSTEIN 54

5 Synagogue Bodies: Building Policy and Conservation Issues EDWARD JAMILLY 84

6 'Eden in Albion': A History of the *Mikveh* in Britain SHARMAN KADISH 101

7 Jewish Cemeteries in the West of England BERNARD SUSSER 155

8 'Four Per Cent Philanthropy': Social Architecture for East London Jewry, 1850–1914 LESLEY FRASER 167

9 'All Manner of Workmanship': Interior Decoration in British Synagogues EDWARD JAMILLY 193

10 Alternative Uses for 'Redundant' Synagogues STEPHEN ROSENBERG 209

Index 225

LIST OF ILLUSTRATIONS

	Interior of the New West End Synagogue, St Petersburgh Place, London	*frontispiece*
1.1	Swansea Synagogue, Goat Street	2
1.2	London, Borough New Synagogue	3
1.3	London, East London Synagogue	4
1.4	London, the New Synagogue, Egerton Road	6
1.5	London, the New Synagogue, Egerton Road	7
1.6	London, St Petersburgh Place	8
1.7	Liverpool, Prince's Road Old Hebrew Congregation	9
1.8	London, synagogue entrance, 42 Old Montagu Street	16
2.1	London, Bevis Marks Synagogue	20
2.2	London, Bevis Marks Synagogue	21
2.3	London, Dollis Hill Synagogue	23
2.4	Manchester, the Great Synagogue	26
2.5	London, St John's Wood Synagogue	26
2.6	Liverpool, Prince's Road Synagogue	28
2.7	London, Finchley Synagogue	32
3.1	Jewish settlement at Cologne and Colchester	39–40
3.2	Jewish buildings at Lincoln	41
3.3	Foundations of Jewish or possibly Jewish buildings in London, Lincoln and Bristol	42
3.4	Jewish buildings at Rouen and Norwich	45
3.5	Cologne Synagogue, excavations	47–8
3.6	The Foundry Yard structure at Colchester	49
4.1	Amsterdam, the Sephardi Synagogue of 1639	55
4.2	Amsterdam, Grote Sjoel	56
4.3	Amsterdam, the Sephardi Synagogue of 1671–75	57
4.4	London, Bevis Marks Synagogue	58
4.5–4.14	London, the Great Synagogue	61–77
5.1	London, Bevis Marks Synagogue	86
5.2	London, the New West End Synagogue	89
5.3	London, Kehillat Yaakov Synagogue	90
5.4	London, Great Garden Street Federation Synagogue	91
5.5	London, St John's Wood Synagogue	93
5.6	London, Liberal Jewish Synagogue	94
5.7	Analysis of congregations	95
5.8	London, Spitalfields Great Synagogue	97
5.9	London, Spital Square Poltava Synagogue	98

6.1	South London *Mikveh*	103
6.2	South London *Mikveh*	103
6.3	Bristol, Jacob's Well	106
6.4	Bristol, Jacob's Well	107
6.5	Cheltenham, Montpellier Baths	112
6.6	Canterbury *Mikveh*	113
6.7	London, Lacey's Baths	116
6.8	London, Schewzik's Russian Vapour Baths	118
6.9	Leeds, Albert Grove *Mikveh*	120
6.10	Grimsby *Mikveh*	121
6.11	Cardiff *Mikveh*	123
6.12	London, Edgware *Mikveh*	129
6.13	South London *Mikveh*	133
6.14	Liverpool *Mikveh*, Childwall Synagogue	134
7.1	Penzance Cemetery	156
7.2	Plymouth Hoe Cemetery – before clearance	157
7.3	Plymouth Hoe Cemetery – after clearance	157
7.4	Bath Cemetery	159
7.5	Cheltenham Cemetery	160
7.6	Plymouth Hoe Cemetery	160
7.7	Snuff-box presented to Aaron Nathan	161
7.8	Plymouth Hoe Cemetery	162
8.1	London, Jews' Hospital, *c.*1806	168
8.2	London, Jews' Hospital, *c.*1815	169
8.3	London, Soup Kitchen for the Jewish Poor	172
8.4–8.7	London, Jews' Free School, Bell Lane	174–7
8.8	London, Cressy House	183
8.9	London, Charlotte de Rothschild Dwellings	186
9.1	London, the Great Synagogue	194
9.2	Exeter Synagogue	197
9.3	London, the New Synagogue, Great St Helen's	199
9.4–9.6	London, the New West End Synagogue, St Petersburgh Place	200–3
9.7	West London Reform Synagogue	204
9.8	Ceremonial objects	206
10.1	Edinburgh Synagogue	212
10.2	Edinburgh Synagogue	212
10.3	Manchester, Spanish and Portuguese Synagogue	213
10.4	London, Brondesbury Synagogue	215
10.5–10.7	London, Dollis Hill Synagogue	216–18
10.8–10.11	London, Cricklewood Synagogue	220–3

Tables

3.1 Jews' Houses Mentioned in Rentals 43
3.2 Synagogue Rentals 45
3.3 Phasing of Medieval German Synagogues 46

Appendices

6.1 The Chief Rabbi's Survey of 1845: Provision of
    Mikvaot 144
6.2 Distribution of *Mikvaot* for Women in London,
    1897–1992 145
6.3 Directory of *Mikvaot* in the UK and Ireland,
    1656–1995 146

ACKNOWLEDGMENTS

This publication was made possible through the generous support of the Kessler Foundation, the *Jewish Chronicle* and the Acacia Charitable Trust.

The editor would particularly like to thank Alex Rosenzweig and Dr Tony Kushner for their advice and support. She would also like to thank Rabbi Dr Bernard Susser for compiling the Index and Edward Jamilly for assisting in the design and layout of the book.

GLOSSARY

The following terms, unless otherwise indicated, are transliterations from the Hebrew.

Almemar   Term for *Bima*, of Arabic derivation.

Almira   Eastern term for synagogue Ark or *Aron Kodesh*, literally wardrobe.

Aron Kodesh, Aron HaKodesh   Holy Ark, focal point of synagogue in which Scrolls of the Law are housed.

Ashkenazi, Ashkenazim   Jews originating in central and eastern Europe, following the German or Polish rite.

Barmitzva   The age of religious majority, reached by a Jewish boy at 13.

Beth Din   Jewish ecclesiastical court.

Beth Hamedrash   Religious study hall.

Bima   Reading desk, traditionally centrally placed in Ashkenazi synagogues.

Chanukia, Chanukiot   Eight-branched or cupped candelabra lit on the festival of Chanuka.

Chasid, Chasidim   Adherents of *Chasidut* (Chasidism), pietistic religious movement founded in eastern Europe in the eighteenth century and divided into various sects, each following a particular dynastic rabbinical leader or *rebbe*, e.g. Lubavitch, Satmar, Sassov.

Chevra, Chevrot   Prayer circle, religious fraternity.

Chevra kadisha   Burial society, which prepares the dead for burial.

Cohen, Cohanim   Descendants of the Temple priesthood who perform specific functions in the synagogue service.

Dayan, Dayanim   Judge(s) in a Jewish ecclesiastical court.

Geniza, Genizot   Repository for used prayer books and other religious appurtenances, usually on synagogue premises.

Haham   Chief Rabbi of the Spanish and Portuguese Community in Britain.

Halakha   Orthodox Jewish law.

Hechal   Eastern term for Ark.

Kashrut   The Jewish dietary laws.

Kehilla   A self-governing religious community of Jews.

Kelim Mikveh, Kelim Mikvaot or *Mikvat Kelim*   Small ritual bath for sanctifying cooking and eating utensils.

Kiddush   Blessing made over wine on Sabbaths and festivals.

Kosher   Fit for consumption or use according to Jewish dietary laws.

Magen David   Shield of David emblem.

Mahamad   Board of Elders of the Spanish and Portuguese Synagogue.

Mechitza   Partition in a synagogue between the men's and women's sections. Often in the form of a latticed grille or fine curtain.

Menora   Candelabrum. See *Chanukia*.

Mezuza, Mezuzot   Parchment scroll with selected scriptural verses placed in container and affixed to doorposts and gates of houses occupied by Jews.

Mikveh, Mikvaot   Ritual bath used for performance of ritual immersion.

Minyan, Minyanim   Quorum of ten males, over the age of 13, required for collective worship.

Mizrakh   Direction for prayer facing Jerusalem, usually to the east or south-east, to which synagogues are traditionally orientated.

Mohel, Mohelim   Communal official qualified to perform circumcision.

Ner Tamid   Perpetual lamp hung over the Ark in a synagogue.

Ohel   Prayer hall at burial ground.

Parokhet   Embroidered curtain covering the Ark in a synagogue.

Posul   Ritually unfit.

Rav, Rabbonim   Rabbi(s).

Rebbetzin (Yiddish)   Rabbi's wife.

Rimonim   Finials placed on the handles of *Torah* scrolls, often worked in silver with bells.

Rosh Chodesh   New moon, beginning of the Jewish month according to the lunar calendar.

Sephardi, Sephardim   Jews originating from the Iberian Peninsula.

Sefer Torah, Sifrei Torah   Scrolls of the Law containing the Pentateuch, kept in the synagogue Ark and used in public worship.

Shechita   Jewish ritual slaughter.

Shochet, Shochtim   Ritual slaughterer(s).

Shofar   Ram's horn trumpet blown to mark the Jewish New Year.

Shtetl (Yiddish)   Township.

Shtiebel, Shtiebels, Shtieblakh (Yiddish)   Small synagogue, often in a private house.

Shul/Shool (Yiddish)   Synagogue.

Talmud Torah   Elementary religious school for boys.

Tebah (Teva)   Sephardi term for *Bima*.

Teshuva   Rabbinical responsum.

Tevila   Ritual immersion.

Torah   The Pentateuch; used generally to apply to Jewish religious sources and tradition.

Tsedaka   Charity, a religious obligation.

Yeshiva, Yeshivot   Traditional religious academy for young men.

Yom Kippur   Day of Atonement; the holiest day in the Jewish religious calendar.

NOTES ON CONTRIBUTORS

Clarence Epstein is undertaking a PhD at the University of Edinburgh on the architectural development of churches in Montreal; he also lectures on Georgian architecture. Born in Canada, he was educated at McGill University, at the Courtauld Institute of Art in London and conducted research in Cambridge. In 1990 he was awarded a Queen's Scholarship to study in Venice where he became interested in the architectural history of the synagogue.

Lesley Fraser graduated in history from the University of Edinburgh. She now works for the London Region of English Heritage, after five years as the Assistant Conservation Officer at the London Borough of Tower Hamlets. She completed the Architectural Association Postgraduate Diploma in Building Conservation in 1991 with a dissertation on 'The Architecture of the Jewish community in London *c.* 1850–1900'.

Anthony Harris is a recent graduate in photography from the University of Westminster. He was a winner of the 1993 Agfa Bursary for his final-year project on London synagogue buildings. A selection of his pictures are featured in *Building Jerusalem*.

Raphael M. J. Isserlin studied archaeology at Leeds and at Oxford Universities and works as an archaeologist for a local authority in the south of England.

Edward Jamilly, RIBA, is a practising architect in London who has been actively involved in the conservation and restoration of a number of period buildings. He has published articles on the history of synagogue architecture in *Transactions of the Jewish Historical Society of England* (1958), in S. S. Levin (ed.), *A Century of Anglo-Jewish Life, 1870–1970* (1973), Cecil Roth (ed.), *Jewish Art* (1961), *Quest* (1965) and the *Victorian Society Annual 1991*. He is chairman of the Working Party on Jewish Monuments in the UK and Ireland.

Sharman Kadish was educated at London and Oxford Universities. She is author of *Bolsheviks and British Jews* (1992) and *'A Good Jew and A Good Englishman': The Jewish Lads' & Girls' Brigade 1895–1995* (1995). In 1991 she organized the 'Future of Jewish Monuments in the British Isles' conference and founded the Working Party on Jewish Monuments in the UK and Ireland. She is now based at the Center for Jewish Art, Hebrew University of Jerusalem, Israel.

Carol Herselle Krinsky is Professor of Fine Arts at New York University. She is author of, *inter alia, Rockefeller Center* (1978) and *Synagogues of Europe* (1985). A past president of the American Society of Architectural Historians and the Committee for the Preservation of Architectural Records, she is currently on the Board of Directors of the International Survey of Jewish Monuments and a member of the Jewish Heritage Council of the World Monuments Fund.

Stephen Rosenberg, FRIBA, has been senior partner since 1964 of architects Rosenberg and Gentle, who carried out the Cricklewood Synagogue conversion scheme in 1989. He is a committee member of the Anglo-Israel Archaeological Society and has acted as adviser and surveyor to archaeological digs at Lachish, Shilo and Tel Chanaton.

Beverley-Jane Stewart, FRSA, holds a degree in art and education from the University of London. She has worked as an art teacher in London and has exhibited at the Royal Festival Hall, the Guildhall and the Ben Uri Art Gallery. In 1980 she won the *Evening Standard* award at the GLC 'Spirit of London' exhibition. She has recently executed a series of original oil paintings of British synagogue interiors and has had her work exhibited in the London Museum at the Barbican.

Bernard Susser was educated at Jews' College London and Exeter University. Formerly Rabbi of the Brighton and Hove Hebrew Congregation, he is the author of *An Account of the Old Jewish Cemetery on Plymouth Hoe* (1972), *The Jews of South West England* (1993), *The History of the Willesden and Brondesbury Synagogue* (1994) and *How to Read and Record a Jewish Tombstone* (1995).

1

INTRODUCTION

SHARMAN KADISH

I will not cease from mental fight,
Nor shall my sword sleep in my hand,
Till we have built Jerusalem
In England's green and pleasant land.

These famous lines in the hymn 'Jerusalem', written by the English poet
and painter William Blake (1757–1827), and set to music by Hubert
Parry, have come to assume the status almost of a second national
anthem. 'Jerusalem' conveys a quintessential Englishness, a combination
of patriotic fervour tempered by social conscience.

Jews too have been part of the English scene at least since the seventeenth century. Unlike any other Jewish community in Europe, we have
enjoyed a history of continuous settlement in Britain since the Readmission
by Oliver Cromwell in 1656. Britain may be credited with the invention
of the Blood Libel and may have expelled its Jewry in the medieval
period (1290), but in modern times we have escaped the displacement
and expulsion so common on the European mainland. During the Second
World War, a mere 20 miles of the English Channel saved Anglo-Jewry
from annihilation.

This comparatively settled history – from the first Sephardi influx in
the days of Menasseh ben Israel, through the mass immigration of east
European Ashkenazim between 1881 and 1914, down to those lucky,
but too few, refugees from Nazi persecution in the 1930s – today results
in a community of about 300,000, and a rare heritage of Jewish monuments throughout the land. Evidence of Jewish settlement, in the form
both of archaeology and of surviving synagogues, cemeteries, *mikvaot*
(ritual baths) and even of buildings with secular Jewish connotations,
may be found in town and country; for example in London, which has
consistently been home to two-thirds of British Jewry in the modern
period, and in the remote valleys of the South Wales coalfields; in
northern industrial centres such as Manchester, Leeds and Glasgow and
in sleepy southern seaports and market towns which had their heyday in
the late eighteenth and early nineteenth centuries: Chatham and Sheerness or Exeter and Plymouth. Jewish communities have cropped up in
the most unexpected places: on the most westerly tip of Cornwall
(Penzance and Falmouth), at Cork and Limerick in Ireland.

Nevertheless, a great deal – far too much – of the Jewish architectural
heritage in Britain has been lost, and what survives is extremely vulnerable.

1.1   Swansea Synagogue, Goat Street
(Henry J. Baliss, 1859); casualty of an air
raid in February 1941.   *London Museum of Jewish Life*

Enormous physical destruction has already taken place. Synagogues have fallen victim to wartime bombing or, more usually, to Jewish demographic shift and urban renewal. Today, only two synagogues remain from the Georgian period, at Exeter and Plymouth. Wholesale destruction has taken place not only in the East End of London, the primary area of immigration, but also in Red Bank and Cheetham Hill (Manchester), the Leylands (Leeds) and the Gorbals (Glasgow). The north of England and the Welsh valleys have been equally denuded of their historic Jewish buildings. Of many early synagogues, no pictorial record survives in the form of architects' plans or contemporary illustrations; in some cases, even the name of the architect has been lost. Nor have there been attempts to document the existence of Jewish congregations in Britain, or even to photograph threatened buildings before they disappear.

1.2   London, Borough New Synagogue, Wansey Street, SE17 (H. H. Collins, 1867); the interior before demolition in 1970. *Greater London Record Office*

The vulnerability of the Jewish architectural heritage in Britain may be graphically illustrated by reference to the history of our most venerable monument: the Bevis Marks Synagogue in the City of London. Built in 1701 to a design by a Quaker architect, Joseph Avis, and reputedly modelled on the Spanish and Portuguese Great Synagogue in Amsterdam (but as likely influenced by the local Wren churches[1]), Bevis Marks stands testimony to the longevity of the Jewish presence in England. Yet few people are aware that it was saved from almost certain destruction in the nineteenth century only through the far-sighted efforts of a group of Victorian Jewish gentlemen. In 1885 they set up the quaintly named Anti-Demolition League to stop the board of management selling its building in order to effect economies. In 1928 the synagogue was designated a Grade I listed monument of outstanding national importance.[2]

In April 1992 a massive IRA bomb destroyed the Baltic Exchange, and extensive damage was done to the very heart of that area on the fringes of the City which was the cradle of London Jewry. The Bevis Marks Synagogue did not emerge unscathed. Ironically, it was the presence of scaffolding inside the building, needed for the much criticized restoration

work on the timber floor, which averted complete disaster. Structural and external damage was sustained, and the eighteenth-century blue leaded glass windows shattered, but the ark and interior fittings remained largely intact. Even so, the cost of repairs was estimated to be £200,000; government subsidies have picked up part of the bill, and the rest of the money will have to be raised through the synagogue's own restoration appeal. Unfortunately, in April 1993, with restoration work almost complete, a second blast rocked the City almost on the anniversary of the 1992 bombing. This time the damage to Bevis Marks was less serious.

The work of the IRA has been a setback we could well have done without. But at least it was not self-inflicted. In 1987 the United Synagogue, the largest London-based synagogue organization in Britain, with a membership of some 39,000, sold the magnificent East London Synagogue in Stepney Green (Davis and Emanuel, 1877) to property developers – for a knock-down price. The developers, or rather speculators, unsuccessfully attempted to resell the site and subsequently went bust. Today the building stands derelict and vandalized, a monument to Anglo-Jewry's indifference to its rich cultural heritage.[3]

The scale of the United Synagogue's current financial crisis – a deficit of nine million pounds, made public in the 1992 Kalms Report[4] – is such that none of the remaining Victorian synagogues owned by the United in London can be regarded as safe from a similar fate. All too often in the past, the United Synagogue has indulged in *ad hoc* quick-fix sales of so-called surplus assets, especially of 'redundant' synagogues with 'deficit' congregations and of ritual silver. It remains to be seen whether the sobering facts of a depressed property market, highlighted in the report, will act as a disincentive for such ill-considered sales in the future.

The United Synagogue still owns two fine Victorian 'cathedral' synagogues in the capital: the New West End Synagogue, St Petersburgh Place, Bayswater (1878), which was designed by George Audsley in collaboration with Nathan S. Joseph, architect to the United Synagogue;[5] and the Hampstead Synagogue, Dennington Park Road (1892), designed by Nathan's nephew Delissa Joseph. The New West End is of particular interest in this context because it may be regarded as the up-market contemporary of the East London. It is built to a similar ground-plan, but marble and gold-leaf replace the simple red brickwork used at Stepney Green, reflecting the wealth and social pretensions of its fashionable West End clientele. Both of these synagogues enjoy Department of National Heritage listed status; both are designated Grade II, and moves are afoot to upgrade their status to Grade II*, with the enhanced protection and access to government grants which that implies.

Unfortunately, the 1915 New Synagogue in Egerton Road, Stamford Hill, is already at risk. This synagogue is of greater historical significance than its vintage suggests, for it is essentially a replica of the New Synagogue in Great St Helen's, close to Bevis Marks in the City, built in 1838 and one of the three founding congregations of the United Synagogue created by Act of Parliament in 1870. The Stamford Hill New retains some original fixtures, most importantly the oak panelled ark. The sale of this synagogue and adjacent buildings by the United Synagogue to the Bobover Chasidim in the neighbourhood, negotiated over a five-year

1.3   London, East London Synagogue, Stepney Green, E1 (Davis and Emanuel, 1877); the Ark in 1902. *Southampton University Library*

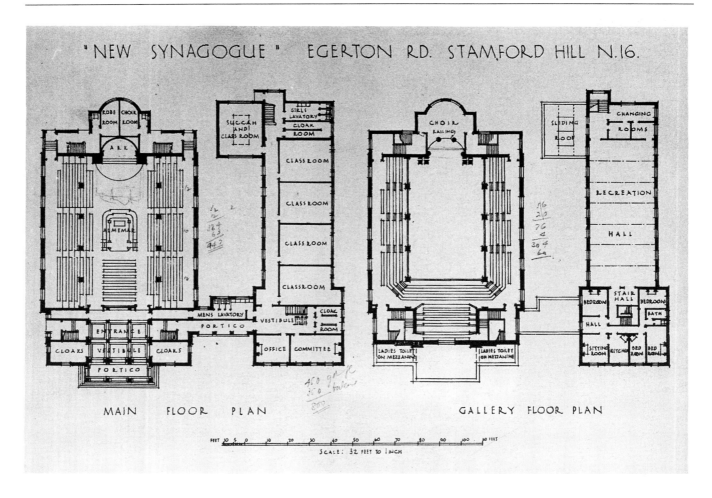

term, has recently run into difficulty. The United Synagogue is threatening the Chasidim with legal action for failing to complete the exchange of contracts.[6]

Like the East London Synagogue, Egerton Road became Grade II listed only after the sale had been set in motion. Both cases demonstrate that listing, and the restrictions it imposes, can reduce the market value of a building and act as a deterrent to a potential purchaser. In order to be beneficial, I would contend that listing must take place well before a change of ownership is contemplated.

Another London United building threatened with redundancy is the Dollis Hill Synagogue, designed (1938) by Owen Williams. It is the only 'modern' synagogue anywhere in the country to have been put on the national monuments list; but do its innovative pleated concrete walls, or other such hi-tec features of even more contemporary buildings, qualify for such protection? This is a subject which needs further consideration.[7]

The problem of redundancy is not confined to the United Synagogue, nor indeed to London Jewry. The contraction of Anglo-Jewry nationwide and its increasing centralization in suburban London and Manchester mean that the future of several more of our dwindling stock of fine

Victorian synagogues must now be in doubt. Manchester's Spanish and Portuguese Synagogue (Edward Salomons, 1874) was rescued through the valiant efforts of Bill Williams, the late Werner Mayer and others and turned into the city's Jewish Museum.[8] Sadly, its neighbour, the Manchester Great Synagogue (Thomas Bird, 1857), was sacrificed to the demolition squad. The Garnethill Synagogue in Glasgow (John McLeod in association with Nathan Joseph, 1879) is now home to the Scottish Jewish Archives Centre as well as to its resident congregation and grant aid by Historic Scotland is helping to secure its future. The work of Alf Dunitz in raising funds for the restoration of the rare Georgian synagogue at Exeter in the early 1980s should also be mentioned. However, Singers Hill, Birmingham (Yeoville Thomason, 1856), Prince's Road, Liverpool (W. and G. Audsley, 1874), and Middle Street, Brighton (Thomas Lainson, 1874–75), all give cause for concern. Faced with falling membership and sparse attendance, the congregations at Singers Hill and at Linnaeus Street, Hull (B. S. Jacobs, 1902), have sought to delist their buildings with a view to demolition and sale of the site. Permission has been withheld.

Against this grim picture of apparent Jewish decline in a recession-racked Britain must be set moves made on a national scale since the late

1.6   London, St Petersburgh Place; the Rothschild rose window (Erwin Bossanyi, 1935). *Anthony Harris*

1.7   Liverpool, Prince's Road Old Hebrew
Congregation (W. and G. Audsley, 1874).
Beverley-Jane Stewart

1980s to arrest the disappearance of our historic Jewish landmarks. In July 1990 the 'Preserving the Jewish Heritage' conference at Southampton University, organized by Dr Tony Kushner, brought together over 50 concerned academics, archivists, curators, conservationists and communal leaders to examine the fast-disappearing heritage of Jewish archives, artifacts and buildings in the United Kingdom. The Southampton conference represented the first nationwide attempt to coordinate action on Jewish heritage conservation in Britain, which until then had been the preserve of local projects (most notably, the pioneering Manchester Jewish Museum and the London Museum of Jewish Life).

In November 1990 the Jewish Heritage Council of the World Monuments Fund (a privately funded American-based organization concerned with conservation projects worldwide) hosted an international symposium in New York on 'The Future of Jewish Monuments'. I was privileged to represent the UK at this conference, which demonstrated how the battle to save the Jewish architectural heritage is being waged in other parts of the world and how, by comparison, Britain was hopelessly behind. And it provided me with the inspiration to organize our own British 'Future of Jewish Monuments' conference in London, which took place in October 1991. The London conference, held under the joint aegis of the Centre for Metropolitan History of the University of London and the Yakar Educational Foundation, was unprecedented in bringing individuals and groups involved in documenting and restoring Jewish monuments in London, Manchester, Scotland, Wales and Ireland together with experts from national governmental and voluntary conservation bodies: English Heritage, the Royal Commission on the Historical Monuments of England, the Council for the Care of Churches and the Victorian Society. Representatives of the World Monuments Fund and the International Council on Monuments and Sites (ICOMOS) also took part, addressing an audience of over 100 people.[9]

To ensure that the momentum generated by the 'Future of Jewish Monuments' conference was not lost, the Working Party on Jewish Monuments in the United Kingdom and Ireland was set up in December 1991. Architect Edward Jamilly recently succeeded me as chairman; the Working Party has about a dozen members and meets in London three times a year. It enjoys the support of the Centre for Metropolitan History and liaises with the Working Party on Jewish Archives, chaired by Tony Kushner, which came into existence in 1990. Our funds are deposited with the Jewish Memorial Council, London, a registered charity, and we have received financial assistance from the Kessler Foundation and the Acacia Charitable Trust.

Since its inception, the Working Party has proved beyond doubt the need for its existence and the importance of the aims it has set itself. It acts as a clearing-house for the exchange of information on Jewish monuments, both sacred and secular, throughout Britain and Ireland. It functions as a watchdog, monitoring the condition of Jewish sites and pinpointing monuments at risk. Already these have included the above-mentioned New Synagogue in London and Singers Hill in Birmingham, where we successfully opposed delisting. We have been consulted by Westminster City Council about a planning application for alterations at the site of the West London Reform Synagogue, Upper Berkeley Street (Davis and Emanuel, 1870). Our two architect members duly studied the plans and made recommendations.

The Working Party has and will continue to demand accountability from communal organizations regarding the future of important sites. We have drawn up a 'Code of Practice' for the orderly removal of fixtures and fittings in cases where a synagogue is forced to close. This is being circulated for the practical guidance of synagogue bodies and individual congregations. We would like to see the compilation of a central inventory of ritual art objects and furnishings from redundant and threatened synagogues in Britain. When objects are recycled in a new synagogue, their provenance will thus have been recorded. The creation of such an inventory, open to inspection by professionals and by responsible members of the public, would also reduce the risk of theft, not to mention attempts — not unknown — by communal organizations to 'sell off the family silver'. In sum, we urge the leaders of British Jewry to put conservation on the communal agenda and to adopt a responsible conservation policy which strikes a balance between safeguarding our architectural heritage and contemporary communal need.

Basic to our strategy from the outset has been to enlist the support of the general conservation agencies in our work. Until very recently the Jewish contribution to the British heritage had been all but ignored, through ignorance rather than deliberate marginalization of minority cultures. Now a representative of English Heritage, Susie Barson, sits on the Working Party. Her contribution is invaluable since English Heritage, which is associated with the Department of National Heritage, has the authority to advance grant aid for restoration work, to recommend sites for listing and to enforce listed building control. She has drawn up *Guidelines for Listing Synagogues* for use within English Heritage itself.

This is a great step forward. When I first became concerned with heritage conservation through the shocking fate of the East London Synagogue at the end of 1987, a mere three synagogues in London and an undetermined number in the rest of the country were listed buildings, compared with literally hundreds of churches. Today, a further seven working London synagogues have listed status, two more which have undergone a change of use, plus the Jewish Soup Kitchen in Whitechapel and the Stepney Jewish Schools, significantly the first secular Jewish buildings to be listed.[10] Thanks to the diligence of a volunteer research worker, Barbara Blum, who patiently searched through the lists of the other regional divisions of English Heritage, we now know that there are at least 21 other listed synagogues elsewhere in England. Scotland, Wales and Ireland, which are of course outside the jurisdiction of English Heritage, have yet to be dealt with.

Simply listing a building is, of course, no insurance policy against fire, flood or vandalism. Nor does listing entirely guarantee full protection in the legal sense owing to the anomaly known as the 'ecclesiastical exemption', whereby 'working churches' (and therefore synagogues) have enjoyed certain immunity from listed building control. In practice, this meant that alterations could be made to the exterior and, especially, to the interior of a house of worship without consultation with English

Heritage. In 1992 the Department of National Heritage produced a consultation paper recommending restrictions on the ecclesiastical exemption. The Working Party on Jewish Monuments was asked to comment on this document and fully endorsed the proposals. We went further by suggesting that controls ought to be extended to cover the interior of ecclesiastical buildings because, in the case of synagogues, the interior, with its furnishings, stained glass, wood and brasswork, is often of far greater interest than the exterior, which is generally plain and discreetly placed. We were therefore gratified when the ministry issued new regulations curtailing the ecclesiastical exemption and requiring 'church organizations' – including Jewish ones – to adopt a code of practice in relation to their historic buildings. It is envisaged that the Working Party on Jewish Monuments will have a future role to play in this area.[11]

Experience has taught us that listing, if carried out early enough, may serve as a deterrent against asset-stripping by synagogue organizations and the predatory intentions of property developers. Progress is now being made in establishing criteria for Jewish monuments deemed worthy of listing on either architectural or historical grounds, be they large or small, sacred or secular, redundant or undergoing a change of use. This is an essential prerequisite for arriving at a rational conservation policy. The experience and expertise to be found in the general conservation agencies are crucial to our purpose.

Not all buildings can be considered for listing, however; still fewer can be preserved. But they can be researched and documented. The Working Party aims to promote appreciation of the Jewish architectural heritage both within and without the Jewish community. To this end, we are preparing publications in the field of Jewish art and architecture in Britain. Back in 1988, a search of the literature revealed the paltry total of four serious articles on Jewish architecture in Britain published in the preceding 40 years. Two of these were written by architect Edward Jamilly, and the other two by design historian Judy Glasman. They are both now members of the Working Party. Clearly, the definitive history of Jewish art and architecture in Britain has yet to be written. A start is now being made. As a result of the conferences, *The Jewish Heritage in British History: Englishness and Jewishness*, edited by Tony Kushner, was published by Frank Cass in 1992.[12]

Building Jerusalem is the first book entirely devoted to a consideration of the Jewish contribution to the architectural fabric of Britain. All of the major Jewish building types are represented – synagogues, cemeteries, *mikvaot*, as well as Jewish communal and secular buildings which served a social function – in a scholarly collection of essays by academics and practising architects, writing from a variety of interdisciplinary standpoints. Carol Herselle Krinsky, Professor of Fine Arts at New York University and author of *Synagogues of Europe* (New York and Cambridge, MA, 1985), provides a transatlantic perspective on the British-Jewish architectural heritage and the general importance of preservation efforts. Raphael Isserlin rediscovers the archaeological legacy of medieval Anglo-Jewry, a small but significant outpost of the continental communities of Rouen and the Rhineland, with the help of documentary evidence, excavated remains and 'above ground' archaeology. Art historian Clarence Epstein uses the architectural evolution of the now lost eighteenth-century Ashkenazi Great Synagogue in London to explore the existence – or lack – of a uniquely 'Jewish' style of architecture in Europe. Architect Edward Jamilly, who published his first research on Anglo-Jewish architects and architecture back in 1955, is the link between a preceding generation of Jewish scholars working in this country who took an interest in Jewish art, Cecil Roth, Vivian Lipman[13] and Helen Rosenau, and the younger generation active in the 1990s. In his two contributions, he assesses the record of the various synagogue organizations in Britain on conservation issues and examines the interior space of extant synagogue buildings: layout, furnishings, decor and ritual objects. Fellow architect Stephen Rosenberg provides some practical suggestions, based on his own experience, for the sympathetic conversion of redundant synagogue buildings to other uses.

My own paper investigates perhaps the quintessential and certainly the most neglected Jewish building type: the *mikveh*. The copious footnoting indicates the considerable 'digging around' which was necessary to compile this inevitably incomplete history of the *mikveh* in Britain. The resulting essay would probably be described as socio-historical rather than architectural, reflecting the bias in the available and scarce sources. My approach is very different from that of the Frankfurt Jewish Museum, which held an exhibition, accompanied by a comprehensive catalogue,[14] on the history of German *mikvaot* in the autumn of 1992.

Rabbi Dr Bernard Susser, an authority on the Jews of Devon and Cornwall, uses the local burial grounds to extrapolate some remarkable sociological data on the communities in the West Country and draws attention to the particular problems of preserving disused cemeteries which are threatened both by natural decay and by vandalism. Finally, Lesley Fraser, who works for English Heritage, broadens the scope of *Building Jerusalem* to embrace the social architecture built in the Victorian period for the Jewish working classes in the East End of London. Her chapter includes schools, hospitals, a refuge and soup kitchen as well as philanthropic housing developments for the Jewish poor. She highlights the need to conserve at least a few specimens of 'down-market' secular building which can serve as a salutory educational antidote to Jewish high or sacred art.

Building Jerusalem is illustrated by plans, drawings and photographs selected by the contributors. We have deliberately ensured that little-known monuments or those which have been lost are represented alongside famous landmarks like Bevis Marks. A young photographer, Anthony Harris, who completed a project on synagogues for his degree course at the former Central London Polytechnic, has provided some fine plates of major London synagogues. Beverley-Jane Stewart has produced a series of colourful oil paintings of synagogue interiors.

As this book will, I hope, demonstrate, the scope for research into Jewish monuments in Britain and for comparisons with other countries is large indeed. Ultimately, I would like the Working Party on Jewish Monuments to form the nucleus of a team of researchers to conduct a nationwide survey of extant Jewish monuments on a region-by-region basis and to publish its findings in the form of a research handbook. Alternative methods of documentation – written, pictorial, photographic and computerized (especially the application of computer-aided design and virtual-reality technology) – may be considered and techniques should be standardized to ensure compatibility with generally recognized guidelines, such as the National Monuments Record's Core Data Standard. The limited number of Jewish monuments and sites in the UK and Ireland, as compared for example with Anglican churches, means that such a project may be of finite duration.

Perhaps the model most relevant to the Jewish experience, however, is not the established church but Protestant Nonconformity. After all, until the mid-nineteenth century Jews were regarded, in the legal sense at least, as just another dissenting church. The removal of civil and political disabilities suffered by British Jews was linked more closely to the Dissenters than to the Catholics. It is perhaps not surprising then that, architecturally speaking, Jewish buildings in Britain have some features in common with the free churches. Both share a congregational form of worship and a portable tradition which can flourish quite independently of its physical surroundings. As an architectural historian of Nonconformity has written:

> the Free Churches . . . are more likely to regard their places of sanctuary as the moveable Tent of Meeting (it is not without significance that we talk of Chapels and Meeting-houses) rather than the fixed Temple which probably has more influence in the understanding of . . . Parish Churches.[15]

It may be contended that throughout Jewish history the *Mishkan* (Tabernacle) in the wilderness, the concept of *Torah* anchored to no one place, has assumed greater significance than that of the *Beth HaMikdash*, the Holy Temple in Jerusalem. Metaphysical ideas, the sanctification of people, faith itself, take precedence over the importance of place.[16] A synagogue's 'holiness' is entirely dependent on its function as house of worship, assembly and learning. Unlike a church it need not be 'deconsecrated' when it has outgrown its useful life for the community – although the classical Jewish sources do specify that it may only be sold for a 'suitable' respectful use and the proceeds used for a higher religious purpose.

Theology aside, Jews and Nonconformist Christians in Britain both largely eschewed the Gothic Revival, which became *the* architectural style of the established church in the Victorian period. Romanesque and neo-classical forms were generally preferred, notwithstanding the search for a peculiarly 'Jewish' style reflected in the elaborate 'orientalism' favoured by Jews in the last decades of the nineteenth century. Like many synagogues, chapels built by Nonconformist denominations frequently adhered to a centralized ground-plan with galleries and staircases, in contrast to the cruciform plan and central aisle found in Anglican churches.

To turn to a more prosaic matter: research costs money. The Working Party on Jewish Monuments recognizes the inescapable need for funds. So far we have raised in the region of £3,000 in sponsorship, the Kessler Foundation being our largest benefactor (£1,500), enabling us to hold the original London conference, to produce a volume of conference abstracts, to plan our future publication programme and to function on a day-to-day administrative basis. The publication of this book would not have been possible without our sponsors' support. Nevertheless, our budget is modest indeed. The current debate on the Kalms Report highlights the need for sensible funding throughout the Jewish community. At the end of the day, buildings are an expensive resource. Only serious investment by the Jewish community itself will secure our architectural heritage for the future. We would certainly welcome the creation of a nationwide conservation fund.

But money alone is not sufficient. Maximizing the potential of communal resources in the form of property and imaginative solutions to the problem of seemingly redundant but historic buildings are equally important. The sale of Woburn House, the operational headquarters of Anglo-Jewry, in the near future could provide the ideal opportunity. The Kalms Report made an eminently sensible suggestion in this regard. Why not relocate United Synagogue Head Office, the Chief Rabbinate and Beth Din in an important and centrally placed London synagogue building rather than in commercial office accommodation? I would go further: perhaps St Petersburgh Place or Dennington Park could play a communal role similar to that of the Great Synagogue, Duke's Place, before the Second World War.[17] On the other hand, the decision to transfer the Jewish Museum to Camden Town strikes me as absurd. One million pounds of private charity have been spent on renovating a listed town house in an area of London which has little or no connection with the history of the Jewish community in the metropolis. Why could not London have followed the excellent example provided by Manchester – where the city's Jewish museum is housed in a major Jewish landmark, the former Spanish and Portuguese synagogue? Or continental examples such as Frankfurt, whose Jewish museum is housed in an elegant former Rothschild mansion, or, better still, Amsterdam, Prague, Toledo and Venice, where museum complexes have been created centred on the old synagogues of the historic Jewish quarters? In this way, Jewish artifacts are displayed in an appropriate setting, while the objective of the conservation of important sites is simultaneously being achieved. In contrast, the London Jewish Museum project is, sad to say, a prime example, not of underfunding, but of the misuse of scarce resources.

In conclusion, a few words to justify the importance of the work we are trying to do. Experience has taught us already that neither the economic climate nor certain fixed attitudes within Anglo-Jewry make our task an easy one. Trying to convey the importance of heritage conservation, indeed of cultural, artistic and educational issues in general, in 1990s Britain is a struggle. However, there are some encouraging signs. Conservation of the historic built environment can only benefit from current preoccupations with environmentalism and 'green' politics. After all, the conservation lobby enjoys the patronage of the highest in the land – the Prince of Wales. Moreover, the 'heritage industry' is gradually opening up to the reality of a multi-cultural society. 'English' Heritage encompasses not only medieval cathedrals and stately homes but also industrial archaeology, working-class housing and the heritage of minority cultures which today are an integral part of the social fabric of British society.

Within the Jewish community itself a younger generation is emerging which is more secure and less self-conscious than its elders, and is no longer content to be relegated to the margins. We want our history and culture to be taken seriously. But we cannot demand that society take us seriously unless we, as a community, take ourselves seriously. For too long there has been a reluctance amongst British Jews to attach any intrinsic importance to the physical evidence of our link with Britain. Perhaps, permit me to speculate, this is a symptom of a psychological state, linked with the perennial Jewish feeling that maybe some day we will have to move on. It is an irony that the greatest progress towards the documentation and preservation of Jewish monuments has been made in those parts of Europe whose Jewish communities were destroyed in the Nazi Holocaust. In Britain we are in a uniquely fortunate position: possessing both Jewish monuments *and* Jews. Our monuments need not be memorials, but a living heritage. Surely understanding the Jewish past is the key to a healthy Jewish identity. Pride in our architectural heritage is a potent expression of our faith in the future.

1.8   London, 42 Old Montagu Street, E1; synagogue entrance in 1971. *Greater London Record Office*

NOTES

1. See Epstein, this volume.
2. See Lucien Wolf, 'Origin of the Jewish Historical Society of England (Presidential Address 15 Jan. 1912)', *Transactions of the Jewish Historical Society of England (TJHSE)*, 1911–14 (1915), pp. 206–21, esp. p. 214; Albert Hyamson, *The Sephardim of England* (London, 1st edn 1951), pp. 372–7.
3. See Sharman Kadish, 'Squandered Heritage: Jewish Buildings in Britain', in *Immigrants and Minorities*, Vol. 10, Nos. 1–2 (March–July 1991), pp. 147–65, and in Tony Kushner (ed.), *The Jewish Heritage in British History* (London, 1992), pp.147–65.
4. Stanley Kalms, *United Synagogue Review: A Time for Change* (London, 1992).
5. On the Audsleys, see 'The Synagogue of the Old Hebrew Congregation, Liverpool', *Shoppell's Owners and Builders Magazine*, Vol. 2, No. 5 (May 1908), cover and pp. 8–9. I am grateful to Bernard Newman, research student with Professor J. M. Crook (architectural history) at Royal Holloway College, University of London, for this reference.
6. See Jamilly, Ch.9, this volume, and *Jewish Chronicle (JC)*, 19 Feb. 1993. Since this was written, it appears that a compromise has been reached, because the alternative was conversion of the synagogue into a mosque, *JC*, 2 and 16 Sept., 9 Dec. 1994 and 6 Jan. 1995.
7. See Rosenberg, this volume.
8. Tony Kushner, 'Looking back with nostalgia? The Jewish Museums of England', *Immigrants and Minorities*, Vol. 6, No. 2 (July 1987), pp. 200–11. Linnaeus Street was purchased by a private individual, the late Jack Lennard, in 1993 with a view to conversion into a Jewish museum.
9. *The Future of Jewish Monuments in the British Isles: 13 October 1991 Conference Abstracts* (Northants, 1992).
10. The listed synagogues in London are:
    Grade I: Bevis Marks (1701) (S&P);
    Grade II*: New West End (1878) (US);
    Grade II: Dollis Hill (1938), East London (1877), Hampstead (1892), New (1915) all US; Lauderdale Road (1896) (S&P), New London, Abbey Road (1882) (Masorti), West London Reform (1870), Sandy's Row (chapel 1766, converted into synagogue 1867) (Independent).
    Princelet Street, Grade II* (Huguenot house 1719, converted 1870) and Spitalfields Great, Grade II (chapel 1743, converted 1897) are no longer in use as synagogues.
    Synagogues and former synagogues in the following towns are listed: Birmingham, Bradford, Brighton (two), Cheltenham, Epsom, Exeter, Falmouth, Hull, Leeds, Liverpool (three), Manchester (six), Nottingham, Plymouth, Ramsgate, Reading, Rochester, Sheffield, Torquay; and in Scotland: Glasgow.
11. Department of National Heritage, Consultation Paper: 'Ecclesiastical Exemption from Listed Building Control' (Feb. 1992); Announcement of Code of Practice (17 Dec. 1992).
12. Paul Lindsay, *Synagogues of London* (London, 1992), was published independently of our efforts.
13. V. D. Lipman, 'Historic synagogues in England and Wales: their importance and problems', *L'Eylah*, Vol. 1, No. 9 (Spring 1980), pp. 32–7.
14. Frankfurt Jewish Museum, *Mikwe: Geschichte und Architektur judischer Ritualbader in Deutschland* (Frankfurt, 1992).
15. Kenneth Street, 'Ecclesiastical Exemption, the case for retention', *Chapels Society Newsletter*, No. 7 (Dec. 1992), pp. 77–9; see also Christopher Stell, *Nonconformist Chapels and Meeting Houses in Central England* (London, Royal Commission on the Historical Monuments of England, 1986) and 'Nonconformist (ie Protestant Dissenting) Chapels and Meeting Houses: Guidelines for Listing' (English Heritage internal working paper kindly provided for me by Susie Barson).
16. Michael Turner, 'The Conservation of Jewish Monuments: A Hungarian Case-study', in *Future of Jewish Monuments*, op. cit., p. 17; Helen Rosenau, *Vision of the Temple: The Image of the Temple of Jerusalem in Judaism and Christianity* (London, 1979). The 1990 New York conference included a session on 'Preservation and Jewish Law'; unfortunately, the proceedings have not been published. See also Rosenberg, this volume.
17. See my letters in *JC* 16 Oct. 1992, 3 Dec. 1993, 4 Nov. 1994.

2

BETWEEN EUROPE AND THE NEW WORLD:
Britain's Place in Synagogue Architecture

CAROL HERSELLE KRINSKY

'Every tradition is sealed beneath a monument', wrote Victor Hugo, whose epic *Notre Dame de Paris* represented the great metropolitan cathedral as the heart of a community's life. But his words also apply to the traditions of others – to the religious precincts of China or the Yucatan, to prehistoric earth sculptures in North America, to the great mosques of Damascus, Kairouan, Córdoba and Asian cities, and of course to the Temple in Jerusalem. At a lesser degree of holiness stand synagogues which, for all their relative modesty in comparison with the divinely ordained Temple, are central institutions for Judaism around the world.

Jews, whose faith proscribes the worship of graven images, have sometimes avoided making *any* images. They have nevertheless welcomed beauty and splendour, as indeed the Temples built by Solomon and Herod confirm, and have often created magnificent architecture when politics and economics allowed. Even before the relatively recent advent of toleration and civil equality in the nineteenth century, Jewish congregations employed architects eminent enough to be active in the prestigious ateliers of Worms and Prague cathedrals, and to work for local rulers, as at Karlsruhe and Wołpa. Synagogue interiors could be as colourful and lavishly endowed as churches, a fact recorded in photographs of some of the now destroyed wooden synagogues in Poland and other Slavic lands, and still evident in the extant synagogues of Venice. Puritanical austerity or indifference to artistic and architectural beauty may have characterized individual Jews or even entire communities, but concern to beautify the house of prayer has more often than not been demonstrated when choice in the matter was possible.

To be sure, many synagogues offer little of visual interest. Judaism is a congregational religion, and some congregations cannot afford more than simple houses of worship. Moreover, in theory at least, a synagogue building is superfluous. It is a locus for prayer and community life, but that need not imply anything grandly architectural; in this respect, the synagogue is fundamentally different from the divinely ordered Temple. A *minyan* (ten adult male Jews required for the full recitation of the prayer service) can meet anywhere from a prison to a palace. Of course, for the sake of convenience, for calling to mind the necessity of prayer, for group prestige, Jews have built synagogues when they could. These appear to be all but universal needs, and Jews are not atypical human beings. The differences between a visually attractive synagogue and a humble structure result from the social, aesthetic and religious outlook of a congregation's leaders, from the group's economic resources and from the artistic talent available.

Whatever the degree of beauty and grandeur in a building, it remains as clearly a cultural document as any photograph or parchment. It is for this reason that sensitive and educated people have worked hard to preserve historic buildings around the world. No more than a moment is needed to recall some of the nineteenth century's most conspicuous men of letters — men whom we might have regarded as reliant only on the written word — who felt that historic architecture embodied otherwise unknowable aspects of human history. One thinks at once of John Ruskin and William Morris, Victor Hugo and Prosper Mérimée. Although they primarily concerned themselves with great buildings, from the church of La Madeleine at Vézelay to the Doge's Palace of Venice, they also wrote on behalf of more modest structures recognizing that some buildings were precious not because they were universally known, or of the highest quality in every detail, or built by well-loved patrons, but because they recorded the social situation of those who commissioned the architecture, the possibilities in technology available at a certain period, the potential for exaltation or constriction given by manipulating space and light, or any number of impressions and feelings difficult to convey in words. Just as the sculpture on a medieval cathedral could be a picture Bible for the illiterate, buildings have been vehicles of expression and understanding for many who never saw the pertinent books.

Synagogues offer excellent case studies in this regard. The location alone of Britain's oldest extant synagogue, the Spanish and Portuguese Bevis Marks Synagogue in east London, tells us immediately that in 1699, when building began, no Jewish house of worship was permitted within the City. Nor was the synagogue permitted to front upon the public street. A young person accustomed to the late twentieth century's polite expressions of toleration may be shocked by these facts into an understanding of the constraints on minorities, past or present. One hopes that this will affect his civic behaviour for the better. The same building tells us that, while the Sephardi Jews were willing to spend generously on dignified interior furnishings, theirs was a small community which was under some landholding and fiscal constraints that made a more ambitious building impossible. This lesson, too, might not be learned so well from books alone. The name of the architect, Joseph Avis, suggests that there were no Jewish architects in Britain at the time, and the fact that he was a Quaker makes us wonder whether architects affiliated with the Church of England had declined to work for the Jews or were thought of as less willing to do so than a Nonconformist. The synagogue's modest exterior is made of materials arranged in patterns reminiscent of other late Stuart and early Georgian buildings, both religious and secular. True, it did not look like most established churches, since it lacks a tower and street-side

2.1   London, Bevis Marks Synagogue
(Joseph Avis, 1701); exterior. *Spanish &*
Portuguese Jews Congregation, London

2.2 London, Bevis Marks Synagogue;
watercolour by I. M. Belisario, 1812.
Spanish & Portuguese Jews Congregation, London

façade. So Judaism was to be differentiated from Christianity by being discreet (this was the case on the Continent as well); but the use of the stone-trimmed brick vernacular shows that Jews were not considered to be wholly unlike their fellow Londoners.[1]

The Great Synagogue of London, built almost a century later, testifies to the stability and growth of the Jewish community, in this case the numerically dominant Ashkenazi branch. By this time Jews must have been seen as respectable clients for an architect as well known as James Spiller, and as people interested in contemporary architecture, since the interior, with galleries flanking a central ground-floor seating space, was akin to that of churches. Before the largely late-nineteenth-century notion of Jews as a 'race', intrinsically different from Christians, rather than a transnational group that clung to an old religion, synagogues everywhere tended to look like other religious buildings in style, with only liturgically driven differences in plan. The use of late-eighteenth-century form and style here shows that there was no fixed tradition stemming from the Bevis Marks Synagogue. Each congregation commissioned what it liked and could afford, and experimented with up-to-date fashions. Those familiar with the cultural distinctions among Jews will not be surprised that the Ashkenazim differentiated themselves from the Sephardim in synagogue design, and in other ways as well.

These early examples suggest the scope of the historical insight offered by synagogue architecture. From the nineteenth and twentieth centuries there are plenty of examples, in Great Britain, on the Continent and in North America, of synagogues designed by inferior architects, although it is tactful not to name them. Since people do not willingly employ inferior designers, the buildings tell us that the clients were poorly informed about design issues, had insufficient funds to engage better architects or felt that they ought to employ co-religionists who had entered the profession. All these factors did, in fact, play a role in the design of less than admirable synagogues; the same could be said of many churches and civic buildings, of course.

Jews, after all, had rarely been numerous enough in western cities before the 1830s to erect conspicuous structures. (Their buildings were more noticeable in the towns of eastern Europe where, in some cases, they formed a majority of the population.) The large seventeenth- and eighteenth-century synagogues of Amsterdam were exceptionally visible, but were isolated on an island which, if not exactly a 'ghetto', was designated for Jewish residence. Usually, the Jews employed local builders, not artistic designers. Often, too, a synagogue would be built – and many still are – as the gift of one major donor, which meant that the congregation had to accept his choice. These factors help to explain why few synagogue building committees or rabbis had extensive experience in judging the merits of architecture. The budget of many synagogues was severely constrained, especially in the absence of donors enthusiastic about building (or wishing, as childless people often did, to memorialize themselves through permanent donations to the community). And there was no guarantee that a Jew who decided to study architecture would be more talented than the average member of his profession. There had been little opportunity for Jews to design and build before the mid-nineteenth century; few Gentile clients wished to deal with Jewish rather than Christian architects, and few Christian architects would take on a Jewish lad as an apprentice, so that few Jews could even become architects. This situation persisted until the 1920s, and indeed until after the Second World War in both Great Britain and the United States. Small wonder, then, that some synagogues seemed made up of uncoordinated details rather than guided by a harmonious vision. Small wonder that some architects and their clients mistook overblown elaboration as the way to make a synagogue worthy of its status as a temporary sanctuary pending the rebuilding of the Temple.

But beauty is not always the point, difficult though it is for an art historian to say so. Indeed, I now regret my lack of thoughtful activity on behalf of the East London Synagogue – magnificent, or at least grandiloquent, before its neglect – although intervention from abroad might have been unwelcome. A synagogue need not be a work of great art in order to be a significant historical document. We can examine even prosaic twentieth-century synagogues – and not all are prosaic – for signs of community life and aspiration, or for evidence of what the Jewish community cares about in design and building.

A search for synagogues today in the suburbs of major English cities generally yields results less visually exciting than those to be found in

American suburbs. (There are so few suburban examples on the Continent that no precise comparison can be made, although there are many comparably *sized* post-war synagogues.) It is impossible to generalize about the reasons, and in any case aesthetic judgments are fallible and individual. If we look to history for suggestions, we think once again about financial constraints. During the 1930s, such considerations so limited the congregation at Dollis Hill that its members turned to the efficient engineer of reinforced concrete, Sir E. Owen Williams, for an economical building. Williams' synagogue at Dollis Hill turned out to be one of the most interesting and progressive religious buildings of the inter-war years in the United Kingdom, thanks more to the designer's power than to guidance from the worshippers who, then as now, were mainly interested in function and economy. And today, Jewish communities of limited means can commission good architecture if they have the will to do so. Talented architects have worked on synagogues recently, for example Eric Lyons (Belsize Square, London, in the 1950s) and Yorke Rosenberg Mardall (Belfast, 1964). It happens that these firms include Jewish principals or partners, but sometimes the desire to employ a co-religionist would appear to have limited a synagogue's aesthetic potential, as an architect is not necessarily good merely because he is Jewish. Perhaps the problem is the lack of a clear vision of what is wanted, whether it is economy, or modesty in external appearance, or adherence to a previous model, or haste in execution. Clients inexperi-

2.3   London, Dollis Hill Synagogue (Owen Williams, 1938). *Beverley-Jane Stewart*

enced in commissioning buildings, architects unfamiliar with the building type, congregations unused to experiencing elevating religious surroundings, lack of prior aesthetic education, reticence about being in the minority – any of these factors can cause a diminution of quality in architecture.

Americans seem to be educated differently, and see their place in society somewhat differently as well – at least insofar as someone who is not a sociologist can generalize. Americans at school hear the inclusive phrase 'Protestants, Catholics and Jews' on occasions when religion is mentioned in public; we expect soon to enlarge the scope with Muslims, Hindus, Buddhists, and others. We live in a country where an established church has been prohibited by the Constitution, our fundamental document of government, and where religions are legally equal. Despite lingering anti-Semitism and simple ignorance, Jews in the United States regard themselves as equal to other citizens and entitled to build as boldly and as beautifully as anyone else. Increasingly, congregations have turned to excellent and/or prominent architects for new synagogues, Frank Lloyd Wright being the best-known internationally, along with Philip Johnson, Harrison and Abramovitz, Minoru Yamasaki, Robert A. M. Stern and others.

American Jews are disproportionately enrolled in university-level educational programmes, and these usually include exposure to the history of art and architecture. Architectural walking tours are offered in many cities; landmarks societies and commissions have become as prominent in the USA as in Britain; architectural guidebooks sell briskly, and television occasionally offers architectural education. Our tax laws include benefits for those who contribute to such worthy causes as religious construction projects. Our social hierarchy elevates those who concern themselves with the arts, and the newer the arts programmes in a given city, the easier it is for Jews – even *nouveaux riches* – to participate. It is therefore understandable that Jews, who count many architects, engineers and property developers among their number, are also concerned clients in religious architecture. In a country where equality is preached, if not always practised, Jewish resources and knowledge have been put usefully to work on behalf of synagogue architecture.

It is perhaps less relevant to compare the situation in Germany, even though post-war synagogues there are often close in size to those of post-war Britain. In Germany, new synagogues have been paid for out of reparations money or other extra-congregational means, and some decisions seem to have been made on behalf of, but not entirely by, the individual congregation concerned. Until recently, the architects were all Christians working on behalf of a minority which many were taught as children to hate; those who designed synagogues may have sympathized with Jews, but they worked in an emotional situation entirely different from that in the United Kingdom or North America. Post-war synagogues elsewhere in Europe have been too few to allow for generalizations, but nowhere in Britain is there a design as assertive as the synagogue of Livorno by the Jewish architect Angelo de Castro (1962) or as uncompromisingly stylish as that designed by Ionel Schein for the lower storeys of a block of flats in rue Gaston de Caillavet, Paris (1980).[2]

Reading a building requires some guidance at first, just as reading a book does, but frequently the visual record is more memorable than the verbal. 'A picture is worth a thousand words' did not become a cliché for nothing. The mere sight of a historic synagogue evokes reactions ranging from filial piety to endorsing the State of Israel's mission of in-gathering the Jewish exiles. American and British Jews with scant interest in practising their religion can often be found visiting continental synagogues, which can reinforce their ethnic identity. The ruins of synagogues in countries overrun by the Nazis, who destroyed Jewish buildings along with Jews, can move visitors of any religion to tears, and can instruct the young about history in ways that statistics, however shocking, cannot.

This is not to say that every old building with Jewish associations needs to be preserved. Preservation, after all, requires considerable resources: for preliminary survey work, for conservation and repair, for refitting if a new purpose is deemed advisable, for continuing maintenance, for staffing. In times when financial forecasts alarm many of us, and when human needs are evident, we may hesitate to spend money for culture, for history, for bricks and mortar. But it is equally certain that people of all faiths care about the visual record of minorities; it is the degree of preservation, not preservation itself, about which people disagree.

In England, for example, one cannot understand the history of Jews only from buildings old enough to be listed when the Royal Commission on Historic Monuments began its work, or from categories select enough to ensure protection under the law. Moreover, it seems curious to an American outsider that Christians employed by government and private amenity societies have been the primary decision-makers about preserving the tangible aspects of Jewish history. It is not that the Christians are ignorant or hostile, but that the scholars and enthusiasts for history and architecture in Great Britain already have a great deal of work to do, and without encouragement and help they may be unable to add to their schedules a concern for minority buildings, or at least the best or most revealing ones. They will need careful instruction in the history and meaning of these buildings. It would seem economical in terms of time, and desirable for the sake of history, for British Jews to take the initiative.

The synagogue in Bevis Marks was built by the forerunners of what is now a small Spanish and Portuguese minority within British Jewry. It tells us nothing about the central and eastern European immigrants who came to Great Britain in the mid-nineteenth century, or those who arrived in the great wave of immigration from 1881 up to the First World War. It says nothing about the early years of penury and effort, the attitude of immigrants to traditional Judaism, later social mobility and assimilation, or other such essential ingredients of British Jewish life. For this, one needs to see at least one relatively lavish and one modest synagogue in the East End of London. In Princelet Street there is an example of the latter, being used well as a heritage centre for educational purposes; but a most instructive example of the former was allowed to decay in Rectory Square, Stepney Green.[3]

London, of course, is not the only city of Jewish interest in Great Britain. For the full understanding of the growth and development of

2.4   Manchester, the Great Synagogue
(Thomas Bird, 1857). Illustrated Times (*2 May
1857*)

2.5   London, St John's Wood
Synagogue (H. H. Collins, 1882); the
interior showing metalwork, in 1975.
Greater London Record Office

THE JEWISH SYNAGOGUE IN COURSE OF ERECTION AT MANCHESTER

provincial cities, it would seem essential to preserve a visual record of the local Jews. Regrettably, the handsome Great Synagogue of Manchester, built in 1857, was demolished: a major loss.[4] This imposing building, with a marble-clad façade upon a brick body, should not have surprised anyone who knew about the role of Jews, especially those of German origin, in developing the city in the mid-nineteenth century. This synagogue was built at about the same time as those of Paris (1852), Mannheim (1855), Berlin (1854), Hamburg (1857), Brno (1855) and Budapest (1859).[5] It could have surprised others accustomed only to the pseudo-Moorish and eclectic synagogues typical of a later generation which came to separate Jews visually from other British citizens. The architect, Thomas Bird, designed a classical façade, with twin towers topped by cupolas flanking a grand columned porch reached by broad steps. Stairs adroitly concealed at the sides led to the women's gallery, while the lower floor, entered behind a vestibule, appeared as stately and spacious as a town hall or large dissenting church, and was well lit by tall round-arched windows.

While Bird is said to have looked to the relatively recent New Synagogue of 1838 in London for his plan, this does not imply a fixed tradition. It is just that he had had no experience in synagogue design, was working for a congregation with a ritual like that used in the model, and by using the model saved himself and his clients a good deal of time. This dignified Renaissance-based monument shows that the local Jews felt that their house of prayer and community affiliation should be part of the local mainstream, yet consciously unlike the contemporary neo-Gothic churches favoured by the Church of England, and not yet in any of the neo-medieval styles which became nearly universal soon afterwards. The Jews were, one might say, building yet another dissenting church. In this case, they employed the architect who had just completed the Town Hall close by the synagogue in the same road. Even if the Jews were forced to choose this municipal designer – and we do not know whether or not they were – they had the services of a practitioner who worked for prestigious clients in the majority culture as well as for the Jews.

A generation later, large numbers of new immigrants, many of them poor and ill-versed in such favoured languages as English and German, gathered for prayer in synagogues whose unfamiliar architectural forms, especially the Moorish, suggested that these were indeed exotic strangers whose integration into British life was considered impossible or undesirable by both natives and newcomers.[6] The significance of the differing architectural styles before the First World War would have been made obvious had the Great Synagogue of Manchester remained standing, for it afforded a great contrast with others in the city, including the smaller Spanish and Portuguese Synagogue of 1874, now the Jewish Museum in Cheetham Hill Road. Its colourful striped accents on darkened brick, its multitude of small arches, and its references to southern Italian Romanesque antecedents that evoke the worshippers' Mediterranean roots (although few local Jews apparently claimed Italy as a homeland) make perfectly clear the internal demarcations among the Jewish congregations of Manchester. Having more than one surviving building from a given period thus demonstrates the independence of Jewish congregations, and, perhaps of even greater importance, shows that there is no such thing as a monolithic Jewry. While a majority of Jews may rally round a specific cause – that of Israel's continued existence being the primary example – differing synagogues bear witness to the absence of a single mind-set, racially bound attitudes, a unitary voting bloc, or dominating innate tendencies. They reveal, moreover, the continuing development of congregational thinking, not a dogmatically inflexible approach to tradition.

Synagogue architecture also testifies to changing social attitudes down the years. In Liverpool, Hope Place Synagogue was designed by Thomas Wylie in 1857 to have a general disposition comparable with that of the Great Synagogue at Manchester, although the Hope Place building had a dome and many different details.[7] By the time the later synagogue in Prince's Road was opened in 1874 to the design of W. and G. Audsley, even people inclined to a safe conservatism in taste had come to appreciate

2.6 Liverpool, Prince's Road Synagogue (W. and G. Audsley, 1874); the minarets have now been removed.

the expressive potential of designs based on a wider range of sources; compare, too, the southern Italian roots of Manchester's Spanish and Portuguese Synagogue. The building in Prince's Road is an original design based on a number of motifs bound together in a dignified Romanesque exterior, adding to the varied religious architectural accents in the neighbourhood. Its interior is more lively; eclectic design elements suggest the exuberance and expansive possibilities of an old faith in a new setting, and show the growth in wealth and confidence of the congregation. This is a building exuding optimism. Its siting is similar to that of nearby churches, demonstrating that neither here nor in Manchester did Jews need to be kept out of sight; it is large and in the style that the congregation and architect chose, not something imitative or reticent. That the interior is more energetic and better endowed than the exterior is not unusual in either church or synagogue design. Minority religions frequently offer politically judicious modesty outside and a sense of communal generosity inside, where the word 'sanctuary' is used in both its meanings. One need not, however, use this building to perpetuate an image of perennially fearful Jews, for it was erected for an increasingly confident and assimilated congregation. The social situation of Jews in Liverpool was to change again in the last decades of the nineteenth century, when a new and poorer Jewish population came to outnumber those who built the synagogues of Hope Place and Prince's Road, and when there arose a new form of racial anti-Semitism imported from the Continent.

Late nineteenth-century synagogues reveal uncertainty about the image that the Jews wished to convey to themselves and others. The Garnethill Synagogue of Glasgow (1879) expresses, by its substantial size and copious ornament, self-confidence and confidence in the future. In detail, however, it is an unclear combination of old and new, eastern and western. Cast-iron supports, symbolic of nineteenth-century industrial progress, rise toward a coffered barrel vault, a relic of Rome and the Renaissance. Ornament from the Graeco-Roman past mingles with Islamic features such as the horseshoe arch at the focal wall, spanning the ark niche. Other synagogues of this period and later seem equally unresolved in design. Should the Jews present themselves as an exotic eastern people rather than as native British? How eastern were Jews, in any case? Should they accept Moorish as a style somehow related to Jewish art and culture? Should each religious sub-group differentiate itself from others, despite any theological points of reconciliation? Whatever the aesthetic failings of synagogues like this one, the building fabric elicits questions that are still pertinent today. English Christians and Jews bereft of all such buildings would lack reminders that these issues, in modified form, are still with us.

Another reason for preserving selected synagogues has to do with the changing face of Britain's urban population. While the Jews perhaps constituted its most conspicuous minority of continental origin up to about 1950, their place in the public eye has now been taken by immigrants from more distant parts of the globe. Distinct traditions may endure among these newcomers, but inevitably there will be more and more aspects of their lives that conform to British norms. It may be that the monuments to the experience of a previous minority group will prove instructive for newer arrivals, and of practical use as well. Just as disused churches were sometimes turned into synagogues, some synagogues have found or will find a new lease of life as mosques or temples of other religions, pending the construction of purpose-built houses of worship which should some day themselves be candidates for historic preservation.

Some Jews are indifferent to architectural beauty, an indifference fostered by centuries of discrimination and enforced reticence. Most Jews give a high priority to communal activities in the social sphere. Besides the traditional emphasis placed on charity, Jewish communities feel obliged to provide for the specific needs of their less fortunate co-religionists, for example the provision of unleavened bread for Passover or kosher emergency food programmes for Jewish disaster victims. Given all these demands on their resources, the maintenance of old buildings in neighbourhoods from which Jews moved long ago is low on the list of worthwhile causes. Nevertheless, money sometimes appears from unlikely sources when a specific appeal touches a susceptible heart. Not all charitable causes arouse equal compassion in everyone, and there may be some who are more concerned with Jewish monuments than with certain acts of charity. To such people, grandfather's *shul* may be of greater interest than the opportunity for a supposedly old-fashioned person to maintain traditional rituals.

New Yorkers, including those with little religious inclination, have recently offered a good deal of financial assistance to two unlikely monuments, and the Jews of Leeds or London might do the same for monuments to their own history. In 1988, an ordinary New York tenement house of no architectural distinction had its lower floor converted into a museum showing the conditions in which immigrants lived, usually for at least a decade after their arrival in America. The museum is not exclusively devoted to the Jewish immigrant experience, but it has attracted important Jewish support. Located on Orchard Street on the Lower East Side, comparable to London's East End, it presents the social and physical aspects of life as experienced by hundreds of thousands of new Americans. People as far removed from Orchard Street as Pinner is from Petticoat Lane now attend presentations, walking tours and guided visits in order to understand their roots within a multi-ethnic society. Not far away on Eldridge Street stands the oldest purpose-built synagogue in the area, and Jews and Christians have joined together to save it from demolition or certain collapse.[8] Fund-raising appeals have ensured its structural stability; tours and public events inform people about aspects of history only lightly touched on in today's crowded school curricula, and present aspects of religion which are not taught in the public schools at all. The participation of Christians in these efforts comes from the understanding that, in the late twentieth century, sectarian isolation and the absence of a measure of mutual interaction are impossible and perhaps dangerous even if possible. It would not be difficult to apply the lessons of this example to British cities as well, although the specifics of each case are bound to differ.

The message about the importance of Jewish monuments is easier to convey today than it used to be. Traditionally, art historians focused on the work of individual geniuses, on the most exquisite, powerful or 'best' examples of art and architecture. Nowadays we understand that even aesthetically inferior works have much to teach us. Our idea of art history has become more socially inclusive, concentrating less on individual great patrons or singular heroes and more on groups and classes. Marxist, feminist, structuralist and other approaches have been used to expand thought and sometimes even appreciation.

We care today about what the common people did, or built, or loved. This may perhaps be seen as anti-elitism, or as simple enlightened self-interest, given that most of us do not come from the upper classes, and the idea of a Jewish elite is almost meaningless to anyone outside the group. Jewish people have a particular reason to embrace this more comprehensive ideal in scholarship, because we had no Michelangelo, no Bernini and, generally, not much money. Nevertheless, the fact that a minority group could render services valuable enough to induce the ruler of Wołpa to put his court builder to work on the Jews' synagogue is significant in the history of eastern Europe, and not for the Jews alone. That the Jews would expend their scarce resources to erect relatively costly and fireproof stone synagogues in poor towns in eastern Europe tells us about their social values, and may inspire our own. That Sir Moses Montefiore went to the trouble and expense of building a small synagogue on his property at Ramsgate raises several questions. He could have designated a room in his house for the purpose of prayer, but noblemen often built private chapels at their country seats; why should Sir Moses not do the same? Was he trying to emulate the English aristocracy in piety or in the demonstration of his aesthetic sensibilities? Did he expect more Jews to move to the south coast? One can hope, with appropriate research, to uncover information about human nature, individuals of importance, the social and economic situation of groups, inter-class relations, and many more topics, from a study of little-known architecture. The greatest and costliest monuments do not tell us about ordinary life or individuals because ordinary people do not commission them and individuals are subordinated to the project's overall needs. Without physical remains, one often cannot even formulate useful and interesting questions. Without such remains, it is hard to imagine any alternatives to current practice.

Architects today are likely to lecture anyone who will listen on the importance of historical precedent. American architects have been among the most avid buyers of books on synagogue architecture, because they need to know something about the building type before accepting commissions for new synagogues. Architects, who tend to be more visual than verbal in their mode of expression and in gathering information, are normally disinclined to plough through descriptions of unillustrated structures in crumbling copies of nineteenth-century professional journals. Since they interpret images quickly, unlike more verbally oriented people, it is inefficient for them to spend long periods of time on archaic prose. As their thinking and their products must be three-dimensional, it is useful to have examples of architecture of many types,

2.7   London, Finchley Synagogue, Kinloss Gardens, N3 (Dowton and Hurst, 1967). *Anthony Harris*

styles, forms and periods. For lack of control specimens, they may make grievous and costly mistakes.

To our children and grandchildren, *our* childhood is a distant phenomenon, and the Holocaust may be too. Children, however, can be introduced to history, with its ability to suggest alternative courses of action, and with its stimulating differences in aesthetics. This is vital given that we now live in a landscape that is increasingly uniform. If one American town after another has a highway 'strip' with the same fast-food outlets and supermarkets, urban walks and 'town trails' must continue to introduce environmental education to American children. If one British town after another has a High Street with virtually identical shops, British children's potential for imagining alternative environments is sharply limited. If all we know of religious and community settings are prefabricated buildings or – to be more imaginative – brick octagons with clerestory windows, we stunt the formation of new ideas for succeeding generations. There is little wrong with inexpensive prefabrication, or with brick octagons, which tend to create unified congregational spaces while avoiding costly curving walls. But we need alternative models in order to develop other ideas for the future. The French phrase *reculer pour mieux sauter* ('one step back, two steps forward') expresses a phenomenon familiar to art historians which is sometimes called the 'grandfather clause'. Often artists of a second generation rebel against the tenets of the first, while artists of a third generation return to and modify ideas of the first, in turn rejecting those of the second. Today's post-modernist designers have done just that, in synagogues as in other projects. Our cultural good health requires models of many kinds, just as society increasingly needs to encourage the talent and participation of all its members, not just of the majority population.

If it is true that 'every tradition is sealed beneath a monument', are we not in danger of losing essentials of British and Jewish tradition if there are hardly any monuments left?

NOTES

1. For a detailed discussion of Bevis Marks and the Great Synagogue, see Epstein, this volume.
2. For Livorno, see C. H. Krinsky, *Synagogues of Europe: Architecture, History, Meaning* (New York and Cambridge, MA, 1985), pp. 352–6; A. Sacerdoti and L. Fiorentino, *Guida al'Italia ebraica* (Casale Monferrato, 1986), pp. 225–30. For Paris, see 'Centro comunitario e sinagoga a Parigi', *Architettura*, Vol. 28 (June 1982), pp. 408–16.
3. S. Kadish, 'Squandered Heritage: Jewish Buildings in Britain' (cited above in note 3 to the Introduction), esp. pp. 148–53.
4. B. Williams, *The Making of Manchester Jewry, 1740–1875* (Manchester and New York, 1976), pp. 153–6; *Jewish Chronicle*, 8 May 1857.
5. For Paris, rue Notre-Dame de Nazareth: D. Jarrassé, *L'âge d'or des synagogues* (Paris, 1991), pp. 70–1. For Germany in general: Hans-Peter Schwartz (ed.), *Die Arkitektur der Synagoge* (Stuttgart, 1988). For Mannheim: H. Hammer-Schenk, *Synagogen in Deutschland. Geschichte einer Baugattung im 19 und 20 Jahrhunderts, 1780–1933* (Hamburg, 1978), pp. 115–18, 305–7. For Berlin, Reform Temple, Johannisstrasse: ibid., pp. 162–3; R. Bothe (ed.), *Synagogen in Berlin. Zur Geschichte einer zerstörten Architektur* (Berlin, 1983), Vol. I, pp. 83–6. For Hamburg, Kohlhofen: H. Hammer-Schenk, *Hamburgs Synagogen des 19 und frühen 20 Jahrhunderts* (Hamburg, 1978), pp. 27–30. For Brno (Brünn): Hammer-Schenk, *Synagogen in Deutschland*, pp. 119–20. For Budapest, Dohány Street: Krinsky, *Synagogues of Europe*, pp. 157–9, 162–3.
6. The use of the Moorish style for synagogues originated in Germany in the 1830s. It was devised for Ashkenazi Jews and had no connection with medieval Spanish Jewish monuments; instead, it was intended to indicate the eastern origin of the Jews. See Hammer-Schenk, *Synagogen in Deutschland*, pp. 259–309.
7. P. Ettinger, *Hope Place in Liverpool Jewry* (Liverpool, 1931).
8. See *Eldridge Street Project News*, published at 83 Canal Street, New York, NY 10002, USA.

3

BUILDING JERUSALEM IN THE 'ISLANDS OF THE SEA':
The Archaeology of Medieval Anglo-Jewry

RAPHAEL M. J. ISSERLIN

The Jews came to England with William I from Normandy in 1066 and were expelled in 1290 by Edward I. Their sojourn largely overlapped with the Crusades (1096–1291). To the Jews, ruled by other, contesting faiths, Jerusalem remained only a fond aspiration. The 'Jerusalem' that they built was thus a metaphysical one, but there was none the less a need to build houses for living and houses for prayer. This chapter looks at some of the physical aspects, as revealed by archaeology, of this distant 'Jerusalem' – the Jewish settlement in Britain, referred to by medieval Jews as the 'Islands of the Sea' (Isaiah 11:11). The excavated evidence, though enigmatic and fragmentary, can be set alongside what we know through more familiar sources.

HISTORY OF RESEARCH

Interest in Jewish antiquities in Europe probably started in 1519, when Andreas Altdorfer drew the interior of the synagogue at Regensburg before its demolition. English interest in Jewish antiquities began in Bristol when Leland noted remains of a 'Temple or Sinagoge' in 1540; in 1586 Stow recorded Hebrew inscriptions in London. In 1888 a more systematic approach related documented Jewish sites in London to the Ordnance Survey map: 'the ground plan, if successfully plotted out, will be the first which has ever been drawn with such claims to accuracy after the lapse of six hundred years without actual excavations',[1] literally putting London Jews 'on the map'. Such achievements, though not without faults (as subsequent research has shown), deserve recognition. A century later, London Jewry's topography and buildings have now been studied archaeologically.[2] The site of the pillaged London cemetery was examined after the Second World War,[3] and the history of the community has recently been reassessed.[4]

The publication in 1927 of Richard Krautheimer's book on medieval European synagogues,[5] which remains essential reading, prompted renewed interest in England. An example is Lincoln's Jewry: Cecil Roth investigated its history and buildings in 1934;[6] the buildings were surveyed in 1935 by Margaret Wood as part of a wider architectural history, and by Helen Rosenau in 1936. The course of events in Europe during the 1930s and 1940s meant that many of the buildings Krautheimer had discussed – and the communities that worshipped in them – were destroyed. Meanwhile, in Palestine, Eliezer Sukenik analysed Graeco-Roman synagogues and in 1934 clarified their origin (though he is probably better remembered as the father of Dead Sea Scrolls research and of the archaeologist Yigael Yadin).[7] Research continues. French, German and Israeli scholars have been active in studying the physical evidence, and British scholars have worked on textual evidence. The interdisciplinary nature of this research is suggested by the title of a volume published in 1980: *Art et Archéologie des Juifs en France*.[8]

SURVIVAL AND NUMBER OF MONUMENTS ABOVE AND BELOW GROUND

After the Second World War some continental buildings were restored as historical monuments. Though the analysis of standing structures had once been possible, research in mainland Europe is now largely restricted to documentary research and archaeological excavation. This also applies to England, where evidence for synagogues does not survive well despite the fact that it was never occupied by the Nazis. A rarity is the synagogue at Lincoln, now occasionally still used for religious functions after 700 years.[9]

There are two main causes for this paucity of material. Between the Expulsion in 1290 and Readmission in 1656, many medieval buildings, Jewish or otherwise, were adapted to other uses. Frequently synagogues were converted into churches (a special mass was said when this process began).[10] One Jewish building, the *Capitolum Judeorum* in Colchester, converted into the Chapel of St Thomas, was *purgatum*, perhaps a stage in this process.[11] Such buildings were frequently remodelled. Each time a church was altered, less and less of the original superstructure would survive, and in the end only foundations would withstand the attentions of architect and builder. Two examples illustrate this law of diminishing returns. Little remains of the medieval fabric of St Stephen's Church, Coleman Street, London, after Wren's restoration. Of the buried synagogue which preceded it, only one thirteenth-century column-base was recovered by archaeologists, enough to suggest that the architectural decoration was 'Early English'. The synagogue at Bristol fared little better. The Church of St Giles, converted into a warehouse, was noted by Leland in 1540. In its vaults were the remains of brick walls, which may be the remains of the synagogue;[12] the use of brick, though suspiciously late, is not impossible, since it was being reintroduced into thirteenth-century England. As we shall see, such vaults ('undercrofts') may have been a feature of such buildings (though not peculiar to Jewish buildings[13]). It is chiefly this buried stuff of cellars and walls with which we have to content ourselves. A recent review of urban excavation commented that no work in a British town 'has yet firmly identified a recognisable synagogue or even its Jewish quarter . . .'.[14]

Medieval Germany's Jewry has been estimated at 20,000; in France, including Provence, the total was slightly higher, and many synagogues survive.[15] If there were fewer Jews in England than in France or Germany, this might explain our lack of evidence, but we must be cautious. England's Jewry numbered perhaps 16,000 souls at most or even as few as 3,000.[16] The biggest community, London, may have comprised a tenth of the Jewish population of Britain, or alternatively more than half, perhaps 1,500–2,000.[17] Fewer Jews may mean fewer buildings, though at least 117 settlements existed, perhaps as many as 200.[18] All told, physical evidence may be scarce at present, because it survived badly and was, until recently, rarely excavated, but fresh work shows that archaeological evidence for medieval Anglo-Jewry can be recognized.

THE CONTRIBUTION OF DOCUMENTS

Documents in Latin and Hebrew locate properties owned or rented by Jews and non-Jews (houses, synagogues and cemeteries). They depict large and small communities, prosperous and poor ones. Valuable modern surveys which make use of such sources cover Norwich, Oxford, Colchester, Cologne and Rouen.[19] Some surveys have been – or can be – linked to archaeological material.

They depict well-recorded beginnings, better-recorded ends, and datable destruction linking whole communities together. For example, devastation occurred in Europe when the First Crusade started (culminating in 1099 in massacre at Jerusalem). Destruction *en route* of Rhenish synagogues in 1096 can be recognized archaeologically at Cologne and Worms (see Table 3.3, p.46). Similarly, a layer of charcoal four inches thick in one part of Norwich's Jewry may relate to the 1290 expulsion from England.[20] No major later fire horizon is recorded in that area of the medieval city.

BASIC FACTORS OF TOPOGRAPHY

To modern minds the terms 'Jewry' and 'ghetto' mean the same thing: an area where Jews were confined. The word 'ghetto' originated in sixteenth-century Venice, well after our period finishes, and scholars have doubted whether such a phenomenon existed in England before then. In Hereford, however, palisades excavated around the Jewish quarter may be part of an enclosure wall.[21] Surveys show that parts of towns where Jews lived were predominantly but not exclusively Jewish. In London, Jewish *responsa* refer to 'street of the Jews' (*rehov hayehudim*[22]): the English street-name 'Jewry' survives today. Jewish moneylenders and merchants could not always live where they wished. A king might have them live near the centre of commerce to stimulate trade, such as the market. They might choose to live near that source of protection and patronage, the royal castle.[23]

The location of Jews in any one part of town was affected by several needs. One factor was paramount: access to flowing water, such as a spring or stream, to feed the *mikveh*. That Oxford's synagogue lay near the Trill Mill stream, its course now known through excavation, may be significant, as may the location of at least one Jewish house close to the River Walbrook in London. Another need was to remain within walking distance of the synagogue. At Norwich, most people lived within 100 yards of it, and 17 out of 25 Jewish families within 250 yards.[24] This may reflect the need to band together for mutual protection, or an attempt to respect the Sabbath.

THE EVIDENCE OF FINDS

Identifying Jews from archaeological evidence is an exciting possibility. Some Hebrew inscriptions supposedly identifying Jewish buildings are discussed below. But finds other than inscriptions can give to anonymous buildings a Jewish context that might not otherwise be recognized if documentary evidence is meagre or lacking. Whether an interpretation is correct needs careful deliberation.

But what makes finds 'Jewish'? Convincing ones are rare. Some domestic and ceremonial objects would travel with their owners. A *mezuza* fixed to a doorpost would indicate Jewish occupancy, but in England most buildings connected with Jews survive (if at all) only as foundations (a *mezuza* is depicted in a fifteenth-century Italian illustration[25]). Most such 'medieval' material that we possess is unprovenanced: a *shofar* found at Leadenhall Market is not particularly close to the London Jewry;[26] a seal, signifying that a commodity (probably wine) was kosher, cannot be linked with any community.[27]

The examination of debris from rubbish-pits has been used with success to demonstrate food-consumption patterns in post-medieval Amsterdam. Jewish households were inferred from a lack of pig-bones.[28] Scrutiny of such rubbish may enhance our understanding of the history of Jewish cuisine. It has been suggested that the custom of keeping poultry fated for the proverbial chicken soup originated in the backyards of medieval central Europe, and that the cookery of medieval Anglo-Jewry bore strong similarities to that of their French and Italian counterparts.[29] More pertinently, one may be able to demonstrate that Jewish households in England too abstained from unclean food, implying strict religious observance (medieval commentators suggest that in London *kashrut* was generally observed).[30] In order to draw such conclusions, samples need to be dated accurately and must be free from contamination. Material could be churned up from earlier levels when pits were dug in the yard. For example, oystershells were found in pits at one documented Jewish site (Gresham Street, London) – a puzzling state of affairs since oysters, like pork, are forbidden food, and the documentation is not in doubt. The date of these shellfish is unclear, however, and they could have been churned up from Roman layers. Bones of chicken and permitted fish, were not immediately visible, though German and French Jews consumed these, along with stews, on Friday nights and festivals at least. More research is needed before conclusions can be drawn here. However, seeds from the cess-pit of a Jewish household in Milk Street

represent not only the standard fruit salad of a well-to-do medieval
London town-house (plums, cherries, blackberries, raspberries, straw-
berries, apples and pears), but the more exotic: grapes, figs and mulberries.
Such fruits would not ripen readily in England and must have been
imported dried, or in jams, figs implying Mediterranean connections.
The cuisine of this household may have been Sephardi, for figs (and
other fruit) were consumed at New Year by Provençal Jews. Pies, rissoles
and noodles(!) formed more normal Anglo-Jewish fare. As regards
grapes, it is well to remember that vineyards in nearby Champagne were
owned by the great commentator, Rashi.

Other approaches may be useful. Because Jews were introduced for
economic and monetary reasons, archaeological evidence for financial
activity may demonstrate their presence. It is common knowledge that
they lent money, on items or properties taken as security, deeds being
taken as pledges and cleft tally-sticks (*starrs*) recording loans (and stored
in the communal chest). But not always: the Milk Street cess-pit yielded
a seal-matrix, a *starr*, and a set of eight wooden bowls, two knives and the
remains of a linen garment. The seal could be from the deed of a property
taken as security, and the tableware and other items similarly pledged.
Working-capital is represented archaeologically, too. Mapping coin-
hoards helped locate Cologne's Jewish quarter;[31] small hoards were
found in the backyards of houses near the synagogue and *mikveh* (which
have been excavated), reinforcing evidence for Jewish occupancy
around the Judengasse (Jews' Lane) to a remarkable degree. They contain coin from Florence (Figure 3.1(a)).

At Colchester a similar situation obtains. Documents of 1293 list six
Jewish houses, one vacant land-lot and a synagogue. The community
may have been larger at one time, shrinking before the Expulsion.
Documents do not always locate such buildings precisely, but seven
Norman stone houses (often associated with Jews) have been located by
archaeological excavation, by architectural survey and in antiquarian
records.[32] Further, two coin-hoards were found, so large that they are
unlikely to have belonged to any other community. They can be mapped
in 'blank' spots next to the High Street or market, where documents
vaguely locate Jewish houses (Figure 3.1(b)). They include Irish, Scottish
and foreign coin. English Jews lent money to Scottish kings.[33]

One hoard consisted of 12,000 silver pennies, buried *c.* 1248; another
of 14,065 silver coins, deposited in 1256.[34] These numismatic dates for
hoard-closure relate to documented years of economic stress for the
Jewish community,[35] reason enough to bury savings worth £50 and
£58 5s. 5d. respectively.

This brings the number of archaeological sites to nine, eight being
listed in the post-Expulsion documents. The evidence correlates well: it
may be possible to identify Jews from coin-hoards and stone buildings,
and to infer that the community was originally larger. The overlap
between differing sorts of evidence may not, however, be total.

Some evidence remains at best ambivalent. Excavations at Flaxengate,
Lincoln, revealed twelfth- and thirteenth-century stone houses like
those still standing at Jews' Court and Jew's House – sites with known

3.1   Jewish settlement at (a) Cologne
(opposite) and (b) Colchester
(overleaf); buildings of Jewish interest
are shown shaded; coin-hoards mark
likely domestic sites. *Drawings in this chapter by
I. Bell and N. Nethercoat*

3.1 (a) Cologne

Judengasse

① Synagogue

② Mikveh

③ Rathaus

● = Coin-hoards

20m

0

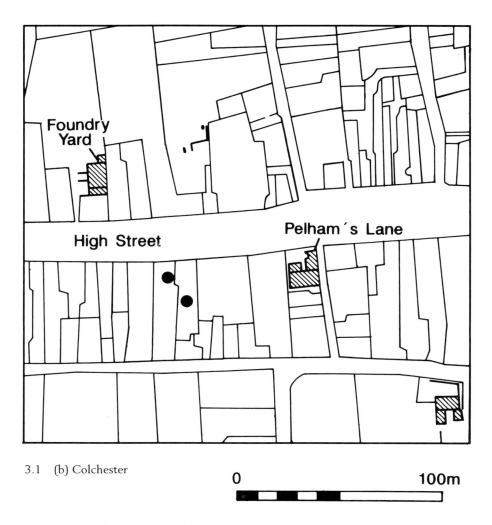

3.1   (b) Colchester

0   100m

● = Coin-hoards

Jewish connections (Figures 3.2, 3.3). Documents suggest that properties adjoining the buildings excavated were owned or inhabited by Jews, and indeed properties were often held *en bloc* by Jews. Nevertheless, documents are silent as to the ownership of the excavated properties.[36] However, pig-bones abounded (even in the twelfth and thirteenth centuries[37]), which is probably significant. If Jews actually lived on these premises (and it is by no means certain that they did), it may have been for so short a time that the fact that they refrained from eating unclean meat would not show up in the melange of excavated food-remains (unless they – or their non-Jewish servants – actually *ate* pork!). Perhaps the site was rented out to non-Jewish tenants – a frequent practice – and they kept the pigs.

Not all Jews were rich or lived in stone houses. Nor were all those people who lived in stone houses, or were rich, Jews. Some were definitely not. One cannot argue confidently from negative evidence. No coin-hoards have been found in the London Jewry, though its location is certain. This may reflect the well-documented poverty to which it was reduced in the years before the Expulsion. The absence of coin-hoards may mean no money, not no Jews. In London, the distribution of other categories of commerce-related artifacts (counters, scales and lead tokens) from domestic sites has been studied.[38] The particularly high quantity of these (together with what are thought to be ritual lamps) is, it seems, statistically significant in indicating Jews. Indeed, several lamps come from the area known as 'Poor Jewry'.

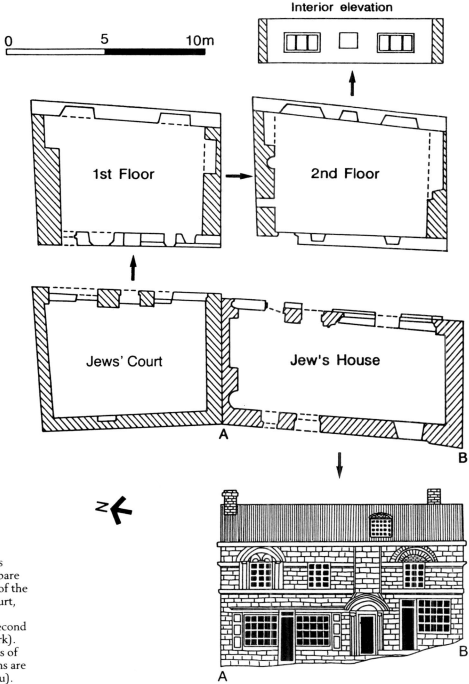

3.2   Standing Jewish buildings at Lincoln: Jews' Court and the Jew's House, at ground floor level (compare Figure 3.3). Also shown are plans of the first and second floors of Jews' Court, together with the elevation of the frontage and the east wall of the second floor (note central niche for the Ark). Shaded areas are surviving portions of the original building; later additions are excluded (after Wood and Rosenau).

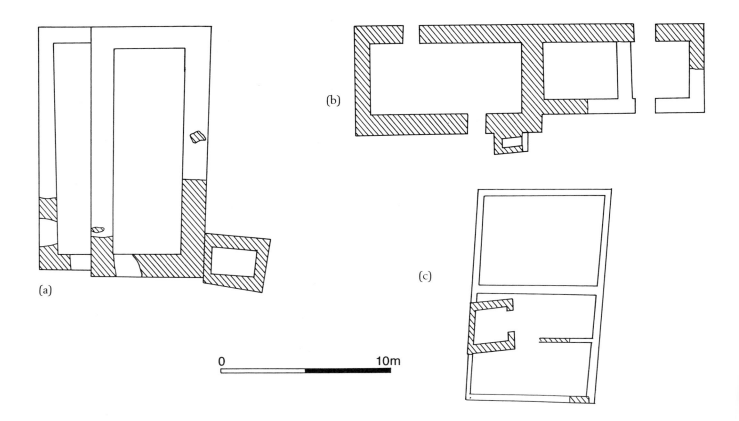

(a)

(b)

(c)

0   10m

3.3   Foundations of Jewish or possibly Jewish buildings revealed by excavation at (a) Gresham Street, London – with what may have been a *mikveh* to rear (after Museum of London); (b) Flaxengate, Lincoln (after Lincoln Archaeological Trust); (c) St Peter's Street, Bristol – note the cellar (after Boore, amended by the author). Shaded areas are surviving portions of the original building; later additions are excluded.

THE EVIDENCE OF INSCRIPTIONS

However, excavated evidence cannot be pressed too closely. Even that most diagnostic of evidence, the Hebrew inscription, has deceived scholars. Stow recorded stones with Hebrew inscriptions incorporated into standing buildings and argued that they originally derived from Jewish houses, which medieval sources mention were demolished. But other medieval sources mention pillaging of the London cemetery (which excavation confirms[39]), and analysis of these inscriptions shows that they were tombstones. One modern survey perpetuates Stow's misinterpretation.[40] This begs a different question – whether there were many Hebrew inscriptions on buildings in England. In medieval France, inscriptions were usually located only above doorways of communal structures such as synagogues, rather than on private houses.[41] Such material rarely survives demolition. One uncommon survival is at the entrance to the Bristol *mikveh* (see Chapter 6 in this volume). Another example of a surviving inscription is on a tombstone from the Northampton cemetery, recently rediscovered in a museum basement after having been 'lost' for over a century![42]

JEWS AND 'JEWS' HOUSES'

The term 'Jew's House' refers to stone buildings of some antiquity and uncertain pedigree.[43] Accurate use of the term depends on documentary proof; accounts of massacres in London and York accentuate the solidity of Jewish houses, implying stone.[44] No late twelfth- or early thirteenth-century stone houses survive at Stamford, though there was in fact a community there. Still (for what it is worth) the façade of one Stamford building (now demolished, but recorded by Samuel Buckler in 1810[45]) was virtually identical with the Jew's House at Lincoln. Documents which would identify the owner do not survive.[46] There is certainly a strong link between Jews and Norman town houses of stone, even so. Lipman's unsurpassed 1967 survey of Norwich,[47] confined to standing buildings and documents, was written before the dramatic growth in urban excavation. A review of the subject should take this newly acquired knowledge into account, reading sense into stubs of wall.

In the late twelfth century, fashionable houses in Lincoln, Southampton, Canterbury and York were no longer being built of timber but of stone. This may reflect growing economic prosperity, as trade and industry revived; many town walls were built at this time. Such houses reflected personal prestige and riches, becoming local landmarks.[48] They highlighted the social stratum which Jews occupied, along with wealthy merchants. Documents describe their vanished rooms and architectural detail: above-ground archaeology.

TABLE 3.1
JEWS' HOUSES MENTIONED IN RENTALS[49]

Town	Rental Value	Date of document	Features noted
Gloucester	13s. 4d.	1253	Hall, chamber, kitchen; of timber; tiled roof
Hereford	20s.	1290	With shop
Lincoln	30s.	1290	With two shops; fair doorway
London	£5	1290	Of stone; with solar

It is to Lincoln that one inevitably turns, as structures survive best there. Though (as hinted earlier) Roth in particular was responsible for putting the buildings into their mainstream religious and social context, their peculiar history has by no means always been recognized, as Hill has observed.[50] They were recorded in 1810 as parts of an English townscape by the artist Samuel Buckler, who remarked upon their antiquity, not their ancestry.[51] The 'Jew's House' (built *c.* 1170–80) probably exemplified the type: thick (2 foot 8 inches) stone walls; an elaborate front doorway, leading to a central passage flanked by shops; stairs leading to the first-floor hall, perhaps via an adjoining rear kitchen[52] (elsewhere in Lincoln the kitchen was a separate building[53]). Next door was 'Jews' Court', possibly a synagogue: stone, much altered, and probably of similar plan. A niche above original floor level in the east wall of the second floor may have been an ark (*Aron*),[54] though authorities disagree as to whether or not the wall is original (Figure 3.2). Another house-synagogue is documented in London.[55] One suspects that the private oratory may have been more common than previously supposed.

After the twelfth century, the decrease in the building of stone houses js notable. One commentator links the short-lived burst of stone building with town liberties no longer being issued.[56] Another links the decline with the Jews' fall from favour.[57] Both explanations reflect the root cause: thirteenth-century economic decline made new houses expensive to build, and became a reason to expel Jews.

Colchester has been referred to in connection with mapping evidence to locate Jewish properties. A more promising example may be Canterbury. Survey has pinpointed over 30 stone houses, of varying size, standing by the early thirteenth century;[58] Platt has specifically not related this large number to Jews.[59] However, there may have been at least 20 Jewish houses, mostly spread along the High Street, some stone.[60] There has been little excavation along the High Street, but twelfth-century stone cellars survive elsewhere in Canterbury,[61] which may augur well for the survival of the Jewish quarter there.

Some of the best evidence comes from London. Analysis of the distribution of certain types of finds has been discussed above. Another type of find reinforces the connection between Jews and stone buildings: the louvre (chimney-pot), which was probably common in stone buildings.[62] Many excavated in London come from sites with Jewish connections.[63] In 1189 a rioter burnt the thatched roof of a Jew's house, causing general conflagration.[64] More unusual information comes from Rabbinic *responsa*. In summer the town's Jews would spend the Sabbath on the roofs of their houses in specially erected canvas tents, where they would receive their visitors,[65] so some roofs were probably flat! At Gresham Street, the foundations of a stone house were excavated: Jewish ownership can be directly proven by documents (Figure 3.3). Its narrow gable-end formed the front wall. The range of rooms ran back from the main street. This site may turn out to have been particularly important for the London community, since documents also locate a synagogue at or near the property. However, the phraseology used makes it unclear whether it was situated in the yard behind the house or on a (vanished) upper floor of the structure excavated (as at Jews' Court, Lincoln). Often synagogues were prudently located in courtyards to the rear of private houses. At Canterbury a synagogue flanked the back wall of the house of Jacob; at Norwich it was situated behind a tenement; at Winchester within the courtyard; at Oxford in the backlands.[66] Further excavation to the rear of the building (underway at the time of writing) may yet help solve this riddle. A stone-lined pit at Gresham Street has been interpreted as a *mikveh* or a strong-room. Full publication is awaited.

Documents have located many tenements and houses in Bristol's Jewry, though commentators wonder if they were built of stone.[67] Some certainly were. Excavation at St Peter's Street revealed the rear portion of a building approximately seven metres square (modern cellars removed the front portion) (Figure 3.3). It was floored with sandstone slabs and divided into two rooms by a timber screen. A small cellar in the rearmost corner of the back-room was filled with debris, and there were indications of burning nearby. The limestone walls of the cellar included a stone cresset lamp of twelfth-century type, reused in its construction. The excavator, aided by documents, concluded that this was a Jew's house.[68]

If so (and the presence of lamps in London were regarded as significant), then one might relate the burning to the riots of 1275. A reason behind the London Building Assize of 1189 was the use of stone in buildings as fire-proofing. More tantalizingly, the cellar might have served as a strong-room for wealth, containing a chest. Documentary references to chests are known: the communal chest or *archa* containing records of loans was more usually placed in a cathedral.[69]

COMMUNAL BUILDINGS: THE HEART OF THE COMMUNITY

We know little about the appearance of medieval Anglo-Jewish communal buildings, although we do know how much synagogues cost to maintain (Table 3.2). The values of synagogues could be far less than the rentals of private houses (which could be opulent: see Table 3.1 above), at Hereford only a fifth (and that included a shop). This may imply that many were of timber.[70] Oxford's was probably of stone; two in London definitely were (remains of one were mentioned earlier). Documents suggest that murals at one (lost) London synagogue were 'of great magnificence'.[71] Resources and ambition dictated what could be done; scruples about whether artwork constituted graven images were overcome. The Ashkenazi communities on the Continent serve as an example of what we yet lack and as a yardstick by which to judge the vanished architecture of medieval Anglo-Jewry. There, lavish communal buildings went up. In Cologne, synagogue windows featured serpents and lions in stained glass, and such decoration gave rise to religious concern.[72] England's best synagogues may have borne artistic comparison with its neighbours, perhaps decorated by the semi-mythical 'Marlibrun of Billingsgate'.[73] Here, as with so much else, we lack absolute proof.

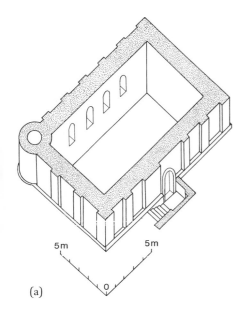

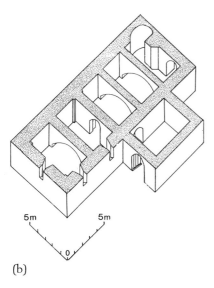

3.4 Jewish buildings at (a) Rouen (the synagogue/*yeshiva*) and (b) Norwich (Music House) reveal a similarity of plan; both may have had a religious function.

TABLE 3.2
SYNAGOGUE RENTALS[74]

Town	Value p.a.
Bristol	3s.
Nottingham	3s. 11d.
Hereford	4s.
Norwich	5s.
Colchester	7s.
Canterbury	11s. 8d.
Oxford	18s. 9d.

In Rouen, whence England's first Jews came to London, a synagogue or a religious academy (*yeshiva*) survives.[75] If this structure (Figure 3.4) is indeed an academy-cum-library (Golb has argued that the plan is similar to the layout of a monastic *scriptorium*), then it is probably where many illuminated manuscripts were produced – and possibly music scores too, such as the work of the twelfth-century Obadiah the Proselyte from Normandy.[76] With this in mind, one can perhaps wonder at the so-called 'Music House' in Norwich, built *c.* 1175, for which a Jewish connection is documented[77] (Roth[78] suggests 'Music' as a corruption of 'Moses'). Perhaps this too was a *yeshiva/scriptorium* rather than a domestic dwelling. The ground-plans are not dissimilar (Figure 3.4).

At Cologne the synagogue, its courtyard and the *mikveh* have been excavated.[79] The synagogue was rebuilt four times (Table 3.3), each time reusing the same site: the Fourth Lateran Council (1215) forbade the building of new synagogues.[80] There was no scope for new wings or side-annexes, as in a church. The floor level was slightly below ground, so that prayers might rise 'out of the depths' (Psalm 130:1). As the ground level rose, and the same wall-lines were maintained, the effect would be accentuated.

TABLE 3.3
PHASING OF MEDIEVAL GERMAN SYNAGOGUES[81]

COLOGNE SYNAGOGUE

Period	Dates	Activities and causes of change
1	*c.* 1000–96	In use; damaged in First Crusade; rebuilt
2	1096–*c.* 1280	Remodelled and in use
3	1280–1349	In use; Jews expelled (readmitted 1372)
4	1372–1426	In use; converted to chapel

WORMS SYNAGOGUE

Period	Dates	Activities and causes of change
1	*c.* 1034–96	In use; damaged in First Crusade; rebuilt
2	1096–1146	In use; damaged in riots; repaired
3	1146–74	In use; damaged in riots; repaired and in use
4	1174/5–1212	Totally rebuilt and in use
5	1212/13–1348	Women's section added and in use
6	1348–55	In use; Black Death; damage; expulsion
7	1355–1620	Readmission; reconstruction and in use

Period 2 of the Cologne building (Figure 3.5a) is particularly pertinent to any understanding of English counterparts: it was to Cologne that the pillaged scrolls and books of the York community were taken for sale in 1190 after their owners had been massacred at Clifford's Tower.[82] The focal point was an ark (*Aron*), housing the Scrolls of the Law, located against the east wall. Benches lined the walls and colonnades ran on either side of the building. A northern wing was probably a separate synagogue for women, as at Worms. In the centre was a *bima* (reading desk), with a cellar underneath – a *geniza* (repository for damaged sacred objects such as the York manuscripts), in which were stored ornate column capitals, detail from the Period 1 building, carved by the same masons who made capitals for Cologne Cathedral.[83] This cellar was, in effect, a small undercroft. In Period 4 the main building was divided into two by a wall running east–west, towards the ark (Figure 3.5b). This makes best sense as low walling to support a *mechitza*, ensuring that traditional proprieties were still observed. It is one of the earliest medieval examples.

The houses at Colchester were discussed earlier. An extramural build-

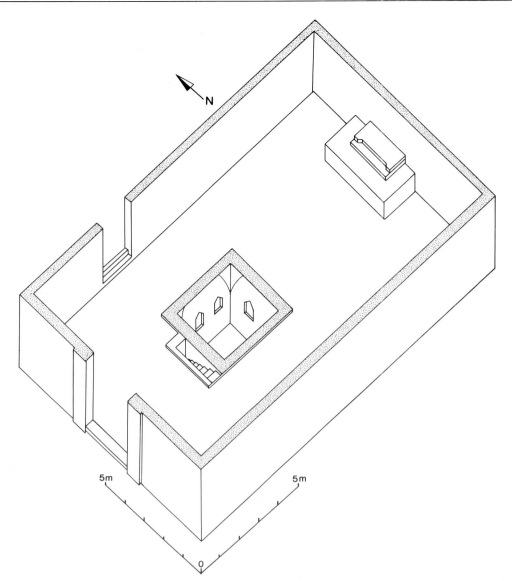

(a)

5m

5m

0

3.5   (a) Cologne Synagogue, excavated (Period 2) – note the central *bima* and the steps down to a cellar beneath it, the foundations for steps up to the Ark at the east end, and the steps down to floor level.

ing (*Capitolum Judeorum/Beth Din* = courthouse[84]) remains a puzzle. Where was the synagogue? It may have been either the enigmatic Foundry Yard structure (recorded before demolition at the turn of the nineteenth century) or the building at Lion Walk. If the synagogue was, as seems most likely, at Foundry Yard, then it was almost the last such purpose-built building to survive above ground in England (Figure 3.6). There is little to distinguish it from an ordinary semi-sunken undercroft, with a hall over, sited to the rear of the tenement. An artist, Mary Benham, recorded a series of three niches, well above ground level, in the eastern wall of the undercroft.[85] The central one seems to be original, while the other two (with detail picked out in brick; compare Bristol, described above) may perhaps be later inserts. Position and siting are consistent with requirements for a simple ark housing the Scrolls of the Law (*Aron*) above the level of the floor. The building was located in a typical position for a synagogue, to the rear of the tenement, out of harm's way. On the other hand, without diagnostic above-ground

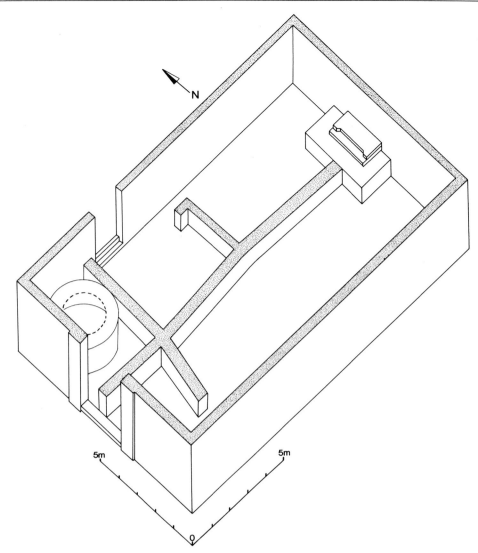

3.5   (b) Cologne Synagogue, excavated (Period 4) – note the central partition (after Doppelfeld).

evidence, one might have to compare the ground-plan with that of a better-known example. In that case, the position of two central piers might suggest the Lion Walk building as a suitable candidate.[86] Central piers are sometimes a synagogue feature, as at Regensburg and Worms; here, however, the east wall with its diagnostic niche for an ark is missing.

Undercrofts may indeed have been a widespread feature of English synagogues, either serving as *genizot* or designed to take the concept of prayer 'from the depths' to great lengths. One possible example from Bristol was referred to earlier. Tantalizing evidence from Canterbury is the '*stone parlour mounted upon a vault and ascended by many stone steps, as the Jewish Synagogues and schools were always built aloft. This was the remaines of a good part of that which was our Canterbury Jewes School or Synagogue*',[87] transformed into part of the County Hotel (demolished in 1927). Its walls were notably thick.

Building a *mikveh* was a *sine qua non*. Access to a certain amount of *living* (that is, free-flowing) water was crucial, although rainwater could

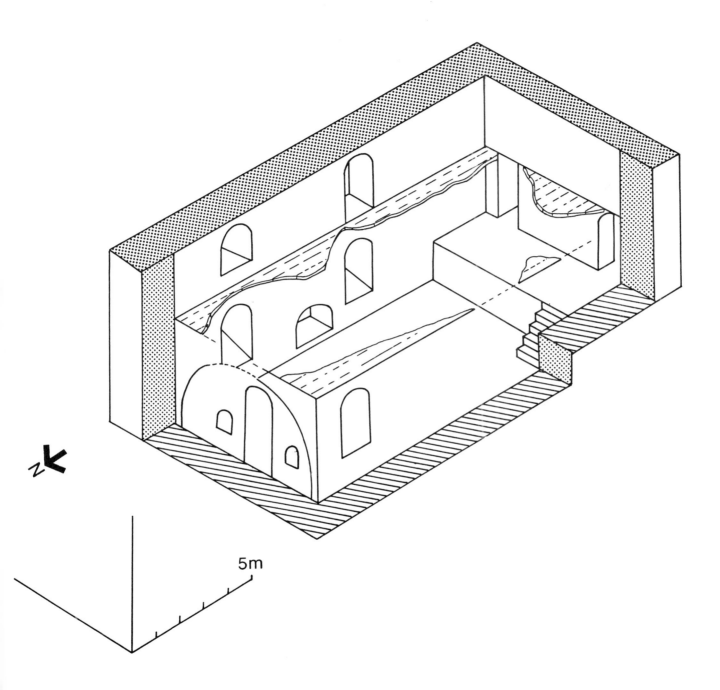

3.6   The Foundry Yard structure at Colchester – note the niches in the east wall, possibly a recess for an Ark (after Crummy).

be used.[88] Reaching a suitable supply could require extraordinary effort, with deep, stone-lined shafts being dug. These could be ornate, as at Cologne or Speyer. In Bristol, adaptation of existing resources sufficed, as there was a ready water-supply in a cave at Jacob's Well. The cave-mouth was suitably embellished with a massive square-headed doorway. Above the lintel was carved the inscription referred to earlier ([*mayim*] *zokhlin* = flowing [water]).[89] A short tunnel with recesses at its sides led down to the water, a layout similar to that at Speyer.

REFORGING THE LINKS

We return to what the concept of 'building Jerusalem' meant to small Jewish communities in distant England. A stray find, the thirteenth-century 'Bodleian Bowl' from Norfolk, probably of French manufacture, has a Hebrew inscription. The likeliest reading is:

> This is the gift of Joseph, the son of the holy Rabbi Yehiel, may the memory of the holy righteous be for a blessing, who answered and asked the congregation as he desired in order to see the face of Ariel as it is written in the Law of Jekuthiel 'and righteousness delivers from death'.

Rabbi Joseph, the son of Rabbi Yehiel, is known from documents in 1258 in connection with property at Stockwell Street in Colchester, and in 1260 he went to Palestine with his father to found a *yeshiva* in Acre. It has been suggested that the purpose of the bowl was to gather funds for that foundation; 'Ariel' implied Jerusalem, 'Jekuthiel', Moses. Whether originally from Norwich[90] or from Colchester,[91] this bowl indicates fond aspirations indeed.

CONCLUSIONS

Houses for living; houses for prayer; houses for living *and* for prayer – all these existed, and some possible examples have been discussed. In one way or another, this is as near to recovering the past of medieval Anglo-Jewry as it is possible to get. Documents, excavated remains, and 'above-ground archaeology' reveal the desire of the Jews to legitimize their presence through the use of the same basic architectural styles as their Christian counterparts – and to remain *à la mode*, by using the very latest styles. Who erected these buildings is not always clear: Jewish builders are known in Europe.[92] In the cases of Rouen and Cologne, however, such work was carried out, it has been suggested, by the same hands that created the cathedrals[93] – and it would not have come cheap.

NOTES

This chapter derives in part from a lecture given to the Archaeology of Medieval Europe conference at York University in 1992. It is a pleasure to acknowledge the assistance of: N. Nethercoat for help with illustrations; J. Bryant of Bristol City Museums; T. Dyson, M. Burch and C. Maloney of the Museum of London; R. Stone of the City of Hereford Archaeological Unit; B. Durham of the Oxford Archaeological Unit; J. Willford of the City of Lincoln Archaeological Unit; B. Ayers of Norwich City Museums; and C. Orton of the Institute of Archaeology, University of London. Though space means that not all the information that they supplied could be used, my debt to them is nevertheless immense, for they produced it at less than a moment's notice. Thanks also go to Dr S. Kadish, to C. R. Wallace and above all to my parents, Dr and Mrs B. S. J. Isserlin, for their support and criticism. Errors are mine alone.

1. J. Jacobs, 'The London Jewry, 1290', *Papers read at the Anglo-Jewish Historical Exhibition, Royal Albert Hall, London, Publications of the Anglo-Jewish Historical Exhibition No. 1* (London, 1888), p. 20, on London.
2. G. Pepper, 'An archaeology of the Jewry in medieval London', *The London Archaeologist*, 1992.

3. W. F. Grimes, *The Excavation of Roman and Medieval London* (London, 1968), pp. 180–1. For the cemetery at York, see J. M. Lilley *et al.*, *The Jewish Burial Ground at Jewbury*, The Archaeology of York, 12/3, The Medieval Cemeteries (York, 1994).

4. J. Hillaby, 'The Thirteenth-century Jewry Revisited', *Transactions of the Jewish Historical Society of England (TJHSE)*, XXXII (1993), pp. 89–158.

5. R. Krautheimer, *Mittelalterliche Synagogen* (Berlin, 1927).

6. C. Roth, *Medieval Lincoln Jewry and its Synagogue* (London, 1934).

7. E. L. Sukenik, *Ancient Synagogues in Palestine and Greece* (Schweich Lectures of the British Academy, 1930: London, 1934).

8. B. Blumenkranz (ed.), *Art et Archéologie des Juifs en France médiévale* (Collection Franco-Judaica 9, Toulouse, 1980).

9. J. T. Willford, 'Shiddukhim – Tenna'im at Jews' Court', *Lincolnshire Past and Present*, 7 (Spring 1992), pp. 5–6.

10. C. H. Krinsky, *Synagogues of Europe: Architecture, History, Meaning* (New York and Cambridge, MA, 1985), p. 17.

11. D. Stephenson, 'Colchester: A Smaller Medieval English Jewry', *Essex Archaeology and History*, 16 (3rd Series, 1984–85), pp. 48–52, at p. 50.

12. M. Adler, 'The Jews of Bristol in Pre-expulsion Days' *TJHSE*, XXII (1928–31), pp. 117–86, at p. 122.

13. P. A. Faulkner, 'Medieval undercrofts and town houses', *Archaeological Journal*, 123 (1966), pp. 120–35.

14. D. M. Palliser, 'The Medieval Period', in J. Schofield and R. Leech (eds), *Britain, Council for British Archaeology Research Report No. 61* (London, 1985), pp. 54–68, at p. 62.

15. A. Grossman, 'The Jews in Byzantium and Medieval Europe', in E. Kedourie (ed.), *Jewish World: Revelation, Prophecy and History* (London, 1979), pp. 168–77, at p. 168; Blumenkranz, op. cit., pp. 57–62.

16. C. Roth, *A History of the Jews in England* (Oxford, 1964), pp. 91, 276.

17. Jacobs, op. cit., p. 39.

18. Roth, *History of the Jews in England*, pp. 277, 282.

19. V. D. Lipman, *The Jews of Medieval Norwich* (London, 1967); C. Roth, 'The Jews of Medieval Oxford', *Oxford Historical Society*, New Series 9 (1951); Stephenson, op. cit.; Z. Asaria (ed.), *Die Juden in Köln von den ältesten Zeiten bis zur Gegenwart* (Cologne, 1959); Blumenkranz, op. cit.

20. Lipman, op. cit., pp. 123, 176.

21. Thomas, forthcoming.

22. I. Epstein, 'Pre-expulsion England in the responsa', *TJHSE*, XIV (1935–39), pp. 187–205, at p. 204.

23. V. D. Lipman, 'Jews and castles in medieval England', *TJHSE*, XXVII (1981–82), pp. 1–20, at p. 15.

24. Lipman, *Jews of Medieval Norwich*, p. 136; see also G. Nahon, 'Quartiers juifs et rues des Juifs', in Blumenkranz (ed.), op. cit., pp. 15–33.

25. Israel Museum, Rothschild Miscellany: MS. 180/51, fol. 126v.

26. Victoria and Albert Museum, *Catalogue of an Exhibition of Anglo-Jewish Art and History in Commemoration of the Tercentenary of the Resettlement of the Jews in the British Isles* (London, 1956), p. 12.

27. C. Roth, 'A medieval Anglo-Jewish Seal?', *TJHSE*, XVII (1953), pp. 283–6.

28. F. G. Izjereef, 'Social Differentiation from Animal Bone Studies', in D. Sarjeantson and T. Waldren (eds), *Diet and Craft in Towns, British Archaeological Reports*, 199 (Oxford, 1989), pp. 41–53.

29. O. Schwarz, *In Search of Plenty: A History of Jewish Food* (London, 1992), pp. 97–8.

30. Epstein, op. cit., p. 204; J. Cooper, *Eat and Be Satisfied: A Social History of Jewish Food* (New Jersey and London, 1993), pp. 80–3, 97, 106, 109, 112; Davis in J. Schofield, P. Allen and C. Taylor, 'Medieval buildings and property development in the area of Cheapside', *Transactions of the London and Middlesex Archaeological Society*, 41 (1990), p. 231; C. Pearl, *Rashi* (London, 1981).

31. J. Schofield *et al.*, op. cit., p. 176; Asaria, op. cit.

32. P. Crummy (ed.), 'Aspects of Anglo-Saxon and Norman Colchester', *Colchester Archaeological Reports*, 1, Council for British Archaeology, Research Report 39 (Colchester, 1981), pp. 69–70.

33. Roth, *History of the Jews in England*, p. 92.

34. N. Crummy (ed.), 'The Coins from Excavations in Colchester 1971–9', *Colchester Archaeological Reports*, 4 (Colchester, 1987), pp. 70–1.

35. Stephenson, op. cit., p. 50.

36. M. K. Jones, 'Medieval Houses at Flaxengate, Lincoln', *The Archaeology of Lincoln*, Vol. 11, No. 1 (London, 1980), p. 4.

37. T. O'Connor, 'Animal Bones from Flaxengate, Lincoln, *c.* 870–1500', *The Archaeology of Lincoln*, Vol. 17, No. 1 (London, 1982), pp. 11, 47.

38. Pepper, op. cit.

39. M. B. Honeybourne, 'The Pre-Expulsion Cemetery of the Jews in London', *TJHSE*, XX (1959–61), pp. 145–59, at pp. 153–4.

40. J. Schofield, *The Building of London from the Conquest to the Great Fire* (London, 1984), p. 157.

41. G. Nahon, 'L'épigraphie', in Blumenkranz (ed.), op. cit., pp. 95–132.

42. M. Roberts, 'A Northampton Jewish Tombstone, *c.* 1259 to 1290, Recently Rediscovered in Northampton Central Museum', *Medieval Archaeology*, 36 (1992), pp. 173–8.

43. C. Roth, 'Jews' Houses', *Antiquity*, 25 (1951), pp. 66–9.

44. Roth, *History of the Jews in England*, p. 11.

45. British Library, Add. MS. 24434, fols. 80, 81.

46. A. Rogers, *The Medieval Buildings of Stamford* (London, 1970).

47. Lipman, *The Jews of Medieval Norwich*, op. cit.

48. C. Platt, *Medieval England* (London, 1979), pp. 71–2; idem, *The English Medieval Town* (London, 1976), pp. 34–5.

49. Sources: Lipman, *Jews of Medieval Norwich*, pp. 23–4; E. R. Samuel, 'Was Moyse's Hall, Bury St Edmunds, A Jews House?', *TJHSE*, XXV (1973–75), pp. 43–7, at p. 44.

50. J. W. F. Hill, *Medieval Lincoln* (Lincoln, 1948).

51. British Library, Add. MS. 24434, fols. 90, 91.

52. M. E. Wood, 'Norman Domestic Architecture', *Archaeological Journal*, 92 (1935), pp. 167–242, at pp. 195–6.

53. Lipman, *Jews of Medieval Norwich*, p. 26.

54. H. Rosenau, 'Note on the Relationship of Jews' Court and the Lincoln Synagogue', *Archaeological Journal*, 93 (1936), pt 1, pp. 51–6.

55. Roth, *History of the Jews in England*, p. 77.

56. Platt, *Medieval England*, p. 72.

57. Crummy (ed.), 'Anglo-Saxon and Norman Colchester', p. 69.

58. W. Urry, *Canterbury under the Angevin Kings* (London, 1967), pp. 193–4.

59. Platt, *Medieval England*, p. 71.

60. M. Adler, 'The Jews of Canterbury', *TJHSE*, VII (1911–14), pp. 19–96, at p. 22; idem, *Jews of Medieval England* (London, 1939), at p. 69.

61. S. S. Frere and P. Bennett, *The Archaeology of Canterbury, Volume VIII. Canterbury Excavations: Intra- and Extra-mural sites, 1949–55 and 1980–84* (Canterbury, 1987), pp. 106–8.

62. M. E. Wood, *The English Medieval House* (London, 1965), pp. 281–2.

63. Pepper, op. cit.

64. Roth, *History of the Jews in England*, p. 191.

65. Epstein, op. cit., p. 204.

66. J. Hillaby, 'The Worcester Jewry, 1158–1290: Portrait of a Lost Community', *Transactions of the Worcester Archaeological Society*, 3rd Ser., 12 (1990), pp. 73–122, at p. 96. R. Serman, 'The Guildhall House – Strong Room or Ritual Bath?', Department of Urban Archaeology Newsletter, Museum of London (Sept. 1990), pp. 12–14.

67. Adler, 'Jews of Bristol', p. 122.

68. E. J. Boore, 'Excavations at St Peter's Street, Bristol, 1975–1976', *Bristol and Avon Archaeology*, 1 (1982), pp. 7–11, at p. 8.

69. Roth, *History of the Jews in England*, p. 29.

70. Samuel, op. cit., p. 44.

71. Roth, *History of the Jews in England*, pp. 43, 117.

72. Krinsky, op. cit., pp. 45–6.

73. Roth, *History of the Jews in England*, p. 115.

74. Data: Samuel, op. cit., p. 44.

75. B. Blumenkranz, 'Les Synagogues', in Blumenkranz (ed.), op. cit., pp. 33–72; N. Golb, 'Exceptionelle découverte à Rouen: les vestiges d'une école hébraïque du XIIe s.', *Archeologia*, 129 (April 1979), pp. 8–33.

76. A. Shiloah, 'The Ritual and Music of the Synagogue', in E. Kedourie (ed.), *Jewish World*, op. cit., pp. 120–27, at p. 124.

77. Wood, *English Medieval House*, pp. 5–6.

78. Roth, *History of the Jews in England*, p. 123.
79. O. Doppelfeld, 'Die Ausgrabungen in Kölner Judenviertel', in Asaria (ed.), op. cit., pp. 71–145.
80. Roth, *History of the Jews in England*, p. 42.
81. Data: Doppelfeld, op. cit.; Krautheimer, op. cit.
82. Roth, *History of the Jews in England*, p. 25.
83. Doppelfeld, op. cit.
84. Stephenson, op. cit., p. 50.
85. Crummy (ed.), 'Anglo-Saxon and Norman Colchester', pp. 54–6.
86. Ibid., p. 53.
87. W. Somner, *Antiquities of Canterbury* (1640), quoted in Adler, 'The Jews of Canterbury', p. 24.
88. Kadish, this volume, pp. 101–54.
89. M. Ponsford *et al.*, 'Archaeology in Bristol 1986–89', *Transactions of the Bristol and Gloucestershire Archaeological Society*, 107 (1989), pp. 243–51, at p. 249.
90. Lipman, *Jews of Medieval Norwich*, pp. 313–15.
91. Stephenson, op. cit., p. 49.
92. Krinsky, op. cit., pp. 45–7.
93. M. Bayle, 'Les monuments juifs de Rouen et l'architecture romane', Blumenkranz (ed.), op. cit., pp. 252–76; Doppelfeld, op. cit.

ADDENDUM

Since this chapter went to press, fieldwork has revealed a square cellared structure at Guildford, Surrey, where a small community is documented. It *may* compare with the Colchester example; there are niches in all four walls. Documentary evidence (and recording of the eastern niche) may establish the matter. Preliminary accounts: *The Independent*, 16 Jan. 1996; *JC*, 19 Jan. 1996. I thank M. Alexander of Guildford Museums for details.

4

COMPROMISING TRADITIONS IN EIGHTEENTH-CENTURY LONDON:

The Architecture of the Great Synagogue, Duke's Place

CLARENCE EPSTEIN

After a noted absence of almost 400 years, Jews reappeared in seventeenth-century England owing in part to the relative toleration of Cromwell's Puritan Revolution. Puritan emphasis on the 'Old Testament' helped to foster the idea of Jews as 'God's people', while Protestant political efforts to thwart Roman Catholicism further deflected religious prejudice away from the Jews. Moreover, the Lord Protector, Oliver Cromwell, recognized the contribution of Jewish merchants to the financial growth of Hamburg and Amsterdam.[1] Menasseh ben Israel, a rabbi from Amsterdam, petitioned Cromwell for freedom of religion, permission to maintain synagogues and public worship.[2] Thus the early Jewish settlers in England were, by and large, Dutch, of Spanish and Portuguese origin (Sephardim). Later, a small Germano-Polish contingent (Ashkenazim) arrived, who were looked down upon by their co-religionists as economically and culturally inferior.[3] The differences in social class stemmed from the higher degree of assimilation experienced by Sephardim in Holland as opposed to the more insular communities which existed in Germany and central Europe. Initially, Ashkenazim complied with Sephardi custom, as the latter administered the only London synagogue, a converted building in Creechurch Lane (1657), in the north-eastern quarter of the City.[4]

Both Dutch and German Jews were familiar with Protestant precepts and were careful to avoid unnecessary clashes with the government. Not surprisingly, they even adapted some of the host country's socio-cultural traits into their own religious traditions. Before settling in Holland, Sephardim had drawn upon Roman Catholic architectural models in the construction of their synagogues, but as it would have been impossible directly to employ these models in anti-Catholic countries, a revised architectural form had to be selected for their place of worship in England. The young community, finding no precedents in London, instinctively looked to the Sephardi centre of Europe, Amsterdam, for inspiration. Dutch Jews had, as a direct result of assimilation, referred to the ecclesiastical buildings of their own country, adopting Protestant church design as a synagogue prototype. To complicate the issue of a definitive architectural precedent, there were as yet no Jewish architects, owing to racial

4.1 Amsterdam, the Sephardi Synagogue of 1639; an engraving of the interior, looking towards the Ark, by I. Veenhuysen. *C. H. Krinsky*, Synagogues of Europe (*New York and Cambridge, MA, 1985*)

discrimination by Christian guilds. As architecture was not a viable profession for Jews, synagogue commissions were awarded to Protestant men. Their basilica-type church plans were conveniently suited to Sephardi worship since they derived from classical prototypes similar to those of the basilican synagogues of medieval Catholic Spain[5] and simultaneously conformed to popular design. This type of plan was employed at the Sephardi Synagogue of Amsterdam (1639; Figure 4.1), a model for Creechurch Lane in London.

Two seventeenth-century Amsterdam synagogues designed by Christian architects were to become models for the younger English congregations: the Grote Sjoel of 1670–71 (Figure 4.2) and the Sephardi Synagogue of 1671–75 (Figure 4.3). While the Grote Sjoel introduced the galleried basilica as it was later seen in synagogue architecture,[6] more influential to early London synagogue design was the Sephardi Synagogue. Hailed as the stateliest synagogue in all Europe, it faced the Grote Sjoel across a

4.2 Amsterdam, Grote Sjoel; the interior showing the *Aron Kodesh*.

C. H. Krinsky, Synagogues of Europe (*New York and Cambridge, MA, 1985*)

canal but was considerably larger and more monumental. Inside, giant unfluted Ionic columns extended from floor to ceiling supporting barrel vaults. Within the aisles created by the giant Ionic order, free-standing smaller columns supported the women's galleries, further emphasizing the building's large scale. On the exterior, buttresses curving outward at the base alluded to those believed to have been used in the Temple of Jerusalem.

Not coincidentally, one of the individuals responsible for introducing Dutch-Jewish ecclesiastical models to England was Jacob Judah Leon (1603–75), a rabbi, craftsman and model-builder who had influenced, if not contributed to, the design of the Sephardi Synagogue of 1671–75. His acclaimed replica of Solomon's Temple (1642) 'opened the eyes of the Jewish and also to a large degree of the Christian reading public to the value of Jewish tradition in architectural thought'.[7] Curiosity was aroused by his visit to London in 1675, during which Templo (as he was called) presented a model to the court of Charles II.[8] He was privileged to carry a letter of introduction from the Dutchman Christian Huygens to Sir Christopher Wren, the most celebrated English architect of his time:

> This bearer is a Jew by birth and profession, and I am bound to him for some instruction I had from him, long agoe, in the Hebrew literature. This

4.3 Amsterdam, the Sephardi Synagogue of 1671–75; an engraving by Romeyn de Hooghe on the Dedication Day. *C. H. Krinsky,* Synagogues of Europe *(New York and Cambridge, MA, 1985)*

maketh me grant him the addresses he desireth of me, his intention being to shew England a curious model of the Temple of Salomon, he hath been about to contrive these many years, where he doth presume to have demonstrated and corrected an infinite number of errors and paralogismes of our most learned schollars, who have meddled with the exposition of that holy fabrick, and most specially of the Jesuit Villalpandus, who, as you know, Sir, has handled the matter 'ingenti cum fastu et apparatu, ut solent isti'.[9]

The facility for communicating Dutch ideas to Britain relied on mutual cultural familiarity, magnified after the accession of William of Orange to the British throne in 1688; Holland and Britain were now ruled by the same king. During this period of affiliation, increasing numbers of Jews migrated to England from the Low Countries, consequently over-crowding the Creechurch Lane premises and prompting the need for additional synagogue space.[10] The Sephardim opted for a site in a discreet lane in Plough Yard, Bevis Marks, as Jews were not yet permitted to build a house of worship on a public street. Here a new synagogue – 'the first

specifically constructed for the purpose in England since the thirteenth century'[11] – was consecrated in 1701. By this time, Wren's numerous ecclesiastical schemes had set the standard for many church commissions, as well as those for the first synagogues.

Joseph Avis, a Quaker carpenter who had worked on a Wren church, St Bride's, Fleet Street (1670–84),[12] was chosen as the builder of Bevis Marks. Hiring a fellow Nonconformist such as Avis seemed more feasible than approaching a 'society' architect like Wren, who might have refused the commission altogether. Avis realized the necessity for creating a sober exterior so as not to offend Gentile passers-by. Bevis Marks was rectangular in form, 80 by 50 feet, with a similar plan to that of the Sephardi Synagogue of 1671–75. Elevations in red brick with painted stone dressings divided the two storeys of the synagogue; arched windows located on every side provided excellent lighting to the interior.

The stately Bevis Marks emerged as the most imitated synagogue in England for the next 60 years. Within, smooth plaster walls crowned by a richly detailed cornice carry around the prayer hall, and grandiose chandeliers are suspended from rosettes in the ceiling. The north and south elevations each contain five windows, possibly alluding to the Ten Commandments. Mounted on the east wall, built in wood with Corinthian decoration, is the *Aron Kodesh*, whose container for the Holy Scriptures was claimed to resemble a Renaissance church façade, as its two levels were connected by scrolls (Figure 4.4).[13] To the west, opposite the *Aron Kodesh*, is an elevated, oval *bima*. Tuscan columns[14] support the galleries around the north, south and west sides of the hall. These galleries display an ornament rare in England, although, not surprisingly, St Bride's featured similar decorative motifs.[15] Avis's twisted balusters on the three principal features – *Aron Kodesh*, *bima* and pews – might have been modelled on the winding columns purported to have been used in Solomon's Temple. While the arrangement of these features adhered to an ancient prototype,[16] Bevis Marks' plan combined aspects of the Amsterdam synagogues with Wren's church designs and would directly influence the construction scheme of the Great Synagogue.

THE MOVE TO DUKE'S PLACE

Prosperity was fairly distributed within the numerically small Sephardi group, whereas economic success in the growing Ashkenazi community was less evident.[17] Many members of the latter were uneducated and unskilled but carried over from the central European ghettoes a strong Jewish tradition. The conspicuous garments worn by pious Ashkenazim aroused negative attention from the public and even from Sephardim. The few wealthy German Ashkenazim who settled in London did not persist with traditional convention; instead they readily assimilated into the English mainstream.

Two of these rich Germans, Abraham Franks and Benjamin Levy, were the only Ashkenazim among the original 12 'Jew Brokers' in London. Their families were to be active participants in the history of the Great Synagogue. Through Levy's munificence a cemetery was acquired, clearly asserting the Ashkenazi desire for independence from the controlling

4.4   London, Bevis Marks Synagogue (Joseph Avis, 1701); the *Aron Kodesh*.
Anthony Harris

Sephardi congregation. Differences in religious ritual finally prompted the separation of the two factions. By the 1690s, with Ashkenazi numbers on the rise,[18] a small congregation held services in rented quarters in Duke's Place, Aldgate, less than 300 yards away from Bevis Marks.[19] Little is known about the group's initial activities,[20] but the area would develop into the core of London's Jewish quarter.[21] Levy's brother-in-law, Moses Hart (1675–1756), a successful stock and commodity broker,[22] attended the Duke's Place services and eventually became the group's spokesperson. His brother, Aaron Hart (1670–1756), arrived in England around 1692 and became rabbi of the congregation.[23] Thanks to Aaron's religious leadership and Moses's financial support, the Hart family assumed an anchoring role in the development of the fledgling Ashkenazi community.

Control of the Great Synagogue by individual patron families such as the Harts would become a recurring pattern during the eighteenth century, inevitably determining the development of the synagogue's architecture. The consequences of familial domination in a religious institution were bitter-sweet; patrons guaranteed the survival of the congregation, but overwhelming control by one group instigated the secession of other individuals whose own ideologies conflicted with those in control. As Ashkenazim were to discover, decentralization was counterproductive to their cause. The severing of ties by the first dissenters, the 'Hamburg group', weakened an already unstable power base. In 1706 the Hambro Synagogue[24] was established across the city by a wealthy German, Marcus Moses. Hart is known to have vehemently challenged Marcus Moses when the latter appealed to the Court of Aldermen for the erection of a synagogue. However emphatic, Hart failed to prevent the creation of another independent Ashkenazi *kehilla* in London.[25]

On the surface, Hart's attempts at solidarity seemed virtuous[26] but his reasons for challenging the Hambro group were rooted in the desire to gain overall control of the Ashkenazim, thus affirming his status as a community leader to the Protestant elite. While affluence alone qualified Jews like Hart for elevated social standing,[27] successful integration with the community at large required the modification of certain traditional religious practices, thereby effectively determining a course for radical assimilation. Most Ashkenazim before migrating to England had lived in ghettoes where the 'boundaries' of the locality helped to preserve Jewish tradition. In their new surroundings, however, the utter absence of the ghetto spirit,[28] caused by the embrace of secular values, brought modifications in lifestyle. This tendency was most visible in activities connected with the arts. Hart readily conformed to the conventions of English upper-middle class society, as he was known to wear a fashionable powdered wig and entertained frequently in his large home at Isleworth in Surrey. On his walls hung works of art by northern masters, including subjects related to Jesus, St Francis, St Lawrence as well as an interior depiction of the Jesuit Church at Antwerp.[29] His collection of works of Christian imagery was ironic for one so active in Jewish community affairs.[30]

With the accession of the Elector of Hanover as George I in 1714,

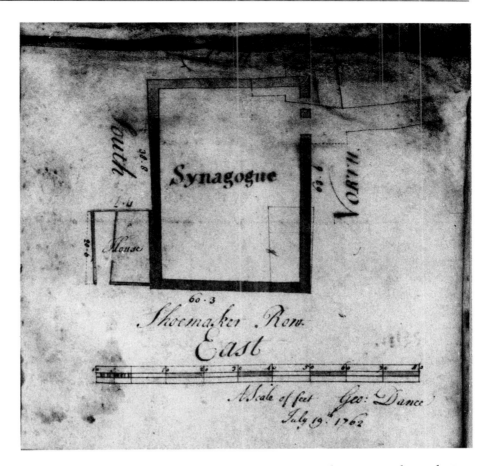

4.5   London, the Great Synagogue; a
drawing (for a lease), dated 19 July
1762. *Corporation of London Records Office*

Britain's diplomatic relations with Germany greatly improved, escalating the migration of central European Jews to Britain. This influx resulted in the numerical domination of Ashkenazim over Sephardim, prompting the need to accommodate a growing congregation – a concern to which Moses Hart ably responded. In 1720, as if his personal wealth was not enough, Hart won a lottery;[31] but within two years he unselfishly put the monies to good use by reconstructing the Great Synagogue entirely at his own expense. In the early 1720s some bordering properties were acquired on the south-east corner of Duke's Place, abutting on Shoemaker Row, which were to be incorporated into the building plan.[32] We have very little architectural information about this 'first expressly constructed synagogue for the Ashkenazim',[33] although a drawing for a lease (Figure 4.5)[34] confirms that it stood on Corporation of London land.[35] The building was box-like, roughly 64 feet long by 60 feet wide, more nearly square in plan than Bevis Marks. At the south-east corner of the property stood a small house of approximately 21 by 18 feet. A yard at the north-west corner made accessible the principal entrance from both Duke's Place Court and Broad Court.

Contemporary commentary reveals that the Sephardi prototype played a significant role in the early development of English Ashkenazi synagogues. In 1738 D'Blossiers Tovey remarked how the Great Synagogue was 'built after the same model as the Portuguese synagogue' but 'not half so big'.[36] His observation is unclear, since the plan of 1765,

SECTION

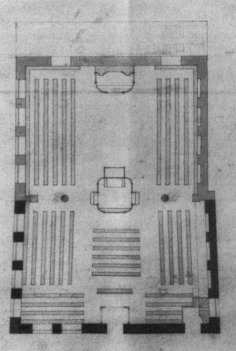

PLAN

A Scale of feet

May the 8th 1769
We do hereby acknowledge that this is one of the Drawings
refer'd to in the agreement the Day signed by us to perform
and compleatly finishing an intended new Cathedral Building to
the Episcopal Church and Dated there of

Witness our hands

4.6 London, the Great Synagogue; plan and section from the surveyor's plans of 1765. *Greater London Record Office*

which also displays the boundaries of the older interior (Figure 4.6), includes only one gallery, at the west end. Because domestic obligations hindered women's regular participation at services, it would not have been unusual for the Germano-Polish congregation to displace them to the rear of the building, as would have often been the case in their native countries. Clearly D'Blossiers Tovey's sweeping observations offered no architectural insight, but it is important to note the conscious intention of correlating the two religious buildings.

ALTERATIONS OF 1765–66

Until 1765, English synagogues outside London, such as the Ashkenazi Synagogue in Plymouth (1762), adhered to Dutch-Sephardi architectural prototypes. Indeed as far away as Newport, Rhode Island, the Yeshuat Yisrael Synagogue (1759–63) was designed by Peter Harrison[37] under the guidance of Amsterdam Rabbi Isaac Touro.[38] During this same period, the Great Synagogue emerged as the central Ashkenazi base in the country and its major rebuilding schemes were determined by, and reflected the character of, the wealthy families who headed its administration. Family patriarch Abraham Franks had been a warden of the

4.6(a) The *Aron Kodesh*, detail of Figure 4.6

synagogue in 1722 concurrent with his position as one of London's 12 'Jew Brokers'. The Franks and Hart families were related through the marriage of Abraham's son Aaron (1685–1777) to Hart's daughter Bilah. Aaron Franks, a gem merchant, chose to live alongside his father-in-law in a mansion at Isleworth, where he is known to have entertained the prominent socialite Horace Walpole among others. Indeed, the Harts and Franks were some of the first Ashkenazim to associate with the English elite, quickly realizing that philanthropic effort[39] promoted social advancement, as well as increasing their political influence in the City.

Following Moses Hart's death in 1756, Aaron Franks assumed a greater role in synagogue affairs and soon became head of the congregation. Although Hart and his son-in-law had been close associates, their contributions to the synagogue represented distinct eras in its development. Hart's efforts were unprecedented; he officiated during a period of limited social activity when only three synagogues served the whole of London. By the 1750s,[40] when the Franks family assumed control of the Great, close to 6,000 Ashkenazim had immigrated. In the late 1760s, major Jewish houses of worship were gaining notoriety in the City and 'the synagogal physiognomy achieved the definitive form which it was to retain for the next hundred years'.[41] Within this framework, the Great Synagogue assumed a commanding position and its activities were monitored by all other congregations.

In 1761, shortly after the accession of George III, another factional secession similar to the Hambro group threatened the Great Synagogue's jurisdiction. No sooner had the dissenters incorporated as the New Synagogue[42] than the Great protested and placed the founders in a state of excommunication. Although never as large as the Great, the New Synagogue was soon to rival the Hambro. This second major secession can further explain why it was necessary for the Great Synagogue to undergo expansion in 1766. Since the 1722 reconstruction, more than 40 years earlier, the building in Duke's Place had remained unchanged. In order to maintain a dominant position within the community and to avoid losing more members to the smaller synagogues, action was taken to enlarge the building. The financial input made by the Franks family was to become vital in this undertaking.[43]

To assess the role played by wealthy Ashkenazi families in synagogal affairs, it is necessary to understand something of the manner in which these families worked to preserve their social and financial position. Illustrative is the act of arranged marriages: wedding within one's social class, a trait shared by the English aristocracy, protected the financial interests of the family. It came as no surprise when Aaron Franks's daughter Phila, married her first cousin Moses, youngest brother of Naphtali Franks. In this instance, the marriage served also to create important links between Jewish and English society. The couple lived in a Palladian villa in Teddington, designed by Moses's friend, the leading academic architect Sir William Chambers,[44] who was simultaneously working on the Royal Gardens at Kew. Chambers's designs for the house were concurrent with plans to rebuild the synagogue. Although there was no connection between Chambers and the Great Synagogue commission of 1765, his affiliation with the Franks family indicated that strong relations were forming between members of the architectural profession and wealthy Jewish patrons. These associations helped to secure a reputable architect for the expansion project.

Aaron Franks's transactions in the City brought him into contact with civic builders; thus it seemed reasonable for him to commission the City Surveyor, George Dance, Senior, who was familiar with the synagogue because it stood on Corporation of London land. The lease of 1760[45] mentioned Aaron Franks by name and includes a signed drawing by Dance Sr, further proof of their interaction. Also discussed in the lease was a tenement located on the north-west side of the building, and two rooms constructed over a passage leading to Broad Court, likely to have become offices and residences.[46] In addition to the City's property, abutting land was acquired from Edward and Elizabeth Holmes.[47] The trustees requested Dance Sr to raze the building on the Holmes's property, adding a considerable synagogue extension in its place.

Dance Sr was the first professional architect to be commissioned for work on an English synagogue. However, the unstated contribution to the project by his son, George Dance, Junior, is an issue which must be raised. Less than five years before the synagogue work, Dance Jr was taking part in a Grand Tour of the Continent.[48] When he returned to England in 1764, his ageing father was eager to take him on as assistant, and at first both father and son shared various commissions. Taking into consideration the relatively modest scale of the synagogue project, it appears likely that Dance Sr allowed his son the opportunity to gain practical experience by undertaking the work, all the while freeing up his own time to attend to more pressing obligations as City Surveyor. On the previous occasion when the younger George was given free rein to design, his creations were striking. Almost simultaneous with the Great Synagogue project, though commencing slightly earlier, was his work at All Hallows, London Wall (1765), a church which was to represent one of the first and most impressive expressions of neo-classical design in the country.[49] Accustomed to the limited funds imposed on the All Hallows project, the young architect would have found the synagogue's modest budget a familiar constraint. The similarity of the neo-classical language employed at both church and synagogue further suggests a significant contribution by the young Dance to the latter's reconstruction. The enlargement scheme marked an unprecedented break from Bevis Marks, showing how Dance's work was pivotal in redefining the course of synagogue design in London.

Before Dorothy Stroud's reference to a number of plans, sections and elevations,[50] little was known about the interior of the 1765–66 synagogue. The drawings illustrate how the interior of the original structure was left relatively unchanged while the recently acquired property underwent the most drastic renovation. A wall dividing the pre-existing building from the newly acquired one was torn down so as to combine both spaces, increasing the total area by approximately 50 feet (see Figure 4.6). As a result, the Ashkenazi building became the biggest Jewish place of worship in London, exceeding Bevis Marks and even larger than the Parish Church of St James, Duke's Place. Shortly after the alterations, *The New and Historical Survey of London* remarked:

> On the west side [of Shoemaker Row] is the Synagogue of the Dutch Jews [*sic*] . . . This synagogue is just now enlarged with an addition of a building in brick that makes it as large again as it was before; and has approached so near to the Church of St James, Duke's Place, that the congregations may be heard from each other.[51]

A roughly basilican plan resulted from the merging of the two buildings.[52] The four windows facing Duke Street were repeated on the new addition, bringing the total to eight. As there were no windows on the opposite side, Dance continued the blind arch motif, employing mouldings above and below, so as to visually align the arches. He provided two entrances to the synagogue hall: one in the rear wall opposite the *Aron Kodesh* and another in the corner, with a staircase leading up to the women's gallery. On the same side of the main doorway were situated two windows, while additional ones flanked the *Aron Kodesh*. Faintly drawn in the plan, behind the Ark wall, was a set of staircases, one possibly leading to proposed additional galleries and another to the basement. A small rectangular room planned as a vestry is also faintly visible on the scheme but was not executed concurrently with the other additions.

The key components of the hall – *Aron Kodesh* and *bima* – were placed on the central axis with no pew or other furnishing between them. The necessity to increase seating made it all the more unusual for pews not to be introduced in front of the *Aron Kodesh*; however, additional seats were placed behind the *bima*.[53] The gap between the *Aron Kodesh* and *bima* suggests the intention[54] to maintain an unobstructed line between the two main religious components to allow for the ceremonial procession of the *Sifrei Torah* during services. By placing the *bima* in the centre of the plan, Dance visually connected both halves of the synagogue. The *bima* was flanked by two giant unfluted Corinthian columns and pilasters, each close to 25 feet high. These columns sustaining the breastsummer, acted as the major structural supports but broke up the field of vision along the central axis. Corinthian columns *in antis* were a feature frequently employed by the young Dance, who used the giant order in his prize-winning designs produced in Italy for the Parma Academy competition (1763). In addition, the synagogue's few columns carried a small pre-existing 'entablature', which at first glance seems unusual. But the selective omission of architectural features had been similarly evident in Dance's work at All Hallows,[55] where the Ionic columns did not carry a full entablature, the architrave being excluded.

Situated to the right of the principal entrance and accessed by a winding staircase was the ladies' gallery. Bordered by traditional latticed grilles, this elevated seating arrangement was added to both sides of the pre-existing section but not to the newer half, so as to avoid obstructing the view of the *Aron Kodesh* (Figure 4.7). The gallery extended nearly 30 feet along one side but did not continue to the corner, since a pre-existing window (illuminating the stairwell) had to be accommodated. Nine-foot-high Doric columns supported the gallery, markedly distinct

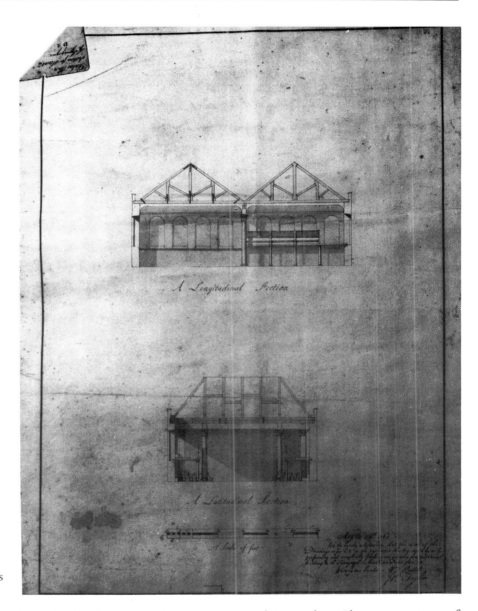

4.7 London, the Great Synagogue; sections of the interior from the surveyor's plans of 1765. *Greater London Record Office*

from the hall's impressive, giant Corinthian order. Clear separation of these structural members was reminiscent of the Sephardi Synagogue of 1671–75 in Amsterdam but was an equally apparent feature of many galleried London churches.

The ceiling plan[56] remained very simple (Figure 4.8). A coved ceiling divided into rectangular compartments contained a total of ten rosettes from which hung candelabra. The two largest ones were placed in the centre of each main section of the hall. The rosettes in the newer ceiling section were arranged closer together to allow for increased skylight space. Four more skylights were added next to the original two in the older section, each measuring six square feet. At ground level, eight windows facing Shoemaker Row (Duke Street) profited from optimal light entry. The sunbeams illustrated in the drawings (Figures 4.6 and 4.7) are shown dramatically penetrating the centre of the hall, illu-

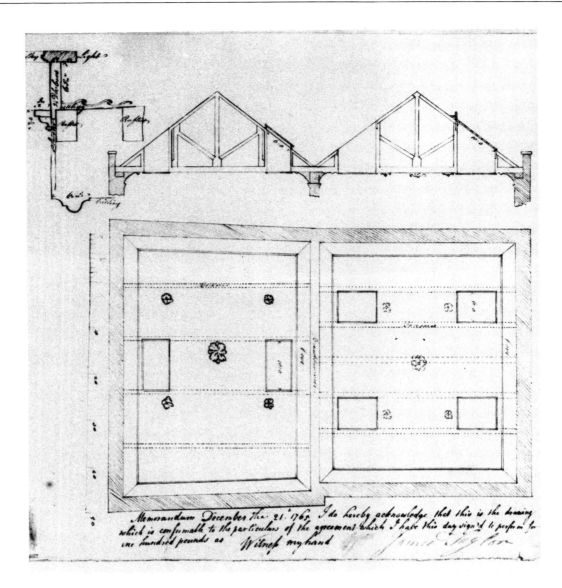

4.8   London, the Great Synagogue; the ceiling plan of 1765. *Sir John Soane's Museum*

minating objects in their path. The light source appears to have been overemphasized so much that the perspective of columns and *Aron Kodesh* is deceivingly rendered. But ultimately the combination of windows and skylights provided excellent illumination for a building so awkwardly positioned.

The younger Dance was not only attempting to enlarge the space but created moreover a unified and permanent setting. The outstanding feature in the plan was an originally conceived *Aron Kodesh* to be integrated into the wall, extending upward almost to ceiling height (Figure 4.6(a)). The lower half was protected by a balustrade; a set of doors flanked by Corinthian pilasters and capped by a semicircular pediment clearly signified the location of the *Sifrei Torah*. Finials were placed above the segmental arch and were supported on either side by small Doric pilasters. In the centre of this upper section were two tablet forms, no doubt the space allotted for the Hebrew inscription of the Ten Commandments. In terms of its neo-classical severity, Dance's design

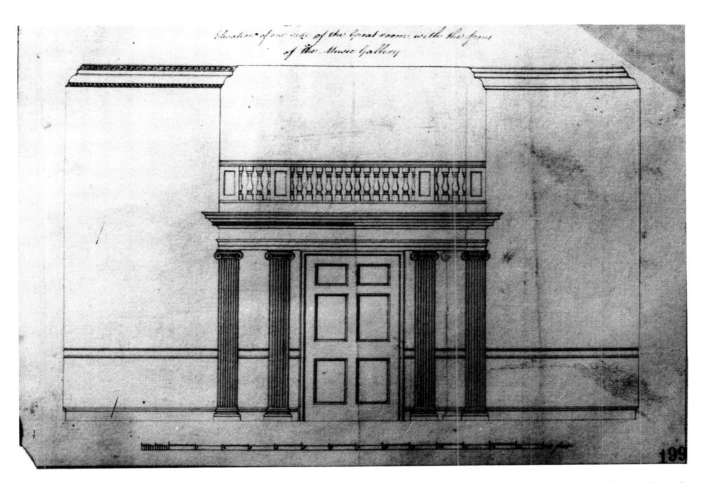

4.9   London, the Great Synagogue;
elevation of the Great Room with the
front of the Music Gallery (1765?).
Greater London Record Office

indicated the impact of travels abroad, and considering how church designs were most recent to his memory, it is all the more credible that Christianized associations should also surface in the plan for the synagogue. Until 1766 the Sephardi Synagogue of 1671–75, stylistically relayed in London through Bevis Marks, remained the prototype for English synagogues; Dance's participation was crucial to the evolution of the Great Synagogue, for it redirected the course of British synagogue design away from the dominant Dutch-Sephardi model.

Included in the Dance Portfolio was a drawing titled 'Elevation of one side of the Great Room with the Front of the Music Gallery' (Figure 4.9).[57] The marked difference in draughtsmanship and the simplicity of the design suggest that this drawing was not executed by the same hand as others in the set (compare with Figures 4.6 and 4.7). Stroud mistakenly assumes that the 'Great Room' was the actual prayer hall, but the low ceiling height (13 feet) renders her supposition impossible.[58] The 'Great Room' was used as a separate space for social functions such as weddings and *barmitzvot*. A conventional door flanked on either side by Ionic pilasters forms the centre of this assembly hall. Pilasters support an entablature above which a music gallery with front balustrade is presented. This side of the room is only 21 feet long; the gallery itself is a compact ten feet long by six feet high. On the wall, above the pilasters, are undecorated bands with enriched cornice mouldings, some of dogtooth design. The drawing of the 'Great Room' is elementary and uncomplicated, probably executed by an assistant in Dance's office.

Immediately before Dance's alteration scheme, David Tevele Schiff was appointed Rabbi of the Great Synagogue. Schiff was descended from a long line of rabbinical scholars and was unhappy with the state of Jewish theological discourse in England, believing that he was becoming associated with a group of men whose secular interests far outweighed their religious commitment. These affluent men thought that by giving financial support to the congregation they were justified a hand in its affairs. Schiff had no choice but to temper his personal views and conform to the anglicized constitution of his congregation. At the synagogue's consecration in August 1766, *The Annual Register* reported:

> This afternoon, the ceremony of the dedication of the new-built synagogue in Duke's Place was performed with the greatest pomp and solemnity in which the chief and other eminent rabbis belonging to the Portuguese Jewish nation assisted; when the prayer for their Majesties and the Royal Family, which was always read in their liturgy, was at this time pronounced in English by the Chief Rabbi . . .

Reciting festive prayers in English at the service as well as permitting the playing of one of Handel's Coronation Anthems[59] further exhibited Schiff's compliance with the lay leaders' wishes. It was evident from the presence of the wardens of Bevis Marks at the consecration that they had accepted the role of the Great Synagogue as the principal Ashkenazi congregation in Britain. More and more Jews were moving to London, assimilation was on the increase and the consolidation of newly established congregations in the provinces was taking place.[60] This last development was crucial for securing the cardinal position of the Great Synagogue within English Jewry, as was apparent from Schiff's inaugural title: 'Chief Rabbi of London and the Provinces'.[61]

RECONSTRUCTION OF 1788–90

Between the 1765–66 alterations and the 1788–90 reconstruction of the Great Synagogue, England's thriving economy regularly attracted Jewish settlers from the Continent, although along with those from 'respectable' backgrounds there arrived a disproportionate number of poor. Many made the greatest efforts to uphold the faith. Pious men formed study groups for learning Talmud and the Biblical commentaries, but even the less affluent were susceptible to assimilation. A pamphlet distributed in the latter part of the century raised the issue of religious laxity within all Jewish social classes: 'parents permitted their children to go barefooted; men and women came together in dancing academies, where they embraced one another without shame; they dressed like lords and ladies, and could not be distinguished from Gentiles.'[62]

The social composition of the Jewish community was changing as the distinction between Jews and Gentiles was breaking down. The Great Synagogue was greatly affected by the population boom. Aaron Franks died in 1777; in the same year his kinsman Naphtali was elected Head for

Life, representing the synagogue in most of its external administrative affairs.[63] By September 1787, still in debt to Edward Holmes for £1,600, the trustees petitioned the Corporation of London to renew their lease.[64] Despite their having maintained a deficit for an extensive period, plans were initiated in this same year for a full-scale reconstruction. Presumably the claim that major structural repairs were required prompted a petition to the Mayor requesting the authorities to break a lease (intended to expire in 1800), so as to allow for the rebuilding.[65]

Members of distinguished families, including the Franks, donated their time and money to the cause. The Goldsmids, newcomers to contemporary synagogue politics, actively participated in fund-raising, while Judith Hart Levy, a member of a family which had all but lost contact with the synagogue, was to become the key patron. Judith was the daughter of Moses Hart and widow of Elias Levy, son of one of the original 'Jew Brokers', Benjamin Levy. In his lifetime, Elias had played an active role in synagogue affairs but it is doubtful whether his widow maintained any religious affiliation with the Jewish community. Judith reputedly led an impious lifestyle, being known in society circles as the 'Queen of Richmond Green'[66] and the 'Duchess of Albemarle Street'. Her donation of £4,000 towards the reconstruction patently stemmed from family loyalties rather than her own religious conviction.[67]

The Goldsmids, unlike other prominent Ashkenazi families such as the Harts, settled relatively late in England. The critical family members, brothers Abraham (1756–1810) and Benjamin (1755–1808), amassed incredible wealth in the late eighteenth century. Beginning as bill brokers in 1777, by the 1790s they were in a position to replace established bankers in securing large loans to the government.[68] Their reputation as major financiers was well known and their charitable donations to secular institutions widely publicized. Both served as officials, charity managers and patrons of the Great.[69] The political influence of the Goldsmids was applied when Abraham led the City sub-committee around the synagogue grounds, helping to convince them of the necessity for a reconstruction.

Abraham's neighbour in Surrey, Admiral Lord Nelson, counted both brothers among his closest friends.[70] The desire to assert their social status was realized by the magnificence of the Goldsmid residences. Abraham's country home in Morden was a stately three-bay villa with Doric portico and surrounded by landscaped gardens.[71] Benjamin, the older of the two, embarked on a Grand Tour of France, Italy, Germany, Holland and Prussia[72] where he acquired a taste for the arts and a 'cultured' lifestyle. In 1801 designs by James Spiller (d. 1829) for Benjamin's villa at Roehampton (*c.* 1796) were exhibited at the Royal Academy.[73] One author remarked of the building's grandeur:

> Nothing was omitted that could add splendour to his abode of luxury and boundless wealth. Magnificent and costly staircases, vestibules with beautiful and expensive marble pavements, a rich library, a noble dining room, a choice gallery of paintings, gorgeous drawing rooms, unique stables . . . such were some of the features of a residence that was compared with Windsor Castle.[74]

The extravagances of Benjamin's 60-acre freehold included works by established artists, Benjamin West and Joshua Reynolds, an artificial lake as well as a small synagogue.[75] He was considerate enough to allocate a piece of land to the Chief Rabbi to grow wheat for making unleavened bread for Passover. Benjamin maintained close ties with the Great Synagogue, and it is almost certain that his decision to hire James Spiller to design his home several years after the architect's reconstruction of the Great resulted directly from Spiller's contact with the brothers in the City. In 1788–90, concurrently with the synagogue's rebuilding, Spiller was Surveyor to the Royal Exchange Assurance Company,[76] where he might have been introduced to the Goldsmids.

James Spiller was descended from a family of builders. His father was evidently a speculative builder; his brothers Robert and John were in business as masons and sculptors,[77] the latter playing a prominent role in the synagogue project. Early in his career James Spiller worked for James Wyatt,[78] and he began practising architecture soon after leaving Wyatt's office. In the 1790s he became a close friend of Sir John Soane, who greatly influenced the development of his style, often discussing with him issues pertaining to the current state of architecture. From Spiller's letters it is clear that he was never satisfied with the work of others (or even with his own), often complaining to Soane about the degeneracy of the times.[79] He was known to argue with clients and patrons, although his persistent ill-health may perhaps explain his temperamental behaviour. However, at the synagogue he worked without any serious disagreement.[80]

When one considers the importance Spiller attached to ecclesiastical design, as expressed in his writings,[81] the construction of the synagogue appears as an inconsistent strain in his architectural repertoire. His only executed church, St John's, Hackney, was built in 1792–97, immediately after the completion of the Great Synagogue; considerably larger than the synagogue, it was described by Summerson as 'a dark brick monster with umbrageous eaves'.[82] While the Greek-cross plan was typical, the devising of the lighting was highly original. Rather than inserting the majority of windows in every large wall surface, Spiller inconspicuously placed them on the smaller axes of the cross plan. This arrangement created an awkward-looking façade but allowed for an unexpectedly radiant interior.

Spiller's church and his synagogue both had unadorned exteriors, and their interior decorative schemes were vaguely comparable. A church design by Spiller dated 1791,[83] one and a half years after the synagogue's completion, further illustrates his unconventional manner and originality. The coloured drawing was a proposal for St John's, Hackney, and its dissimilarity to the synagogue design suggests that the degree of his participation at the Great has been overstated. Was James Spiller solely responsible for the synagogue design? His brother, John Spiller (1763–94), was active in both the Great Synagogue and St John's commissions.[84] Considering the Soanian qualities of the church – the monumentality and eclecticism of its architectural members – the Adamesque style of the synagogue interior appears antithetical to James's manner. It is feasible that the Spiller brothers participated in varying degrees on each

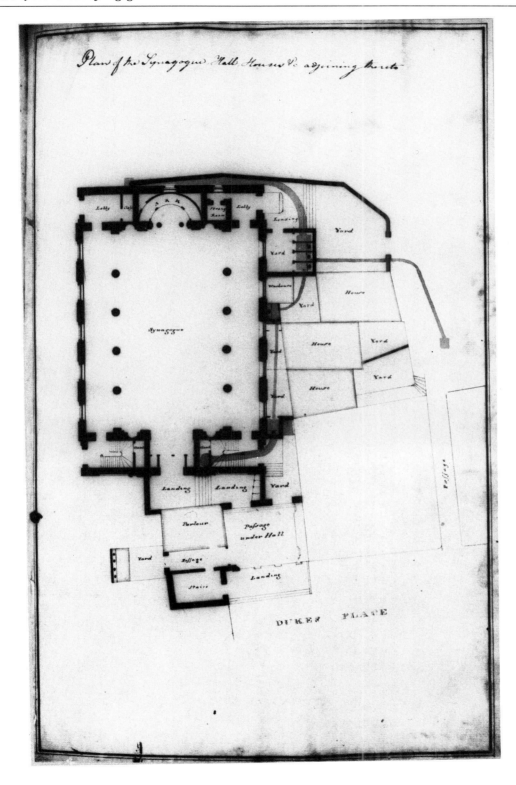

4.10   London, the Great Synagogue; a
1788–90 plan of the synagogue, the hall
and adjoining houses. *Greater London Record Office*

ecclesiastical commission, and that the synagogue construction was a combined effort. According to the Synagogue Building Accounts, John Spiller, not James, was appointed as director of the project, and in the list of paid employees John earned more than James.[85] It is possible that for this contract James drew up the basic plans, acting as liaison with the Goldsmids, and John was more active in their realization. It seems unlikely that James Spiller would have wholly created two ecclesiastical structures which were so closely linked chronologically, yet stylistically inconsistent.

Another misconception regarding the rebuilding stems from the nineteenth-century claim that the new structure was twice the size of the former.[86] The prayer hall, although completely razed and rebuilt, did not drastically increase in size relative to the 1765 project. The synagogue did undergo further expansion during the 1790 reconstruction but much of the acquired property was transformed into additional administrative, social and storage facilities. The plan (Figure 4.10) reveals how Spiller's greatest contribution to the rebuilding scheme was the merging of previously detached spaces of the complex, thus improving overall accessibility. Three houses were acquired from John Weston in Little Duke's Place (alias Mitre Court),[87] as well as additional ground belonging to the City. A later plan of the synagogue[88] shows how the dimensions were similar to those of 1765. The contiguous properties which were incorporated doubled the synagogue space, not the prayer hall itself. Clearly, Dance's 1765–66 alterations to the sanctuary had extended the room to its physical limit, determining the standard shape and size with which the later architect had to comply. Spiller replanned

4.11   London, the Great Synagogue; a wash-drawing of the exterior, looking from Duke's Place. *Jewish Museum, London*

the space in such a manner as to allow the greatest accessibility and to further emphasize the permanence of the structure.

Unlike Dance, Spiller had the opportunity to control the reshaping of the entire complex. He refaced a three-bay house and small building to its side, transforming their restricted frontage into a main entrance in Duke's Place.[89] Several steps led up to a principal level demarcated by a series of three archways enclosed by iron gates. Sash windows on the upper storeys of both buildings were not aligned, although a stringcourse above the principal storey visually connected the two (Figure 4.11). The single doorway in the smaller building accessed offices[90] and a staircase which brought the congregant to a large hall 'purposely appointed for the celebration of weddings of poor Jews'.[91] On the principal storey, a passage led to a large parlour and yard bordering Broad Court (Figure 4.10). From the passage under the hall, a staircase led the congregant up two levels of landings, revealing the principal entrance to the prayer hall. Another yard permitted separate access to the women's gallery and main level. Taking into account the two approaches directly facing Duke Street,[92] there was a total of five entrances to the prayer hall. Indeed the considerable number of exterior entrances to the whole complex suggests that the congregation felt at ease in its environs,[93] in contrast to the restricted location of Bevis Marks which reflected the insecurity of the Jews a century before.

Visible from Duke Street, the unadorned five-bay, two-storey brick façade was flanked by two entrances (Figure 4.12). The storeys were divided by a plain stringcourse with five arches and archivolts on each

4.12   London, the Great Synagogue; the exterior, looking from Duke Street. *Cecil Roth*, The Great Synagogue (*London, 1950*)

The New Jewish SYNAGOGUE, *in* Duke's Street, LONDON.

level. The arches on the lower level incorporated smaller square windows which could be opened to allow for ventilation. Whereas Dance had continued the series of blind arches lengthwise, the recent acquisition of property allowed Spiller to freely design windows for this space. Simplicity and austerity of design were practical for this exterior and comparable to Dance's successful street-front elevation at All Hallows, where the unbroken wall surface was designed to prevent street noises from disturbing the religious services.

The interior of this galleried basilica was far more splendid than its external appearance suggested (Figure 4.13). On either side of the broad nave, four giant unfluted Ionic columns raised on pedestals were carried uninterrupted to the roof. The arrangement of galleries within the inter-columniation was reminiscent of the Grote Sjoel in Amsterdam (see Figure 4.2). The hall seated approximately 500 men on the main floor and 250 women in the galleries,[94] this time with brass latticed grilles visually distinguishing the gallery space from the main area. Women's galleries were more prominent in Spiller's design than in Dance's as was evident by improved access to this level. Furthermore, the galleries were now fully incorporated into the layout, with one being added above the main entrance. Spiller placed the new *Aron Kodesh* in its standard

4.13   London, the Great Synagogue; an engraving by Pugin and Rowlandson of the interior, looking towards the *Aron Kodesh*.
Rudolf Ackermann, Microcosm of London (*London, 1809*)

location, as well as positioning the low, oval *bima* (Figure 4.14) in the centre of the room with pews surrounding it on three sides. A pulpit was incorporated on one side of the *Aron Kodesh*, testimony to Protestant influence and remarkably similar to the one placed at St John's, Hackney, several years later. The pulpit emphasized the aspect of teaching, so fundamental to both Jewish and Protestant worship, while its proximity to the Ark reinforced the connection between education and religion. Introduction of a pulpit and integration of galleries further connected church design (though no one church in particular) with the synagogue.[95]

The wall containing the *Aron Kodesh* was decorated in similar fashion to the high altar wall in a church. Helen Rosenau is correct in correlating the design with Robert Adam's fashionable exedrae at Syon House and Osterley Park,[96] although the application of this form in a religious milieu, as opposed to a residential one, was unique. Divided into three parts by Ionic pilasters, the central wall section, surmounted by swags and garlands, housed the *Aron Kodesh*. Extending into the congregation's space, a low wooden balustrade with curved ends supported large torchères, while the concave area encasing the Torah Scrolls was apsidal in form. Contrary to tradition, the *Aron Kodesh* was consolidated into the total room design. This physical integration of the Ark into the interior scheme perhaps conveyed the Ashkenazim's feeling of security in their English surroundings. The Ark opening was supported by marble-

4.14 London, the Great Synagogue, Duke's Place; the *bima*, photographed in 1931 by Morris Joseph. *Southampton University Library*

ized Corinthian columns *in antis*, all with gilded capitals. The arch soffit was decorated with rosettes surrounded by octagonal mouldings. Within the coffered semi-dome, a hidden light-well and a lunette window directly above provided the same light source. During evening services, the seven brilliant chandeliers[97] suspended from the coved ceiling must have imparted a truly spiritual ambience.

'I have set the Lord always before me' (Psalm 16:8) was inscribed in Hebrew on the *Aron Kodesh* entablature (see Figure 9.1). On a pedestal flanked by urns above the inscription were two tablets displaying the Ten Commandments. By placing these in the same prominent position as in Dance's *Aron Kodesh* design, Spiller directly quoted his predecessor. He could interpret Dance's starkly neo-classical work as well as rely on the suggestions of prominent congregants who had visited various synagogues on the Continent. Whereas Dance did not find inspiration in any one Jewish prototype, Spiller, if guided by any precedents at all, looked to Ashkenazi, not Sephardi, sources.[98] While many features recalled those at the Grote Sjoel in Amsterdam,[99] for example the integration of the *Aron Kodesh* and the style of the galleried basilica, it is highly doubtful whether Spiller ever visited the Dutch building. The Great Synagogue had autonomously become the country's Ashkenazi power base; thus pivotal to the design was its emphasis on grandeur. Conforming to popular fashion was all too crucial since it reinforced the status of Jews as part of the English fabric, most importantly for London's wealthy Ashkenazi community, whose loyal patronage determined the course for religious as well as social reform.

For Dance Jr and Spiller, the Great Synagogue commissions arrived at crucial moments in their careers when they were eager to put their architectural ideas into practice. The evolution of the synagogue scheme from 1765 to 1790 carried a common strain: the fusing of church design with a limited understanding of Jewish tradition. Immediately prior to Dance's alterations, the erection of All Hallows, London Wall had been hailed as the architect's 'first child'. Immediately following Spiller's rebuilding was the execution of St John's, Hackney, his only church commission. The significance of church design was embraced by Dance and reacted to by Spiller. Designs for the synagogue in 1765–66 and 1788–90 stylistically classify this building type within the range of London's contemporary church designs. It is ironic that two Protestant architects were to have such a great influence on English synagogue design, and moreover that these Jewish commissions should also represent some of the earliest ecclesiastical work in their own careers.

As Ashkenazim gradually assimilated into English society the desire to conform overcame the concern to uphold tradition; this caused synagogal practice to be modified. The contribution by prominent families to the various reconstructions of the Great Synagogue was bitter-sweet testimony to the evolution of British synagogue architecture. On the one hand, the erection of a building dedicated to the worship of God was respectable and an indication of their religious allegiance. On the other hand, members of the leading families responsible for development, such as the Harts, Franks and Goldsmids, were concerned more with displaying their wealth than with religious commitment. The repeated reconstructions of the Great Synagogue acted as social markers, reflecting not simply Ashkenazi immigration to London, but more importantly the drastic assimilation of its conspicuously wealthy members. This privileged group, aspiring to imitate the English upper middle class, opted to liken the synagogue to a church. The equation was an attempt to align themselves with the Protestant mainstream and improve their chances of gaining full acceptance within English society. Employing the Dance office in 1765 indicated that their commercial connections within the City were the rudimentary points of contact with Gentiles. Less than 25 years later, the hiring of Spiller proved that the Jews were already seeking a fashionable architect, one who could furnish the congregation with an identity comparable to the Protestant elite. In both cases, the financial undertaking and much of the planning were in the hands of those who acted as synagogue trustees.

Religious apathy during the Georgian period and the search for material success militated against the development of a vibrant Jewish cultural life in England. Ashkenazi decentralization, which resulted in the foundation of the Hambro and New Synagogues, did not stem from theological disagreements within the Great Synagogue but from political ones. Ashkenazim were unable to pool their resources, nor could they contribute towards the promotion of a cohesive community identity. In the absence of strong communal institutions, there was no way to monitor Jewish behaviour. As a result, eighteenth-century English synagogue building followed no continuous tradition. The seeds for radical assimilation were taking root.

NOTES

This essay is based on my dissertation, 'The Great Synagogue, Duke's Place: Architectural Assimilation in Georgian London' (1992), submitted in partial fulfilment of a Master's degree at the Courtauld Institute of Art. I am grateful to Mr John Newman and Professor C. Michael Kauffmann for their supervision and support.

The Great Synagogue was completely destroyed as a result of German bombing in the Second World War.

1. V. D. Lipman (ed.), *Three Centuries of Anglo-Jewish History* (London, 1961), p. 6. For more on the state of commerce during the period, see M. P. Ashley, *The Commercial and Financial Policy of the Cromwellian Protectorate* (Oxford, 1934).
2. In 1655 he brought from Holland a small English pamphlet and presented it 'To his Highnesse the Lord Protector of the Commonwealth of England, Scotland and Ireland. The Humble Adresses of Menasseh ben Israel, a Divine, and Doctor of Physick, in behalfe of the Jewish Nation'. Cecil Roth, *A History of the Jews in England* (Oxford, 1964), p. 161.
3. Sephardim were concerned that the poorer Jews (Ashkenazim) would attract public attention and undermine the grudging toleration that they themselves had achieved.
4. The synagogue was reconstructed in 1675. Cecil Roth, *The Great Synagogue* (London, 1950), p. 2. During this period, Jews were not allowed to purchase property within the City, hence situated themselves on its outskirts.
5. Helen Rosenau, 'The Synagogue and Protestant Church Architecture', *Journal of the Warburg and Courtauld Institutes*, 4 (1940–44), p. 81.
6. C. H. Krinsky, *Synagogues of Europe*, (New York and Cambridge, MA, 1985), p. 389.
7. Helen Rosenau, *Vision of the Temple, The Image of the Temple of Jerusalem in Judaism and Christianity* (London, 1979), p. 135. The work of sixteenth-century Spanish Jesuit Juan Bautista Villalpando was referred to by Templo. A monograph about the Temple appeared on the Continent later in the seventeenth century: M. Leonhardi Christophori Sturmii, *Sciagraphia Templi Hierosolymitana* (Leipzig, 1694).

8. *Catalogue of an exhibition of Anglo-Jewish Art and History*, Victoria and Albert Museum (London, 1956), n.p. It is believed that Templo designed the coat of arms for the Grand Lodge of the English Freemasons, which would link him directly with some of the country's architectural faculty. Roth, *A History of the Jews in England*, p. 226.

9. Taken from Rosenau, *Vision of the Temple*, p. 141, but first published in J. A. Worp, *Briefwisseling*, VI, No. 32 (Rijks Geschiedkundige Publication, 1917), pp. 274–5. The closing remark is that Villalpando handled the matter 'with great show and apparatus, as they [Jesuits] are accustomed to do'.

10. In 1690 a visitor to London noted that the Jews' synagogues 'cannot contain them all'. Norman C. Brett-James, *The Growth of Stuart London* (London, 1935), p. 510.

11. Roth, *History of the Jews in England*, p. 185. It is now the oldest standing synagogue in Britain.

12. Edward Jamilly, 'Anglo-Jewish Architects and Architecture in the Eighteenth and Nineteenth Centuries', *Transactions of the Jewish Historical Society of England (TJHSE)*, XVIII (1953–58), p. 130.

13. Krinsky, *Synagogues of Europe*, p. 413. Contemporary craftsmen often employed components such as scrolls in their decorative repertoires.

14. The columns are described as 'Doric' by the *Royal Commission on Historical Monuments (England) – London (The City)*, IV (London, 1929), p. 10.

15. Helen Rosenau, 'The Architectural Development of the Synagogue', Ph.D. dissertation, Courtauld Institute of Art, University of London (1939), p. 68a. The author made the aesthetic link between the two buildings, although it is uncertain whether she realized that Avis had previously worked on the church.

16. Traditionally the Ark should be detachable from the wall so that in case of emergency it may be quickly removed. *Dictionary of Architecture*, VII (London, 1887), p. 175.

17. 'In the first half of the eighteenth century Sephardim owned three-quarters and the Ashkenazim one-quarter of the wealth of the community.' V. D. Lipman, 'The Development of London Jewry', in S. S. Levin (ed.), *A Century of Anglo-Jewish Life, 1870–1970* (London, 1970), p. 44.

18. By 1695, one quarter of the Jews living in east London were Ashkenazim. *Miscellanies of the Jewish Historical Society of England*, VI, p. 73.

19. Duke's Place was called Duke's Place Court, Little Duke's Place or Broad Court. Cecil Roth, 'The Origins of the Great Synagogue', *Jewish Chronicle Supplement*, 122 (Feb. 1931). For more information regarding the area see 'Vestry Minutes of Parish of St. James, 1725–1785', *Guildhall Library Manuscripts Collection* (MS. 1218–1).

20. The records of the Great Synagogue for its first 25 years of existence do not survive. However, the congregation's situation in Duke's Place suggests a continuous tradition of worship at one spot longer than Bevis Marks. Cecil Roth, *Archives of the United Synagogue, Report and Catalogue* (1930; Greater London Record Office, Acc. 2712), p. 10.

21. Contemporaries used the term 'Duke's Place' to refer to the Jewish community in general. Todd M. Endelman, *The Jews of Georgian England* (Philadelphia, 1979), p. 47.

22. Todd M. Endelman, *Radical Assimilation in English Jewish History 1656–1945* (Bloomington, IN, 1990), p. 34.

23. Aaron Hart attended rabbinical school in Poland, and his timely appearance in England coincides with the establishment of the Ashkenazi synagogue. *Dictionary of National Biography*, IX (1909), p. 55. Moses Hart's position influenced the appointment of his brother to the post of first rabbi of the synagogue.

24. Roth, *Archives of the United Synagogue*, p. 15. Within three years of the Great Synagogue's first reconstruction and in spite of Hart's efforts, the Hambro Synagogue materialized in Church Row, Fenchurch Street. A photograph taken before its 1892 demolition reveals a smaller but similar design to Bevis Marks, but no doubt comparable to the Great in its ritual and liturgical practice.

25. Three documents are held in the *Guildhall Library Manuscripts Collection*, MS. 7731: 'The Proposall of Moses Markes to the Parish to have a Senegogue'; 'The Opinion of Councell against the Senegogue 1725'; '1725 The Court of Aldermen Order against the senegogue'. In the final document it is recorded: 'a peticon of Moses Hart on behalf of himself and the rest of the members of the synagogue of German Jews complaining that one Markus Moses is now building a new synagogue for the Jews in Magpie Alley in Fenchurch Street . . .'.

26. Not only did Ashkenazim break away from the Sephardim, they were now divided among themselves. The physical distance between the two Ashkenazi congregations impeded communication and delayed the formation of mutually beneficial community services.

27. Endelman, *Jews of Georgian England*, p. 148.
28. Roth, *A History of the Jews in England*, p. 172.
29. Endelman, *Radical Assimilation*, p. 36.
30. *Jewish Chronicle* (JC), April 1890. Moses Hart's name derived from a remodelling of his father's name, Hartwig Moses; the family name, Pheibush, which Aaron (R. Pheibush) had kept before his arrival in London, was dropped altogether, clearly a sign of anglicization; Aaron, often referred to as the 'high priest', and Moses, undisputed leader, provide further association with their Biblical namesakes. It is entertaining to think that a painting of *Moses and Aaron Supporting the Ten Commandments* hung above the Ark at the Great. In addition, the illustration on the title-page of the *1791 Synagogue Takkanot* (body of rules) depicts the figures of Moses and Aaron, suggesting yet another association with the Hart brothers.
31. Cecil Roth, 'The Rise of Provincial Jewry', *Jewish Monthly* (London, 1950), p. 16.
32. Shoemaker Row was later renamed Duke Street.
33. Cecil Roth, 'The Great Synagogue – A Destroyed Building's Historical Associations', *JC*, 20 June 1941, p. 6.
34. As the lease is dated 7 Nov. 1760 (prior to the 1765–66 alterations) it can be assumed that the plan illustrated the 1722 dimensions of the building.
35. 'Lease from the mayor of London to Mr Aaron Franks and others of the Synagogue of Duke's Place', *Comptroller's City Lands Deeds*, Box 3, No. 17, Corporation of London Records Office (CLRO). The lease is dated 7 Nov. 1760 and was to run from Christmas 1760 for 40 years, expiring in 1800. The drawing is signed and dated 19 July 1762.
36. D'Blossiers Tovey, *Anglia Judaica* (1738), p. 301.
37. John Summerson, *Architecture in Britain 1530–1830* (London, 1983 edn), p. 556. Harrison had once been a pupil of Sir John Vanbrugh.
38. A. W. Brenner, 'Synagogue Architecture', *Brickbuilder*, Vol. 16, No. 7 (Feb. 1907), p. 25.
39. Moses Hart willed £1,000 to the London Hospital. *Gentleman's Magazine* (May 1756), p. 595: Abraham Franks was a governor of the Foundling Hospital.
40. Endelman, *Radical Assimilation*, p. 34.
41. Cecil Roth, 'The Lesser known Synagogues of the Eighteenth Century', *JHSE Miscellanies Part III* (London, 1937), p. 1.
42. The alternative place of worship was located in Bricklayers' Hall, Leadenhall Street, in the building of 'The Worshipful Company of Tylers and Bricklayers'. See also 'Agreement between Moses Jacobs and George Wright [builder] for construction of synagogue on site of Bricklayers' Hall'. United Synagogue Archives, Deeds 1759–1814, p. 58.
43. Endelman, *Radical Assimilation*, p. 39. The Franks family donated at least £1,000 towards the 1765–66 alterations.
44. Malcolm Brown, 'Anglo-Jewish Country Houses from the Resettlement to 1800', *TJHSE*, 1981–82, XXVIII (1984), p. 27. The house was built in 1765.
45. For details of the lease, see Notes 34 and 35 above.
46. *City Lands Journal*, Vol. 52, 22 Oct. 1760, CLRO.
47. A contiguous plot of ground in Broad Court was purchased from the couple on behalf of the congregation on 23 March 1765. Roth, *Great Synagogue*, p. 131.
48. There is no documentation which suggests that Dance Jr had any encounters with Jews while abroad. There is some correspondence within the Dance family relating to Tabitha Mendez (1725–1811), a rich but unlovely Jewess whom Nathaniel, George's brother, had some relationship with. Dorothy Stroud, *George Dance Architect* (London, 1971), p. 66.
49. Dan Cruickshank, *A Guide to the Georgian Buildings of Britain and Ireland* (London, 1985), p. 112.
50. See Stroud, *George Dance*, pp. 77–8. The footnote in her text, labelled '*', should read: C.R.O. Surveyor's Miscellaneous 18th Century Plans, Nos. 265, 268; also 199.
51. Roth, *Great Synagogue*, p. 131. Note their misleading description as 'Dutch' Jews; it probably referred to 'Deutsch' meaning German, or is perhaps an ignorant racial generalization.
52. The plan is dated 8 May 1765 and signed by William Pettit and James Taylor. *Surveyor's Miscellaneous Plans (Dance Portfolio)*, No. 265, CLRO.
53. The irregular distribution of pews on either side of the hall was due to the asymmetrical floor plan caused by merging two different buildings.
54. In the nineteenth century, pews were added between the *Aron Kodesh* and *bima*.
55. Stroud, *George Dance*, p. 75.
56. There is also a detail for a roof in the upper left-hand corner. The plan maintains

James Taylor's signature and probably William Pettit's (although illegible). The plan is dated 21 Dec. 1765. *Dance Drawing, Portfolio 7*, A.L.S.D., Sir John Soane's Museum.

57. On the verso is written: 'Dukes Place Des^{gn} for Music Gall^y in New Build^g bef. Synag. D2', *Surveyor's Miscellaneous Plans (Dance Portfolio)*, No. 199. According to Stroud (op. cit., p. 78), the plan carries a note signed by William Pettit and James Taylor, artisans, and is dated 8 May 1765. No evidence of that note has been found.

58. The variation in types of scale to those evident in the other synagogue plans further disproves Stroud's claim.

59. Jamilly, 'Synagogue Art and Architecture', p. 76.

60. Roth, *Great Synagogue*, p. 139.

61. D. C. Duschinsky, *The Rabbinate of the Great Synagogue – London from 1756–1842* (London, 1971), p. 84.

62. Roth, *Great Synagogue*, p. 141.

63. In 1774 Naphtali had negotiated with Edward Holmes (whose land the synagogue occupied) regarding the balance owed for his property. As synagogue funds had been exhausted because of the cost of alterations less than seven years previously, the trustees had no choice but to mortgage the place of worship to Holmes.

64. 'A Petition of Napthali Franks Esq. [*sic*] to renew a lease of Ground and Buildings on the East Side of Shoemaker Row', *City Lands Journal*, Vol. 79, 14 Sept. 1787, p. 174, CLRO. Also mentioned was an indentured lease with Edward Holmes dated 9 Oct. 1777.

65. 'On the 14th of September last we rec'd a petition from Napthali Franks Esq [*sic*], the surviving lessee, setting forth that the time of renewal had escaped the attention of the lessees, and that the part of the synagogue held under the city was in dangerous condition, and necessary to be rebuilt, and therefore requesting permission to review the said lease . . . and having referred to a sub-committee, they reported, that they had viewed the premises and had been attended by Mr Abraham Goldsmid who informed them, that it was intended forthwith to rebuild or substantially repair the whole of the synagogue, the other thereof being freehold . . .' *City Lands Journal*, Vol. 79, 20 Dec. 1787, p. 256, CLRO. In January 1788 a new 40-year lease was granted. 'Surrender of a Lease of a Synagogue – Adjoining in Shoemaker Row London', 24 Jan. 1788, *Comptroller City Lands Deeds*, Box 3, No. 17.

66. Roth, 'The Origins of the Great Synagogue', p. 2.

67. In addition to her personal contribution, a sum of approximately £5,000, left in trust by others, including her father, was appended to the fund. Building Accounts (1790–93), Greater London Record Office, United Synagogue Archives, Acc. 2712/I/B/23.

68. *Dictionary of National Biography*, VIII (1908), p. 80.

69. Following the reconstruction, loans by members of the Goldsmid family totalled more than £800. Greater London Record Office, United Synagogue Archives, Acc. 2712/I/B/23.

70. Pamela Fletcher Jones, *The Jews of Britain* (Gloucestershire, 1990), p. 134.

71. See the illustration in Endelman, *Jews of Georgian England*.

72. Levy Alexander, *Memoirs of the Life and Commercial Connections, public and private, of the late Benjamin Goldsmid, esq. of Roehampton containing A Cursory View of the Jewish Society and Manners* (London, 1808), p. 24.

73. Algernon Graves (ed.), *The Royal Academy of Arts, A Complete Dictionary of Contributors and their work from its foundation in 1769 to 1904*, VII (London, 1906), p. 220. The work was attributed to 'Spiller, John . . . Architect', but 'John' should certainly be 'James'. The architect contributed various works to the Academy in 1780, 1792, 1801 (including Goldsmid's villa) and 1805. Designs for the Great Synagogue were never exhibited.

74. James Picciotto, *Sketches of Anglo-Jewish History* (London, 1956), p. 242. There is a sketch at Sir John Soane's Museum for the decoration of one of the rooms (F. 14); although Soanian features are evident in the design, it was drawn by Spiller.

75. Endelman, *Radical Assimilation*, p. 39.

76. Howard Colvin, *A Biographical Dictionary of British Architects 1600–1840* (London, 1978), p. 564.

77. Ibid., p. 772.

78. Arthur T. Bolton (ed.), *The Portrait of Sir John Soane, R.A.* (London, 1927), p. 155.

79. Ibid., p. 101.

80. Jamilly, 'Synagogue Art and Architecture', p. 77.

81. Spiller frequently complained about the subordinate state of contemporary church design. He was the author of a pamphlet titled *A Letter to John Soane, Esq. . . . on the*

subject of the New Churches (1822), which strongly criticized the design of churches built under the Act of 1818. At Sir John Soane's Museum there is a small collection of Spiller's unexecuted church designs (XLVII, Nos. 22–31).

82. John Summerson, *Georgian London* (London, 1988), p. 207.

83. The drawing is dated 20 June 1791 (verso). Sir John Soane's Museum (47/10/31).

84. *Redgrave's Dictionary of Artists* (1878) states that John Spiller was born in 1763. No other record has been discovered which supports an alternative date of birth. John Spiller was a pupil of the sculptor Charles Bacon. Further adding to the confusion between the two brothers, in the Royal Academy's *Dictionary of Contributors* (see Note 73), James Spiller is recorded as 'Spiller, John . . . Architect', while his brother is noted as 'Spiller, John, Junr. . . . Sculptor' (p. 220). Both of their residences were listed as Highbury Place, Islington.
    John Spiller was noted as the mason for the St John's project in a letter dated 20 Oct. 1820 (Sir John Soane's Museum, Private Correspondence, X.D.1, letter 3). He died while construction of the church was in progress.

85. In large letters at the front of the Accounts Ledger was written: 'Account of Moneys Recievd [*sic*] and Paid to Mr L de Symons Treasurer for Building the Great Synagogue in Duke's Place London under the Direction of Mr Jon Spiller Surveyor which was consecrated on Friday . . . being the 26th Day of March 1790.' In the list of payees, 'Jon Spiller Mason' earned £621 7s., and further down the list, 'James Spiller Surveyor' was recorded as being paid £541 15s.

86. *Laws of the Great Synagogue* (London, 1863), p. IV.

87. Building Accounts (1790–93), Greater London Record Office, Acc. 2712/I/B/23. The document discusses annuities to John Weston for 53 years after which the properties would belong to the synagogue. One of these houses may have been converted into the *mikveh*; see Kadish, this volume.

88. 'Lease of a part of a synagogue and a small building adjoining on the West side of Duke Street late Shoemaker Row . . .', 30 April 1844. *Comptroller's City Lands Deeds*, Box 173, No. 37.

89. The buildings were independently constructed as is clearly discernible from their uneven window heights.

90. See the plan in Portfolio Volume 1, Surveyor's City Lands Plans, No. 37, CLRO.

91. C. F. Partington, *National History and Views of London and its Environs*, II (London, 1834), p. 207.

92. One of the entrances also accessed a strong-room.

93. 1790 was the 500th year after the expulsion of the Jews from England. The relatively accessible design of the Great Synagogue reflected the degree of toleration which they had achieved.

94. Unlike the practice in the Sephardi Synagogue in Amsterdam, poor men never sat in the galleries; instead they were accommodated behind a bar at the rear of the hall, close to the main entrance but separate from the more affluent members' seats.

95. During the eighteenth century, the Chief Rabbi was hailed as the 'High Priest' and the synagogue known as the 'Jewish Church in England'. Gentile visitors to the area commented on the 'Christian' pomp of the ceremony, and it was true that in many ways the synagogue's ritual forms looked to non-Jewish archetypes just as it had for its architecture.

96. Rosenau, 'Architectural Development of the Synagogue', p. 82.

97. Partington, *National History and Views of London*, II, p. 207.

98. Interest in synagogue design resulted from a drawing of a Dutch synagogue in *Gentleman's Magazine* (1788). Jamilly, 'Anglo-Jewish Architects and Architecture', p. 130.

99. Krinsky, *Synagogues of Europe*, p. 389.

5

SYNAGOGUE BODIES:
Building Policy and Conservation Issues

EDWARD JAMILLY

Hardly any authenticated pre-Expulsion monuments of Jewish life and worship exist; those that do owe their survival to local authorities (where they have become part of the history of a town), to institutions, or to a succession of private owners (starting with robber barons!) who have succeeded in finding alternative uses.

Synagogue bodies are a recent phenomenon. Only the Sephardim can claim an organization originating from the Resettlement of 1656. Although the first of its constituent synagogues can be traced back to 1692, the United Synagogue, often regarded as the leading body, came into being as late as 1870.

The Reform secession took place earlier, in 1840, and Samuel Montagu brought the Federation into being in 1887. Liberal and Progressive synagogues to the left and the Orthodox Union to the right (popularly known as the Adath) are creations of the early decades of the twentieth century, while the Masorti movement is a mere 30 years old. The extent to which these bodies have protected buildings in their custody is discussed here.

A HISTORY OF LOSS AND NEGLECT

Most of the synagogues constructed in England since the Resettlement have disappeared. Some fell victim to shrinking and migrating congregations and schisms before being demolished or sold for other uses. Others were rebuilt to accommodate growing congregations. Bombing of the East End of London during the Second World War took its toll: the Great Synagogue in Duke's Place, which would be a Grade I building today, was gutted; buildings of social history such as the Jews' Free School, the Free Reading Room, Jews' Infant School, the Beth Din and Beth HaMedrash were wrecked, as were a number of small synagogues in London and the provinces. Architecturally, the significant losses are the Georgian and Regency synagogues, most of which have gone without trace. For illustrations of important Hanoverian synagogues such as

Exeter, Portsmouth and Liverpool we have to thank the National Buildings Record, public libraries or print-sellers, not Jewish agencies.

Such historical detritus as survives seldom owes its existence to synagogue bodies. For example, the Canterbury Synagogue of 1847, unique as an Egyptian Revival building, was in the stewardship of the Charity Commissioners from 1931 until the opening of the University of Kent in 1965 brought Jewish students and teaching staff to the area, giving it a new lease of life. When that revival faded out, the King's School bought the building in 1982, refurbished it and now uses the Old Synagogue as a music room. A number of European synagogues[1] whose congregations are long since departed have been conscientiously restored by state or municipality; not much of this goes on in the United Kingdom!

There is a depressing picture of neglect by Jewish agencies in Britain. Over 30 years ago I stood on the leaking roof of Exeter Synagogue (built in 1763–64) and tried to interest the Jewish Memorial Council in raising the cost of repairs to cure the damp and rot that pervaded the interior. The estimated cost of a new roof was then under £5,000, a sum far beyond the resources of a small community. After years of neglect £30,000 was spent on repairs from central funds. That is the price of delay. I have rescued prayer books left in the debris of the Bayswater Synagogue, Harrow Road, London. Others have plundered once great synagogues in Manchester and East London as soon as their doors closed.

Standing in the static water tank that the Maiden Lane Synagogue (1829) became, I looked at two and a half walls and tried to envisage how it had been (there are no illustrations). Through the good offices of a scene painter, whose theatrical backdrops hung from the ceiling, I was able to see the interior of the Borough Synagogue much as it was drawn in the *Illustrated London News* in 1867. More imagination was needed during the 1960s in a furniture repository[2] on a hill overlooking Falmouth Harbour to reconstruct the 1808 synagogue as it had been before becoming a cinema. For descriptions and pictures of Victorian synagogues we rely heavily on non-Jewish newspapers and their illustrators, even for important ones in the capital demolished during or after the Second World War, for example Barnsbury, Bayswater and the Central.

Fine Victorian buildings with shrinking congregations are today expiring in such centres as Birmingham, Liverpool and London, their listing regarded more as an irksome restraint than a matter for communal pride. However, not all Jewish monuments are under the control of synagogue bodies, particularly in the provinces. The larger metropolitan bodies and their conservation record are discussed below.

THE SPANISH AND PORTUGUESE CONGREGATION

The oldest of present-day synagogal bodies, the Spanish and Portuguese, almost lost the most venerable 'temple' in England when the elders and congregants decided to demolish and redevelop its site, prompting the formation of the Bevis Marks Anti-Demolition League of 1885, which obtained a reprieve.

The proposed redevelopment arose from the north and westward migration of congregants from Aldgate, resulting in branch synagogues being opened in Wigmore Street (1853), Bryanston Street (1869), Canonbury (1883), Maida Vale (1896) and, in this century, Wembley. Associated synagogues were later founded in Holland Park, Golders Green, Stamford Hill and Harrow.

The mercantile tendencies of the leaders of the congregation were counterbalanced by a small group of outstanding historians and antiquarians, including Lucien Wolf, who headed the Anti-Demolition League. Wilfred Samuel, first chairman of the Jewish Museum London, reconstructed on paper the first synagogue of the Resettlement,[3] with the assistance of Manuel Castello who drew the plan, and researched a great deal else. Haham Gaster described Bevis Marks; Albert Hyamson (a former civil servant in Palestine) wrote the Sephardi history; surveys of old cemeteries in the East End and as far afield as Barbados were undertaken. Dr Lionel Barnett, who chaired the Records Committee, published much congregational material and assembled a scholarly catalogue of synagogue silver and furniture.[4] His son Richard, also a Keeper at the British Museum, chaired the Tercentenary Exhibition

5.1   London, Bevis Marks Synagogue (Joseph Avis, 1701). *Anthony Harris*

Committee in 1956. These scholars provided a body of historiography in which the Spanish and Portuguese congregation could take pride and it has behaved itself ever since, conscientiously maintaining the established London synagogues and assisting others, including the Amsterdam Great Synagogue.

Today, Sephardi charities support a preparatory school and old-age home. Old and new cemeteries and links with overseas communities are kept up by the congregation. Although there is no scheme of planned maintenance, money is set aside for repairs and expended when the need arises. However, the outbreak of timber infestation in Bevis Marks in 1991 and the damage inflicted by the IRA bomb at the Baltic Exchange in the following year were beyond the resources of a congregation of 1,700 members, and it has had to appeal to a wider public for help.[5]

Manchester still maintains three operational synagogues built by local benefactors and independently supported. This city's fourth and oldest Sephardi synagogue has, through the imagination and efforts of Bill Williams, a local non-Jewish historian, become the Manchester Jewish Museum, but that could falter if grants are discontinued.

Nevertheless, the Sephardim's conservation record has not been entirely unblemished. Their rabbinical seminary was transferred to a mean suburban house in London and the fine Victorian collegiate crescent (1866) at Ramsgate demolished and sold off. During the Montefiore centenary celebrations (1985) there was a proposal to remove the bones of the patriarch and his wife from their Ramsgate mausoleum and crate them up for reburial in Israel. Few rabbis would have supported unequivocally the exhumation of thousands of graves, the destruction of headstones and sale of the greater part of the *Nuevo* cemetery in East London during the late Rabbi Dr Solomon Gaon's Hahamate.

The section of Anglo-Jewry most conscious of its past let go for redevelopment its original almshouses in the East End, its vestry offices and school in the City. Branch synagogues were closed in the lifetime of the present *Mahamad*'s[6] grandparents without an adequate pictorial record being made. And who, one wonders, authorized the application of polystyrene tiles to the ceiling of Bevis Marks, a Grade I listed building with excellent acoustics, or a cornice replacement in fibreglass and the wholesale ripping out of timbers undisturbed for 300 years instead of a conservation repair – leaving English Heritage unhappy with the way 'ecclesiastical exemption' was exercised?

The Sephardim have been discussed at some length because they illustrate well the ambivalence of synagogue bodies towards conservation. Their synagogues, though few in number, include three of great architectural interest: at Bevis Marks, in Ramsgate and at Lauderdale Road, London – all listed buildings.

THE UNITED SYNAGOGUE

The United Synagogue is not only a great deal larger and in command (until very recently) of greater funds but more philistine in its attitude towards building conservation. The President reported to his Council in

July 1991 that four million pounds could be realized through the closure or merger of under-used synagogues. 'It is fundamentally wrong,' he said, 'to have spiritually non-viable communities in buildings that are massive, costly to operate and in very little use.'[7]

Who would contradict him, if he was thinking of expensive blunders such as the Marble Arch and Central Synagogues, built at enormous cost some 30 years ago by short-sighted United Synagogue lay leaders in search of aggrandizement? Or the Western Synagogue, for whom a church in Crawford Street was converted and as quickly closed? And there was the unhappy incident of the Bayswater Synagogue that the United Synagogue was drummed into rebuilding in Maida Vale; it lasted a mere 25 years, though it has now happily been turned into a Jewish preparatory school. But an outstanding edifice like the New West End Synagogue[8] deserves to be retained, and even if its congregation diminished the building could perhaps serve a wider community.

The United Synagogue has not been keen to see its synagogues pass to other congregations since the débâcle over the so-called 'Jacobs affair', when its redundant St John's Wood (Abbey Road) Synagogue became the seat of its dissenting minister – although this resulted in a splendid refurbishment. The disposal of the New Synagogue, Stamford Hill to the Bobov community has not run smoothly, and the fate of the East London Synagogue, sold to developers, has reflected little credit on the vendors.[9] There is a tendency to group some independent synagogues with the United Synagogue, but a distinction should be drawn between constituent and affiliated synagogues; some provincial buildings of quality are in the keeping of self-governing congregations.

One cannot help feeling that the United Synagogue is ruled more by financial than spiritual considerations. Local synagogues are urged to be managed as business centres, as the 1992 Kalms Report demonstrated. As younger congregants move to more fashionable areas, so demands are made for new building loans, which can be provided from the proceeds of sale of older buildings. Scant thought is given to the residual congregants or to the future of a redundant building that deserves to be treated with respect for its architecture and history. A dying congregation may revive owing to social change: indeed population shifts during the two world wars opened a few provincial synagogues[10] and closed others. One wonders why the adherents of *shtiebels* unable to obtain planning consent for expansion are not encouraged to join ageing London suburban synagogues, bringing fresh blood and a resurgence of Jewish life.

For its post-war building programme the United Synagogue has shown a pathetic faith in the architectural tastes of the successful businessmen and lawyers appointed as lay leaders. Its officers can hardly know how to treat building interiors sympathetically or we would not have seen the blue-and-white decor and varnished panelling applied throughout the synagogues of the 1930s nor the suburbanization of the interior of Dollis Hill Synagogue. The various attempts made during the last 30 years to persuade the United Synagogue to take the lead in setting up an advisory council for the care of synagogues have met with a cool response. In 1970, when the United Synagogue celebrated its centenary,

5.2   London, the New West End Synagogue, St Petersburgh Place, Bayswater (G. Audsley and N. S. Joseph, 1878). *Anthony Harris*

it caught a brief glimpse of its history and applauded the achievements of its ancestors.[11] Their patrimony is now being sold off, starting with 'the family silver' – much of it inherited from the founding synagogues and on loan to the Jewish Museum – which the Museum was forced to buy. Under financial pressure, accountants are now taking charge, and this development augurs ill for the conservation of worthwhile buildings. Although it has counted as many as 80 member congregations, some would regard the United Synagogue as a diminishing force, losing members to fast-growing groups on the religious left and to the right.

THE FEDERATION AND THE ORTHODOX UNION

Formed as an umbrella organization for the many small *minyanim* and *chevrot* which immigrant Jews created in the East End of London during the last quarter of the nineteenth century, the Federation of Synagogues built some new places of worship of its own, but its leaders seem not to have believed in 'architecture' or perhaps could not afford good architects.

There was a tinselly feel about Federation interiors in the East End. Its principal synagogue in Philpot Street, Stepney, had a pretentious portico badly grafted on to a plain hall; it was bombed during the Blitz on London. The folksy east European interior of Princelet Street Synagogue (1870) – itself a conversion – served as a garment workshop until rescued by the (non-Jewish) Heritage Trust. This and other disused synagogues in the East End have been documented[12] more for reasons of social history than for architectural merit. In its role as a burial society, the Federation's oldest cemetery in Edmonton stands in stark contrast to the well-kept burial grounds of the United Synagogue at Willesden and Bushey; its records seem as haphazard as its maintenance.

There have been recurring problems about finance, and one doubts whether the Federation has anything more than an *ad hoc* policy towards repairs. Conservation is probably quite alien to its ethos, but few of its synagogues are worth a second glance for their architecture, and none of the 32 currently functioning is a listed building.

How much more so does this apply to the Union of Orthodox Hebrew Congregations and its affiliates, now numbering over 40 and based in north and north-west London. For many strictly Orthodox congregations a *minyan* makes a synagogue and they can worship happily in private houses and even tents in the garden, while the 'evangelists' are more

5.3   London, Kehillat Yaakov (Congregation of Jacob) Synagogue, Commercial Road, E1 (1921, rebuilt 1930). *Susie Barson*

5.4   London, Great Garden Street
Federation Synagogue, Greatorex Street,
E1 (1924). *English Heritage*

noticeable in the streets. Chasidic sects are generously supportive of
their institutions, as are followers of respected religious leaders such
as the late Rabbi Eli Munk. Finance is made readily available for their
usually modest buildings, none of which, however, yet qualifies for
conservation.

MASORTI

By contrast the Masorti, although the newest synagogue body, owns one
listed building and could well take over others, as the movement (roughly
equivalent to Conservative Judaism in the United States) is growing fast.
The New London Synagogue started well by carrying out perhaps the
most sensitive refurbishment undertaken in recent years: Misha Black's
1965 renewal of the St John's Wood Synagogue (Abbey Road), formerly
the property of the United Synagogue. This was followed by a North
London branch, accommodated with admirable simplicity in a former
convent chapel at Finchley, and the movement now numbers five
congregations.

REFORM SYNAGOGUES OF GREAT BRITAIN (RSGB)

The Jewish Reform movement came to this country from Germany in
the middle of the nineteenth century. Two of its early synagogues are
listed Grade II, both still open: the small Moorish temple of 1880 in
Bradford and the large Byzantine West London Synagogue (1870) in
Upper Berkeley Street, W1. The frilly horseshoe Gothic of Manchester's
Park Place Synagogue came a little earlier (1854); the classical revival
(with cast-iron structure) of London's second Reform temple in Margaret
Street was earlier still (1849); both are now gone, one through bombing,
the other after replacement. Unfortunately, no pictures of the very first
London Reform synagogue[13] in Burton Street exist.

Most of the Reform synagogues of Great Britain, now 41 in number,
were built since the Second World War, and owing to the autonomy
enjoyed by each congregation, upkeep depends on local funding, which
may not always be adequate. A comprehensive survey of Reform buildings has yet to be made. Their 'flagship', the West London Synagogue,
flourishes – having even expanded its facilities – and is the best of the
synagogue buildings remaining in the West End, although its ceilings,
shaken by wartime bombing, were put back without their original
geometric decorations.[14]

THE LIBERAL AND PROGRESSIVE MOVEMENT

It is perhaps too early to think about conserving Liberal Jewish buildings,
although the St John's Wood congregation was much attached to its
1925 Greek portico opposite Lord's Cricket Ground, retaining it through
two reconstructions of the synagogue that it fronts. The West Central
congregation, after losing a fairly distinguished disused Baptist chapel in

5.5   London, St John's Wood Synagogue,
Abbey Road, NW8 (H. H. Collins, 1882);
after restoration in 1965 by Misha Black.
Greater London Record Office

5.6   London, the Liberal Jewish
Synagogue, St John's Wood Road, NW8
(Ernest Joseph, 1925); the rebuilt
portico (using the original Portland
stone) and the new synagogue complex
behind (Preston Rubins Associates,
1991). *Anthony Harris*

Hill Street, its first (1911) synagogue, has now rebuilt for the second time in Whitfield Street, W1, in combination with flats and offices, a popular formula in recent years for the redevelopment of over-large church sites.

There are currently over a dozen Liberal and Progressive synagogues, some in converted buildings such as the former Methodist church now accommodating the North London Progressive Synagogue in Amhurst Park, N16. As this and other expanding movements grow, there may be considerable potential for adopting redundant synagogues of the 'Establishment'.

THE CARE OF SYNAGOGUES

There is a tendency to look to synagogue bodies for leadership, but the record of the recent administration of the United Synagogue, in particular, hardly inspires confidence in their ability to deal sensitively with conservation issues. On the other hand, the architectural historian alone is insufficient; he or she seldom ventures inside a synagogue but tends to

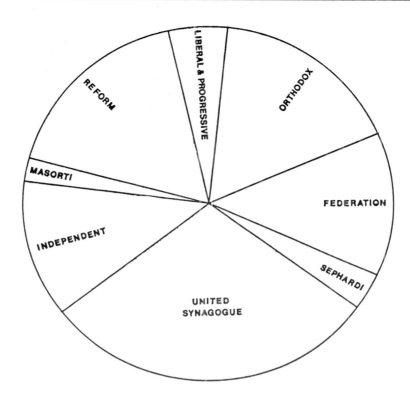

5.7   Pie chart showing the affiliations of British Jews.

conduct research in libraries. There is an absence of comprehensive reference data, such as exist abroad. The definitive gazetteer of Jewish monuments has not yet been published, nor has the architectural history of the English synagogue. Pevsner cannot be relied upon: some of his attributions were wrong, and there are strange, bizarre and beautiful things he never saw – Georgian woodwork in Devon, Byzantine mosaics in the north-east, Castilian friezes in Bayswater, an Egyptian temple in Canterbury and, in ancient cemeteries, the most beautifully cut headstones.

There is a great need for an authoritative advisory body to which synagogues of all shades of observance could refer on the design and conservation of their buildings, possibly based on the Working Party on Jewish Monuments in the United Kingdom and Ireland. The temporal bodies controlling synagogues should be less prone to deciding on the life or death of a synagogue, its alteration or even a change of colouring, as if it belonged to them. These buildings were mostly constructed by public subscription headed by individual philanthropists and the present organizations are 'caretakers', who should take the most skilled advice before determining their future. Insensitive treatment by inexperienced administrators should be avoided.

Paradoxically, as synagogue organizations have neglected to respect their inheritance, there has been growing recognition by non-Jewish bodies of the importance of synagogue buildings to the general architectural heritage of Britain. Cecil Roth, writing in 1947 in the aftermath of the Nazi maelstrom, drew attention to the wholesale destruction of the Jewish artistic patrimony in Europe and went on to say: 'We have delayed study until it was too late; it is well that we should try at least to preserve the memory and turn our attention to what remains while there is still time.'

When I addressed the Jewish Historical Society on the subject of Anglo-Jewish architecture in 1954,[15] there were only three listed synagogues: Bevis Marks, Exeter and Plymouth. Today there are ten listed synagogues in London (the majority listed in the last five years) and some 21 more in England as a whole.[16] The original initiative came principally from the late Dr Vivian Lipman who, when Director of Ancient Monuments, instituted a review that led to the first listings. Ground was also broken by local enthusiasts of the Jewish Historical Society such as Bertram Benas (Liverpool), Alex Jacob (Falmouth) and David Spector (Brighton), and their efforts introduced Jewish artifacts and architecture to statutory conservation bodies at the national level for the first time. The underlying motive has been that 'If you demonstrate the quality of a building, it is less likely to be demolished.'[17]

Much has been achieved in obtaining within a short timespan[18] official recognition of so many synagogues, but synagogue bodies do not yet seem fully conscious of the importance of their holdings, nor are they particularly amenable to outside advice – the prerequisite for successful conservation.

The difficulties of conserving little-used synagogues of quality are compounded by the absence of religious restraints. Although consecrated at its opening (or reopening after alterations or refurbishment), a synagogue has only a temporary sanctity while in use – unlike cemeteries and certain ritual objects (for example a *Sefer Torah*). It does not have to be deconsecrated. Once its congregation has moved away it can be disposed of for other purposes, although the ritual furnishings should be (but have not always been) removed.[19]

Rabbinical opinion holds that Judaism is perpetuated by teaching, not by buildings, and many rabbis regard it as a moral duty to free funds locked up in a redundant building or its site for educational purposes. Although the passing of a fine building and its ghosts may be regretted, the conservationist can look for little support from the clergy. It may often be more productive to seek an alternative use than to oppose closure.[20]

CONSERVATION BY ALTERNATIVE USE

What are the options for redundant synagogues of quality? Some have been adopted by other faiths just as Jews have converted Christian meeting places all over the country for their use. The best-known London example is the Machzike Hadath in Fournier Street, E1, a Huguenot church before it became, in the late Dr Bernard Homa's words, 'a fortress in Anglo-Jewry'. It is now a mosque. Penzance Synagogue was turned into a gospel hall before being annexed by a nearby public house. Synagogues redundant for one Jewish organization could be sold to another, were it not for *shul* politics and pride. A danger within this scenario is that damage may be done to artifacts of which the

5.8 London, the Spitalfields Great Synagogue (Machzike Hadath), Fournier Street and Brick Lane, E1, in 1946; the building was originally a Huguenot Chapel (1740s) and is now a mosque. *Greater London Record Office*

purchasers may disapprove, just as churches have suffered at the hands of different Christian denominations, Catholic, Protestant and Non-conformist. Synagogues have become school halls[21] and workshops. Hull's first synagogue became part of a dock, the second was turned into a warehouse and the third is now a nightclub! Can this really be acceptable? The Jew's House, Lincoln (1170) survives to this day as a shop with living accommodation, as well as a famous Jewish monument.

Churches have successfully converted into offices and studios, have been adapted for flats and various media uses: music, art and drama. As in the case of churches, so too can the best features of synagogues be preserved, while movable furnishings should be transferred and reused as in the past,[22] with a record kept of the provenance of these objects. Imaginative suggestions have been made for the preservation of historic but little-used synagogues, for example that Ramsgate Synagogue be taken apart and reassembled in a populous Jewish area,[23] and that the

5.9 London, Spital Square Poltava (German) Synagogue in the 1920s. The congregation dates back to 1858 and the building was erected in 1886. It was a founder member of the Federation of Synagogues. It was destroyed in the Blitz.

The Federation of Synagogues

attic of Bevis Marks, which is as large as the synagogue hall, be converted to house the Jewish Museum,[24] thus combining the two places most sought after by Jewish tourists to London. Neither idea was followed up by a feasibility study.

THE IMPORTANCE OF RECORDS

If all attempts fail to keep a historic building in use, it is essential to recover records, to take photographs and to make measured drawings and sketches before demolition. The United Synagogue archives committee has placed the responsibility on the honorary officers and hard-pressed synagogue secretaries, but systematic records should be made by professionals and kept centrally where they are available to scholars and the public. The United Synagogue cannot produce plans of all the properties it owns. Many people cannot locate their great-grandparents' graves. Many interesting buildings have gone unrecorded. We cannot find illustrations of over half of the synagogues that have been built in the United Kingdom. It is important not to ignore the internal features of unlikely or unprepossessing buildings, which often house interesting relics of the past. Private synagogues have been incorporated in houses, hospitals and ships. Many *Sifrei Torah* have old silver finials that pre-date them, often with missing bells – there should be a committee for restoring *rimonim*.

The word 'monument' signifies a memorial, a reminder or a record, an appeal to future generations not to neglect or forget the past.[25] During the 1930s Wilfred Samuel and Cecil Roth were the first in Britain to see the need to preserve works of art and craftsmanship that illuminate the Jewish past and its spirit. In the wake of the destruction wrought during the Second World War, restlessness and discontent have given way to a nostalgia for a vanishing past. The case for preserving Jewish monuments has been made many times but never more fiercely than today. A series of conferences, in Southampton, in New York City and in London during recent years, has brought new pressure to bear on synagogue bodies to value and conserve their inheritance.

NOTES

1. In the Czech Republic, Slovakia, Denmark, France, Germany, Holland, Italy and Poland.
2. Julians had left Doric columns and pilasters just visible among the piles of storage. I am informed the building is now a studio.
3. Creechurch Lane; see *Transactions of the Jewish Historical Society of England* (*TJHSE*), X, 1924.
4. *Treasures of a London Temple* (London, 1951).
5. See Sir Peter Levene, 'A new lease of life for Britain's oldest synagogue' (Bevis Marks Appeal pamphlet, 1992). Further minor damage was occasioned by the second IRA bomb in Bishopsgate in April 1993.
6. Board of Elders.
7. Sidney Frosh, as reported in the *Jewish Chronicle* (*JC*), 12 July 1991.
8. See Jamilly, Chapter 9 in this volume, and 'An Introduction to Victorian Synagogues', *Victorian Society Annual*, 1991, pp. 22–35.
9. Sharman Kadish, 'Disused Synagogue a monumental disaster', *JC*, 11 Oct. 1991.
10. For example, Canterbury Synagogue, cited above, closed in 1911 but was reopened to hold services for troops from 1914 onwards. In Basingstoke, a country town previously without a Jewish community, a synagogue was opened during the Great War for military tailors and Jewish soldiers in the locality.
11. See S. S. Levin (ed.), *A Century of Anglo-Jewish Life, 1870–1970* (London, 1970).
12. See Gina Glasman, *East End Synagogues* (Museum of the Jewish East End, now London Museum of Jewish Life, 1987).
13. A converted Baptist chapel had served the congregation from 1842 to 1849.
14. Exempt from contributions under the War Damage Act, ecclesiastical buildings had to content themselves with a 'plain repair' after the Second World War.
15. See *TJHSE*, XVIII (1953–55), pp. 127–41.
16. With the help of English Heritage, particularly Susie Barson of the London Division.
17. Hermione Hobhouse, editor of the Survey of London, as reported in *Building Design*, 21 Aug. 1992.
18. This compares favourably with the national time-scale, from 68 monuments listed in 1882 to 170,000 buildings and 2,000 conservation areas a century later.

19. For example, a photograph taken during the 1970s of the former New Road and Grove Street Synagogue, Whitechapel (1892), then in use as an Asian dress factory, shows the Ark and Decalogue still in place.
20. See Rosenberg, Chapter 10 in this volume.
21. Brondesbury Synagogue was acquired by Kilburn and Brondesbury School for this purpose and now (1995) houses an Islamic centre within its Moorish portals. Canterbury, cited above, is another example.
22. For example, the *bima* from Old Portsmouth Synagogue went to Bournemouth, the Ark to Southsea; Hampstead's Ark is now in Ealing Synagogue. Westminster and other synagogues in Britain house *Sifrei Torah* rescued from Central Europe.
23. Several precedents exist: the transfer of the New Synagogue from Bishopsgate to Stamford Hill by Marcus Samuel; the transfer by another benefactor, Fred Worms, of a Cochin Synagogue to the Israel Museum, in Jerusalem, where the interior of the Vittorio Veneto synagogue has also been reassembled, the gift of Jakob Michael.
24. I am indebted to Rabbi Dr Abraham Levy for this and the previous suggestion. However, the Museum is now transferred to Camden Town, an area with no Jewish connections other than a day school. See Kadish, Introduction, above.
25. Professor Sir Ernst Gombrich's address at the World Monuments Fund European Monuments Forum, Switzerland, 1983.

6

'EDEN IN ALBION':
A History of the *Mikveh* in Britain

SHARMAN KADISH

And a river went out of Eden to water the garden, and from
there it split and became four headwaters.

Genesis 2:10

INTRODUCTION

Since Temple times, and indeed before, the *mikveh* (pl. *mikvaot*; literally,
'a gathering of water') or ritual bath has played an essential role in
the practice of Judaism.[1] Ritual immersion (*tevila*) to achieve spiritual
purification (*tahara*), as opposed to spiritual impurity (*tuma*), has been
practised since the Giving of the Law on Sinai, although its function in
connection with the Temple rite died out with the destruction of the
Second Temple in 68 C.E. However, the *mikveh* has retained a primary
function in the regulation of conjugal relations. To this day, it is used by
Orthodox Jewish women in fulfilment of the laws of family purity
(*taharat haMishpakha*). Immersion in the *mikveh* is also an essential prerequisite to conversion to Judaism for both men and women. It is believed
that the Christian rite of baptism is derived from *mikveh*. There is also a
custom (*minhag*) among strictly Orthodox men, especially Chasidim, to
immerse in the *mikveh* as a means of spiritual purification on the eve of
the Sabbath, New Year and Yom Kippur. A special small pool known as
a *kelim mikveh* is used for the ritual purification of metal and glass utensils,
when bought or obtained from a non-Jew, as a form of 'dedication' for
use by Jews.

The detailed laws (*halakhot*) which apply to the construction of the
mikveh are ultimately derived from the verse: 'Only a spring, and a pit, a
gathering of water, shall be clean' (Leviticus 11:36). Since these laws
have important implications for the design of the *mikveh* it is useful to
summarize them here.[2]

1. The *mikveh* must consist of clear, natural water. This natural water
may be one of two types:
    a) coming out of the ground, that is, a spring (*mayan*) or, in some
    cases, a river derived mainly from springs, or a well (*bor*) of 'living
    water' (*mayim chayim*), or the sea[3]; or
    b) rainwater, snow or melted ice.[4]
The rainwater *mikveh*, as opposed to the *mayan*, is the type most
commonly in use today.

2. The receptacle (*bor*) containing the water, and its ancillary pipework,

can be manmade. It must be fixed; that is, the *mikveh* must be built directly into the ground or be an integral part of a building attached to the ground. In certain circumstances it may be built in an upper storey. The *mikveh* cannot consist of any vessel (*kelei*) that can be disconnected and carried away, or can hold water, such as a tub, vat or barrel (*tephisat yadei adam*), or indeed a prefabricated structure.

3. The water must be gathered or static in one place, that is, not flowing (*zokhlin*); the container must be completely watertight. The only exception to this rule is the *mayan*, a natural spring, or a river derived mainly from springs. A river whose water is derived mainly from rainwater or melted ice and snow does not possess the status of a spring and, since it is flowing, is not a kosher *mikveh*.[5]

4. The water of the *mikveh* cannot be drawn (*shoavin*); that is, it cannot be brought to the *mikveh* through direct human intervention, for example, by pumping (although it can be removed by electric or automatic pump, so long as the pump itself cannot hold any water).

5. The water cannot be channelled to the *mikveh* through any vessel which can become impure (*tomeh*), even if that vessel cannot hold any water. For this reason, it cannot flow to the *mikveh* through pipes made of metal. Thus the pipes are usually sunk in the ground, thereby ensuring that they no longer have the status of vessels, or they are made of earthenware or plastic.

6. When a pool has fulfilled the above requirements (paragraphs 1–5), it is a valid *mikveh* and cannot lose its kosher status by the addition of more ordinary water. Therefore one can add any amount of water to it (but not take it away).

7. A rainwater *mikveh* must contain at least 40 *se'ah* of water, calculated at between 80 and 200 gallons, 24 cubic feet. Forty *se'ah* is traditionally taken to be about twice the volume of the average man, 'the measure of man'. In former times, there was a tendency to build large pool *mikvaot* according to the most generous calculations. The *mikveh* pool is, in any event, large enough for several people to stand in comfortably, with water reaching chest level. There is a further rule, that provided that half of the water in the *mikveh* is kosher (a minimum of 21 *se'ah*) non-valid water may be mixed with it, if it flows over three *tephachim* (about 30 cm of ground).

The most common method used for the construction of *mikvaot* in modern times is based upon the following principle: the construction of a *bor* of natural water *as a source* to give another pool, of tap water, connected with it the status of a *mikveh*. The water in the latter pool can thus be changed as often as required (water in a rainwater *mikveh* is liable to stagnate, unlike that in a *mayan*), or for heating purposes. Generally, rainwater is gathered in a tank on the roof of the structure and conveyed underground, where three separate tanks have been constructed:

a) The *Hashaka* 'kissing' or 'contact' tank. This contains the natural rainwater and is connected to the main pool (c) by means of a hole about two inches in diameter below the water-line, thus enabling the water from one pool to mix freely with the water from the other (the 'kissing' of the waters).

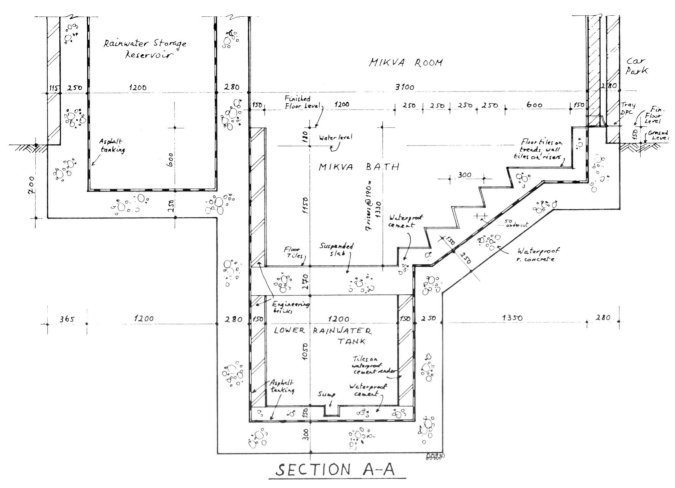

SECTION A-A

6.1 South London *Mikveh*,
Wimbledon (Rabbi Meir Posen, 1991);
plan showing the position of the water
tanks. *Rabbi Meir Posen*

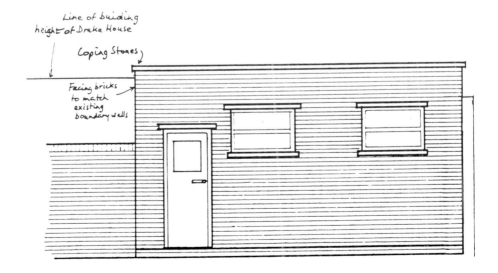

Elevation to Car Park — North-East

6.2 South London *Mikveh*,
Wimbledon (Rabbi Meir Posen, 1991);
the front elevation. *Rabbi Meir Posen*

b) The *Zeria* 'seeding' tank. This is used for passing tap water through it. Tanks (a) and (b) are waterproofed to stop any leakage, which would constitute flow and therefore make the rainwater *mikveh* invalid.

c) The *Mikveh*, which is both waterproofed and tiled and is used for *tevila*. A series of steps leads down into the pool. In actual fact, the *mikveh* used for immersion consists of both *Zeria* and tap water, but it is considered to have been 'added' to the original *bor* by means of the connecting hole and is thus a valid *mikveh* in itself. Most *mikvaot* nowadays only use *Zeria* water and this is heated by immersion radiators connected to the central heating system.

The rabbis of the Talmud attached great importance to the *mikveh*. In the establishment of a new community (*kehilla*), they gave top priority to the building of a *mikveh*, rather than the opening of the synagogue or burial ground or even the acquisition of a *Sefer Torah*.[6] They expressly forbade Jews to move to a town without a *mikveh*. Ideally, the *mikveh* should be located within walking distance, so as not to preclude its use on the Sabbath, when travelling is prohibited. *Mikvaot* may be situated in the basement of a synagogue building, in a separate outhouse in the courtyard of the synagogue, or even in a private house converted to the purpose. Some *mikvaot* have been constructed in public or private bathhouses. The basement *mikveh* was common in medieval Europe, both to make use of underground wells and to conceal its existence from often hostile Gentile authorities. Similarly, the external architecture of the building housing the *mikveh* was, and is still, often discreet so as not to attract unwelcome attention.

Thus the *mikveh* is a fundamentally Jewish building type, but one which has been largely ignored in studies of Jewish architecture – although this is not the case in the realm of archaeology. Some research has been carried out on the ancient *mikveh* and cistern systems in Israel, particularly in Jerusalem and at sites dating from the Second Temple period at Masada, Ma'on and Herodium. However, even in Israel, excavated *mikvaot* were only identified as such in the 1960s – by Yigael Yadin at Masada. Research has also been done on the medieval *mayanot* of the Rhineland, such as those of Worms, Cologne, Speyer and Friedberg.[7] A possible medieval *mikveh* has been discovered at Rouen in France; others are extant at, *inter alia*, Carpentras (1343) and Montpellier (thirteenth century). The *mikvaot* at Besalú and Tomar in the Iberian Peninsular have also been excavated as well as that at the Pinkas Synagogue in Prague. Research into *mikvaot* is therefore a necessity for the architectural historian of Jewish monuments. It is also of value to the general historian of Jewry, for the provision or lack of *mikvaot* is an accurate barometer of the level of religious observance among Jews. The complicated *halakhic* specifications involved in the construction and maintenance of *mikvaot* implies considerable expense and a high degree of communal organization and commitment. Moreover, whereas the keeping of the dietary laws and of the Sabbath indicates public commitment to Judaism, the existence or otherwise of *mikvaot* is a useful gauge for sociologists of the level of private commitment and the religious viability of a given Jewish community.

MIKVAOT IN BRITAIN

In the introduction to his classic *The Rise of Provincial Jewry* Cecil Roth writes:

> It is not easy to say at what stage a Jewish community comes into existence. Is it when the first Jew settles in a town; or when public worship according to the Jewish rite is first held; or when regular services are begun; or when the worshippers become formally organised; or when a room is set aside for prayer at the common expense or when a synagogue is at length built? All of these definitions can serve; and in fact in the accepted accounts one often finds the date of the dedication of the present synagogue given as that of the establishment of the community. A better criterion is the date of the acquisition of a burial ground, which unlike the other manifestations of Jewish religious life requires corporate action and thereby a certain degree of organisation.[8]

Nowhere here is the building of a *mikveh* even considered as marking the legitimate establishment of a Jewish community. Indeed, the existence or otherwise of *mikvaot* in Britain is scarcely alluded to in the standard communal histories. Occasionally the *mikveh* is referred to in passing or as the cause of some long-forgotten communal row.[9] Rarely is information given about the age of a particular *mikveh*, its type, construction, amenities, location or level of use. Either, one may surmise, the *mikveh* was not regarded as significant enough in the life of the community to merit inclusion, or it was considered too 'delicate' a subject for public mention, given its association with sexuality. Perhaps too, without imposing dogmatic constructs on our inquiry, this absence of information may be a function of the operation of gender in historical writing. After all, most of the communal histories of Anglo-Jewry have been written by men, just as most of the architecture has been designed by men. Relegated to the status of a 'women's issue' along with the family and childcare, *mikveh* was ignored. On the other hand, the 'new wave' feminist historians have shown equally little interest in this subject, being largely preoccupied with secular social issues, such as the place of women in the economy and the struggle for equal opportunities. Religion was dismissed as at best irrelevant and at worst oppressive.[10]

As a largely submerged aspect of Jewish architectural and social history, information on *mikvaot* in Britain is difficult to get at and patchy. What follows is an account of the history and provision of *mikvaot* in this country in the medieval and modern periods so far as it can be pieced together from the available sources: physical, illustrative and documentary.

Mikvaot *in medieval England*

With one notable exception, little evidence survives regarding the location of the *mikvaot* which were undoubtedly used by religious Jews settled here between the Norman Conquest and the Expulsion by Edward I in 1290. In London, the largest of the medieval Jewries, there is some inconclusive documentary and archaeological proof that a *mikveh* existed on the site of what is now Gresham Street (formerly Catte

Street), near the Guildhall. Joseph Jacobs, in *The Jews of Angevin England*, which was published a hundred years ago, speculated that the building known as Bakewell Hall

> was once a synagogue or public building of the London Jews. And if so this very possibly explains its somewhat enigmatic name. Bakewell Hall may be a corruption of Bathwell Hall, the bathing-place or mikveh of the London Jewesses, where they used to perform the ritual lavations pre-scribed by Rabbinic law.[11]

The building was apparently in use from *c.* 1220 to the Expulsion. In 1985–86 archaeologists from the Museum of London uncovered on the site 'a unique stone built sunken feature measuring 1.65 m by 1.15 m internally with a depth of 0.40 m . . . composed of greensand blocks with two steps on the western side'. It has been conjectured that this indeed was the *mikveh*. Expert *halakhic* opinion is awaited.

More concrete evidence for the existence of a medieval *mikveh* is available at Bristol. The true identity of the site known as Jacob's Well was rediscovered only as recently as 1987, by the Temple Local History Society, and it is still under investigation.[12]

As part of a project by the local history society to trace Bristol's medieval water courses, the site of the former Hotwells Police Station bicycle shed was excavated to reveal the hot spring which Edward III is known to have presented to the city in 1373. It was then known as Woodwill, but was situated in the area of the medieval Jewry confiscated during the preceding century. The well, the water of which is 53°

6.3   Bristol, Jacob's Well; the entrance to the *mikveh*. *Bristol City Council*

Fahrenheit – not as warm as the 76° of the now lost Hotwell – is situated on the Clifton side of Jacob's Well Road (formerly Woodwell Lane), opposite the pre-Expulsion cemetery. A chamber reached by descending steps was discovered which fills with clear water issuing from a fissure in the rock and leaving via another opening feeding a conduit. There is also a higher exit hole beneath the top step which may have been used as an overflow for *tevila*. Owing to the subsequent connection of the pool to the general water supply, and consequently the siphoning off of water, there is today insufficient water in the *mikveh* for even partial immersion of a person. There is also an unexcavated second chamber which, it is thought, may give access to a *kelim mikveh*, although no medieval glass or metal ware has yet been found.

Not only does the existence of the steps suggest that Jacob's Well was at one time a *mikveh*; this theory is reinforced by the discovery of a partially obscured Hebrew inscription on the lintel supporting the super-structure. The word *zokhlin* has been deciphered, and the rest may read *mayim*, that is, an accurate description of the type of *mikveh* being entered by the user.

The well has been dated as contemporaneous with the site of Lesser St Augustine's, one of the many monastic buildings in medieval Bristol and identified with the original abbey by many experts. Masonry found at both sites is very similar and it is now believed that the acquisition of the spring by the Jewish community must pre-date the foundation of the abbey (1142). As for the Hebrew inscription, the style of the lettering resembles that found in medieval Jewish burial grounds in Germany,

6.4 Bristol, Jacob's Well; the lintel with the Hebrew inscription *zokhlin* (flowing [water]). *Bristol City Council*

such as that of Mainz, dating from 1082. A number of Bristol Jews hailed from that German city.

Thus Jacob's Well is a site of major importance. Not only is it apparently the only medieval *mikveh* yet discovered in Britain (there is a Jacob's Well on the site of a former inn in Trinity Lane, York, and recent excavations of the medieval St John the Baptist Hospital at Oxford yielded elusive evidence of a possible *mikveh* there); it is also likely to be the oldest in Europe, pre-dating similar well-type *mikvaot* in Germany – the earliest of these being at Cologne (1170), discovered in 1956. Lastly, the inscription may represent the earliest pre-Expulsion Hebrew lettering ever to be found in this country.

From the Resettlement to c. 1840

The parent congregations of the post-Resettlement Jewry in London, the Spanish and Portuguese Synagogue at Bevis Marks (1701) and the Ashkenazi Great Synagogue (1790–91, remodelled by James Spiller), both possessed their own *mikvaot*, although the exact location of each has not yet been fully established.

There was a *mikveh* under the control of the Spanish and Portuguese congregation at Creechurch Lane, the precursor to Bevis Marks, in the seventeenth century. It appears from the records that this *mikveh* was originally sited at the synagogue, but it is nowhere identified in contemporary maps and plans of the area.[13] However, an entry for *Rosh Chodesh Nisan* (New Moon, *c.* April) 5424 (1664) in *El Libro de Los Acuerdos* reads as follows:

> Seeing that it is an imperative need in conformity with Din [religious law] that this nation should have a public Bath, with the customary requisites and formalities, without the publicity which the one that has been made in the Synagogue House has had, because of there not being a suitable site, the Sra. widow of Yehudah de Paiva and her sister having requested permission of this Mahamad to have it in her house, and to use it as a public bath of this Kahal [congregation], it was allowed to them, and as a loan whatever uses they might make of the boiler and leaden pipes, and anything else that may be.

A regular salary was paid to the 'bathwoman' from the early days, and we know that 'new river water' was supplied to the *mikveh* in 1698.

In the nineteenth century the *mikveh* was located at 2½ Heneage Lane, right behind the synagogue. The *mikveh* at this address is listed in the *Post Office London Directory* from 1853 onwards and in early editions of the *Jewish Year Book* (1897–1900 inclusive). The names of four 'bath-keepers' are recorded: Mrs Esther/Sarah Paris (to mid-1881), Mrs Emma Haliva (*c.* 1881–86), Mrs Levy Bensky (1897–98) and Mrs Cracower (1898–99); they all lived on the premises. Mrs Haliva was paid by the congregation £18 per annum for carrying out her duties, plus a coal allowance, presumably to heat both the *mikveh* and the house itself. Since the majority of *tevilot* take place at night-time it would be a convenient arrangement to have the lady attendant on the spot. In January 1883 Mrs Haliva was allowed to retain her tenancy of 2½ Heneage Lane, apparently rent-free, but was in return required to surrender her salary and coal allowance of ten tons. However, in January 1886 she was granted an additional five tons to heat the bathhouse.

By January 1882 alternative arrangements for female congregants were under consideration by the *Mahamad*, with a view to abolishing the maintenance of an independent *mikveh*. Some structural alterations to increase water capacity were recommended in the October of that year and the *mikveh* remained in use. Eventually, in 1899, the buildings in Heneage Lane belonging to Bevis Marks, including the *mikveh*, were demolished and the site was leased out for redevelopment. The synagogue looked to *mikvaot* in the now burgeoning Jewish East End (see below) to serve the poor women of the Sephardi community free of charge. Today, no trace remains of the Bevis Marks *mikveh* and no ground-plans of its structure or even of its precise location in the street exist. As far as can be established, there has never been any attempt on the part of the Sephardi community in Britain to replace it with a new communal *mikveh*.

In the eighteenth century the *Mahamad* of Bevis Marks actively discouraged the conversion of Christians to Judaism, a process which would naturally have involved immersion, on the grounds that proselytizing was contrary to the terms of the Resettlement. They tried to enforce this policy among the Ashkenazim and certainly had the support of the Rabbi of the Great Synagogue, Tevele Schiff, who refused to convert Lord George Gordon in 1787.[14] Potential converts were thus sent to Holland – or to Birmingham, as was apparently the case with Lord George. Nevertheless, unauthorized conversions did take place. For example, in 1759–60 a certain Meir Cohen, a member of the Great Synagogue, performed the marriage, at the house of the Rabbi, between a Jew and a foreign proselyte whom he had admitted to the faith and who, according to the records of the Great Synagogue as quoted by Cecil Roth, 'was given the ritual bath in the *mikvah* in the house of Abraham Ben Josele'. Josele was heavily fined for his pains and Cohen was expelled from the congregation.[15]

Another case is cited by Todd Endelman in *The Jews of Georgian England*. In 1816 one Sarah Innes, the non-Jewish wife of Joseph Jonas, was converted according to Jewish practice:

> The father made arrangements with Elimelech Mudahy, who was known to perform clandestine conversions for a fee, to have her converted at the Ashkenazi mikveh in Heneage Lane. The witnesses were Ashkenazim, who were made to swear that they would not reveal any of the circumstances. The father then applied to the Mahamad for permission for his son to marry Sarah bat Israel.[16]

Whilst the essentials of this story are undoubtedly accurate, the reference to the 'Ashkenazi mikveh in Heneage Lane' is probably not. It is unlikely that two *mikvaot* serving both sections of the London Jewish community would have existed in the same narrow street at this period. On the other hand, the precise location of the bathhouse of the Great Synagogue is still unclear. I strongly suspect that it was in a private house at 1 and 2 Mitre Square, behind Duke's Place – 'Mrs Jacobs' Jewish Baths' as advertised in the *Jewish Chronicle* in the mid-Victorian period (see below). Some clues regarding the maintenance of the Great Synagogue's *mikveh* at that period have also come to light.

In July 1846 Chief Rabbi Nathan Adler, whose survey of religious facilities, including *mikvaot*, in Britain we will come to presently, wrote the following letter to 'the President and Wardens of the Great Synagogue':

> Many poor persons having complained to me of the heavy expense to which they are subjected to in making use of the *Mikvah* (the charges ranging from 1/6 to 2/-) I deem it my duty to call your attention to this subject, and to beg that you would make arrangements for granting the poor the free use of the *mikvah*; I have reason to hope that you will the more readily comply with my request when I state that the Portuguese here, as well as most congregations abroad extend such privilege to their poor Brethren, and that the expense thereby incurred would amount to no more than about £10 annually.

The Chief Rabbi's further request that the other City synagogues, that is, the Hambro (1725) and the New (1761, rebuilt in Great St Helen's in 1838), help subsidize this arrangement was followed up: the upshot was that the Great contributed £7 10s., the New and the Hambro £3 15s. each.[17]

Likewise, some information on the maintenance of a provincial *mikveh* in the early nineteenth century has come to light. At Liverpool, from 1816 to 1819 a levy of 3s. per annum was charged on all married congregants of the Old Hebrew Congregation for the upkeep of the *mikveh* in Upper Frederick Street. This *mikveh* was probably built between 1810 and 1816; it may have replaced an earlier one on or near the same site and had a resident 'bath proprietor', probably Ellen Benedict, a daughter of Joseph Hart. She was succeeded by her own daughter, Frances Benedict (to 1880), and she in turn by Julia Rose (1884–90).

It is quite possible that *mikvaot* were constructed in the outlying country houses of the more religiously observant of the eighteenth- and nineteenth-century Anglo-Jewish aristocracy for their private use. Little hard evidence exists. In 1983 there was some short-lived excitement that a *mikveh* had been discovered at Cromwell House, Highgate (1638), reputedly the earliest extant 'country' house owned by Jews in Britain after the Resettlement (the Da Costa family, 1675–1746). However, on inspection the basement was found to contain a large storage tank, but it is unlikely that it ever housed a *mikveh*.[18] Other properties owned by wealthy Sephardim – Da Costas and Cappidocias, for example, in Richmond – were in close proximity to underground springs.[19] East Cliff Lodge, Ramsgate (1790s), purchased by Sir Moses Montefiore in 1831, was built around a quadrangle which contained 'a well of fine water' which may conceivably have provided Lady Judith with the facilities for *tevila*. It is certain, however, that a *mikveh* was built underneath one of the houses which comprised the Judith Lady Montefiore College, established in her memory (Henry Davis, 1866). The site was sold in 1961 and demolished, but plans survive in the archives of the Spanish and Portuguese Congregation.[20] The extant Gothic bathhouse at Gunnersbury, which apparently pre-dates the Rothschilds' acquisition of the estate in 1835, does not look as if it might have lent itself to use as a *mikveh*; records reveal the existence of another bathhouse of later provenance, since demolished, which may have been the structure we are seeking. There was a 'natural spring' in the vicinity in 1829. Research has not yet revealed *mikvaot* at other Rothschild residences, Waddesdon and Tring.

Mikvaot *in Victorian Jewry*

On his appointment as Chief Rabbi of Great Britain and the Empire in 1845, Nathan Adler, in his thoroughly Germanic way, sent out a questionnaire to the Jewish communities which recognized his jurisdiction, seeking data on their numbers and facilities. One of the questions posed was 'Is there a *mikveh?*' The returns on this point are particularly revealing for any assessment of the condition of British Jewry at the start of Queen Victoria's long reign.[21]

A breakdown of the findings given in Appendix 6.1 shows that while one half of the congregations which replied to the question claimed to possess a kosher *mikveh*, that number again did not. Of the latter, no fewer than 13 out of the 19 respondents claimed to have made alternative arrangements: in the case of coastal communities, the sea; at spa towns, natural springs; and, in many other instances, local public and private baths. Although in theory such alternatives could be acceptable, there are in fact both *halakhic* questions to be asked and practical problems to be solved.

The Newcastle community used a public bath which certainly met the requirements satisfactorily, being 'the depth 4½ feet spring water'. On the other hand, the situation at Exeter was far from ideal: it seems that although a *mikveh* had been constructed at the synagogue 'at a cost of not less than £80' (no date was provided, but the building itself dates from 1763 and is one of the two surviving Georgian synagogues in Britain), the bath had been abandoned 'within the last eighteen months' because of technical difficulties due to 'its being built on the second floor and the apparatus to heat the water being above that again and the difficulty of obtaining a supply of water and the injury it produced to the premises'. The public bath resorted to as an alternative was found upon investigation 'to be within two inches of the prescribed rule for size as being *kosher*'. The statement continues: 'But we regret to add that *on account of a trifling extra expense it is not generally used.*'

The spa towns of Bath and Cheltenham, which were made fashionable in the reign of George III, apparently had the advantage of natural *mayanot*. However, according to the local historians of Bath Jewry, there is no evidence in the County Record Office of the most unusual use to which the Roman baths were put.[22] At Cheltenham the Jewish community, which prayed in a fine neo-classical synagogue of 1838 (still standing), used the Montpellier Baths in Bath Road for *tevila*. An admirable engraving and description of this facility, where the famous Cheltenham Salts were also manufactured, are to be found in George Rowe's *Illustrated Cheltenham Guide*, which was published in the same year as the Chief Rabbi's Survey was carried out:

> These Baths have been long celebrated for their medicinal properties, the establishment is very extensive, consisting of fourteen warm baths of various sizes, beautifully fitted up and lined with marble and Dutch tile;

6.5 Cheltenham, Montpellier Baths, from George Rowe's *Illustrated Cheltenham Guide* (Cheltenham, 1845).

one large cold bath, 20 feet by 10, and several smaller ones, with a never failing supply of clear cold water; besides a proper complement of shower, champooing [*sic*], hot air, and steam baths; the whole fitted up on the most approved principles.[23]

The luxuriousness of Montpellier Baths notwithstanding, in the following year Montague Alex, 'surgeon dentist' and leading light of Cheltenham Jewry, wrote to the Chief Rabbi that: 'They were sanctioned by our late Rabbi, but owing to their having very lately undergone an alteration, Mr Pulver [the minister] has been instructed to attend to others that will be altered to suit our wants, and which will soon be ready for our use.' The historian of Cheltenham Jewry comments:

> Where these future baths were, or if their use ever materialised is not evident, but in 1878 the attempt could have been accomplished through the purchase of the house next to the Infants' School opposite the Synagogue. Edward Lowe [president of the synagogue] offered to advance the money at 5½% if the owner was willing to sell. No further mention of the matter is recorded.[24]

Communities at Dover, Jersey and Yarmouth evaded the subject of *mikveh* by reference to the sea. While it is true that the sea is a *halakhically* acceptable solution, it is not necessarily a practical one, owing to the need for privacy and the danger of drowning at night in a cold rough tide. It is unlikely that many Jews took advantage of the sea for immersion, and it is perhaps significant that most of the *kehillot* in seaside resorts claimed to have purpose-built *mikvaot*, although not all of these claims have been independently corroborated for this period.[25] It is also interesting to note that no major urban community claimed to make use of its local river, but they were, we must infer, equipped with rainwater *mikvaot*. The Thames in London, for instance, at high tide, is valid for *tevila* since, like the majority of rivers in the British Isles, it contains mostly seawater.[26]

A particularly interesting example of an early Victorian *mikveh* still survives in the grounds of the Canterbury Synagogue (Marshall of Canterbury, 1848, itself unique in being the only Jewish house of worship ever built in this country in the Egyptian style). According to the *Narrative of the Erection of the New Synagogue at Canterbury* compiled by its first honorary secretary, Jacob Jacobs, the *mikveh* was added in 1851. He writes:

> Since the erection of the Synagogue the filial piety of Messrs Samuel and Joseph La Mert induced them in memory of their late mother liberaly [*sic*] to assist the Congregation in the year 1851 to erect a building on the estate containing a bathroom and dressing room the whole costing the sum of £91 12s. 10d. Messrs La Mert contributing the sum of seventy pounds Mayer Lyons being President.[27]

No record of how long this *mikveh* was in use survives; the synagogue was closed and sold in 1931. It is now the music room and concert hall of the King's School. The *mikveh* has been converted into a rehearsal room.

London, with two-thirds of Anglo-Jewry, was the city best provided with *mikvaot* in the nineteenth century, and remains so. We have already mentioned the *mikvaot* serving Bevis Marks and the Great Synagogue, neither of which shows up in the Chief Rabbi's Survey (the former, being Sephardi, was not under his jurisdiction and the latter, for reasons

6.6 Canterbury *Mikveh* (1851); a drawing by Hubert Pragnell. *D. Cohn-Sherbok,* The Jews of Canterbury, 1760–1931 *(Canterbury, 1984)*

which must remain obscure, failed to respond to this question). As seen, the other City synagogues, the Hambro and the New, paid annual contributions to support the *mikveh* at the Great during the early Victorian period. By this time too, other synagogues had been established in the West End: the Western and the Maiden Lane. According to the Survey, these congregations utilized private *mikveh* facilities, the latter having access to two such establishments, 'belonging to Mrs H. Cohen & Mr & Mrs Raphael' respectively. Judging by advertisements in the Jewish press of the period, there was keen competition for custom among a number of such privately owned *mikvaot* on the eastern fringes of the City.[28] An issue of the *Jewish Chronicle* in May 1854 carries two separate insertions for 'Jewish Baths' appearing side by side: one placed by Mrs Jacobs of 1 and 2 Mitre Square, Aldgate (the Great Synagogue's *mikveh?*), and the other by Mrs R. Woolf of No. 8 Sussex Place, Leadenhall Street, in an area which contained a number of communal institutions at that time including the New Synagogue and the Beth HaMedrash. Mrs Jacobs' reads as follows:

> Mrs Jacobs in thanking the Jewish ladies for their past favours, begs most respectfully to inform them that under the superintendence of the respected Chief Rabbi, Dr Adler, she has had constructed an entirely new suite of Baths, replete with every comfort and convenience. The water has been laid on at considerable expense, and in sufficient quantity to afford a fresh supply for each bather. The rooms are ventilated on Dr Arnott's plan; the Mikvos are lined throughout with marble, and the smaller baths will bear comparison with those usually seen in any bathing establishment in the kingdom. The luxuries of a fire, gas, and good personal attendance, combine to render this Jewish Bathing Establishment as complete as possible. J. Jacobs, therefore, in confidence, hopes that she will meet with the patronage and success she will always make it her endeavour to merit. Letters and Messages punctually attended to.

Mrs Woolf's Baths had evidently also undergone refurbishment with the Chief Rabbi's approval. A further facility, 'Mrs Cantor's' at 9 Jewry Street, Aldgate, was announced in the *Hebrew Observer* in December 1854 and yet another, at 12 Camomile Street, Bishopsgate, in the *Chronicle* two years later. This latter noted that 'Vehicles can be driven up to the door. Bath made ready at a quarter of an hour's notice'.

Nevertheless, it appears that use of the *mikveh* was widely neglected by Jewish women in the early Victorian period. In 1846, Chief Rabbi Adler received a letter concerning the 'non observance of tevila' among 'the poor women' in London. In 1853 he drafted a letter in the following terms to the Reverend Moses Rintel, formerly of Britain and now in Melbourne, Australia:

> I exceedingly regret to hear that there is still no mikveh [written in Hebrew in original] in Melbourne which is of the utmost importance and the very first request for the proper observation of your faith. Indeed, as you are married you must necessarily feel the want of it acutely; It is moreover your duty to watch over the spiritual wants of your congregation. Therefore I trust that you will earnestly [deleted] exert your best effort [endeavours deleted] to cause a mikveh [Heb.] to be established.[29]

As Rabbi Steven Singer, who has written on religion in early Victorian

Anglo-Jewry, comments, 'Apparently, even a Jewish clergyman bred in London could be quite unconcerned about this basic observance of Orthodox Judaism'.[30]

Mikvaot *and Public Baths*

The first issue of the *Jewish Year Book* in 1897 records the existence of no fewer than six private *mikvaot* in the East End of London. By 1914 there were eight such establishments; wartime disruption was presumably responsible for a decline in the early 1920s to two. In 1929 the number had again risen to six, till 1934, before going into irreversible decline.[31]

From 1881 the centre of Jewish gravity in London shifted east-wards with the mass immigration from the Russian Empire, Galicia and Romania, which continued until 1914. During this period some 100,000 Jews, escaping persecution and economic pressures in eastern Europe, settled in the East End of London and in the poorer districts of the expanding industrial towns of the Midlands and north, Manchester, Leeds, Liverpool and Glasgow. The Yiddish-speaking newcomers came, for the most part, from traditional Jewish communities, where the march of modernization, 'enlightenment' and secularization had failed to penetrate very far. They largely shunned the institutions of native Anglo-Jewry, foremost amongst them the United Synagogue (see below), preferring to set up their own *chevrot* (prayer circles) and *shtiebels* (back-room synagogues), where they could recreate the familar world of the *shtetl* or at least of urban Warsaw or Odessa whence they had come. A multiplicity of such *chevrot* sprang up in the East End of London, in Red Bank and Cheetham Hill (Manchester), the Leylands (Leeds) and the Gorbals (Glasgow). Other institutions vital to an independent, fully observant Jewish community were also created: facilities for *shechita* (ritual slaughter), *chevrei kadisha* (burial societies), friendly societies, kosher butchers, bakers and printers – and *mikvaot*. Little is known about the construction or funding of the commercial *mikvaot* in London, except to say that none of those in the East End, as far as can be deter-mined, was based at the address of a known *kehilla*. In the West End, by contrast, two of the *mikvaot* known to have existed between 1897 and the 1930s were privately funded establishments associated with a particular synagogue. One of these was located at 49 Westbourne Park Crescent, near the Bayswater Synagogue (1863), and the other served the largely working-class community of Soho at 14 Manette Street, off Charing Cross Road, the home of the West End Talmud Torah, which was begun by Polish immigrants in 1916 and later joined the Federation of Synagogues (see below). Its predecessor was at Percy Street, off Tottenham Court Road, apparently a private concern, until about 1909.

To return to the East End, my mother recalls regular visits to a private *mikveh* cum bathhouse in a terraced house in Exmouth Street, White-chapel, before the Second World War:

> Every Friday my mother took me to Betts Street [the nearest public bath to where the family lived in Langdale Street]. But there were queues in summer. So we sometimes got the bus to Exmouth Street . . . more refined. . . There was a waiting room, a front parlour, with dark chairs and curtains. You didn't have to wait too long. You had your own hot and cold water taps too . . . we only had a cold water tap in the yard at home . . .[32]

6.7   London, Lacey's Baths, Exmouth Street, E1; an advertising poster. *Aumie Shapiro*

Exmouth Street (also known as 'Lacey's Baths'), and, one would suppose, other such private bathing establishments in the East End, had bathrooms attached to the *mikveh*. Such facilities were essential for the proper fulfilment of the ritual of immersion, which necessitates for women scrupulous cleanliness *before* the actual *tevila* in the *mikveh*. Given that before the turn of the century 'almost no working class family in the East End had the use of any other than a public bath',[33] the importance of alternative facilities for personal hygiene for the Jewish population in general cannot be overestimated.

Before the present century, bathing for pleasure or even for hygiene was a decidedly upper-class pursuit. The *bagnios* and spas of the eighteenth century and the steam, vapour and Turkish baths of the nineteenth were patronized by the social elite, and, even then, such activities were the exception rather than the rule. Richard Metcalfe, author of *The Rise and Progress of Hydropathy in England and Scotland* (1909), observed that, 'Though we hear much talk of baths and bathing, we Christians of Europe are a dirty generation in comparison with some of the people of pagan times'.[34]

The masses were indeed the Great Unwashed! An indoor tap of cold running water for the purposes of cooking, washing up and laundry was a great rarity, let alone a bath, in most working-class homes, in town or country, well into the twentieth century. Periodic outbreaks of cholera and other diseases led to increasing concern among Victorian social reformers.[35] In 1842 Edwin Chadwick published *The Sanitary Condition of the Working Class*, and in October 1844, after a public meeting at the Mansion House, the 'Central Society for the Establishment of Baths and Washhouses for the Labouring Classes' was set up under the chairmanship of William Cotton, Governor of the Bank of England. It was this privately funded body which was responsible for building the first public baths in London at Glass House Yard, East Smithfields (1845) and at George Street, Euston Square (1846). A pilot bathhouse at Upper Frederick Street, Liverpool, had been opened in May 1842. In 1846 Parliament stepped in with the Public Baths and Washhouses Act (Dukinfield's Act), which empowered local boroughs and parishes to provide these facilities, raising capital by borrowing and charging for their use. Managers of gas and water works were given incentives to supply their services at reduced rates or free of charge. In 1847 the first Model Baths were opened at Goulstone Square (later Goulston Street), designed by Price Prichard Baly, to serve the Whitechapel district. With two-thirds of the baths 'of the cheapest class', costing 1d. for a cold bath with towel (compared with 6d. for a 'first class' bath with two towels), the Goulston Street establishment was clearly aimed at the poorest end of the market. Detailed descriptions of the design and layout of these baths may be found in a number of sources – *London Exhibited in 1851*, *The Builder* and *The Times* – but no illustrations or plans of the original building seem to have survived, making it difficult to assess fairly a contemporary verdict that it was 'downright ugly'. Almost rectangular in shape and situated between Goulstone Square and Old Castle Street, the bathhouse was divided into bathing and washhouse facilities. The baths were segregated according to sex, with separate entrances for men and women, and also according to class, there being an equal number of first and second class. The interior used slate for the divisions between the bathing cubicles and the doors, and the baths themselves were of cast iron lined with enamel, sunk into the floor.

> The furniture of each room also comprises – a shower bath, capable of being converted into a vapour bath; a looking glass; a seat with a space therein, into which hot water is introduced for warming a towel. Hot and cold water are introduced by a very simple contrivance through the same aperture in the bath . . . there is but one handle to turn, and an index marks how far it is to be moved, for procuring hot water or cold, or both together . . . there are no less than 96 [baths] and . . . not only can the whole population of Whitechapel be washed to the top of their bent, but there will be no excuse for bodily filth in the neighbourhood.[36]

The concept was clearly imitated elsewhere; in 1854 there were eight such public bathhouses in London alone. However, never self-supporting, the public baths failed to make a real impact, at least until further legislation in the 1890s. They were 'looked upon as coming within the same category as workhouses'.[37] In the late 1860s the Goulston Street Baths were leased to a local speculator named Pilbrow, who allowed them to deteriorate and in 1871 offered them for sale with a view to demolition. Luckily for the inhabitants of Whitechapel, among whom Jews were forming an increasing element, local philanthropists Reverend Samuel Barnett (of Toynbee Hall) and Frederic D. Mocatta, afterwards a director of the Four Percent Industrial Dwellings Company, helped form a committee under the aegis of the Whitechapel Vestry to save the baths; they were modernized (architect: John Hudson) and reopened in 1878. In 1896 swimming baths were added, one for women and two for men.

Thus the Goulston Street Baths were, by the turn of the century, 'possibly the best in London' and were undoubtedly used by many Jews, given that even in the most advanced developments, such as Rothschild Buildings (N. S. Joseph, 1887), where about 80 per cent of families had access to their own sculleries, there was not a single bath in the block. Thus a bath could only be taken either by the fire, in a tin or zinc tub filled with water boiled in a copper on the stove or, more conveniently, given that families were often large, at the public baths. Men would frequent 'Shefshick's', the Russian vapour baths run by Rabbi Benjamin Schewzik in Brick Lane, especially before the Sabbath;[38] women must have preferred the private establishments which, as we have seen, flourished in the neighbourhood. It is relevant in this context that most of the municipal bathhouses – Goulston Street being no exception – provided far more baths for men than for women. According to one estimate made at the turn of the century, only 18 per cent of all baths taken in London's public facilities were by women.

In 1903 Hermann Landau, an active communal worker on behalf of East End Jewry, drew attention to the practice of *mikveh* in his evidence submitted before the Royal Commission on Alien Immigration. This was a rare public utterance on the subject, designed to deflect the popular association between foreign Jews, dirt and disease, prevalent amongst anti-alienists of the day. He stated:

> How many Christians are aware that in the East End many bathing establishments exist, called 'Mikvahs', which I can only translate as 'Ritual Baths'. The minute sanitary observances which every married woman, however poor, undergoes, [are] one reason of the extraordinary health and fecundity of the race, seldom found among other people.

The existence of so many private Jewish baths went against the prevailing trends. A 1918 *Report on Public Baths and Washhouses in the United Kingdom* found not only that every London borough bar one (Finsbury) had a public bath and that every city of over 100,000 inhabitants had likewise, but that these baths were mostly municipal: 'Baths still under the control of philanthropic agencies or private persons are few and far between.'[39] The *mikvaot* of the East End and elsewhere were beyond the scope of the inquiry.

Outside London there are several cases of *mikvaot* being constructed by the local authority for the use of the Jewish community (albeit with subsidies raised by the latter for building and/or maintenance). The Albert Grove *mikveh* in Leeds was opened by the Lord Mayor of the City on 25 October 1905.[40] According to the official programme printed for the occasion, these '"Ladies' Baths", specially designed and constructed in accordance with Jewish Regulations [were] the first of their kind that have been so specially constructed by any Municipal Authority in England'. This claim was incorrect. The Trippett Baths, Wincolmlee, Hull, designed by David Thorp for the Corporation and opened in April 1850, included 'on the ladies' side an excellent plunge bath, called the Jewess's bath – and intended solely, we understand, for the use of the ladies of the Hebrew nation'. In 1919, on the initiative of the Reverend H. M. Bendas of the Hull Old Hebrew Congregation, the 'immersion bath' at the East Hull Baths, Holderness Road, was converted into a *mikveh* at a cost of £25 to the Corporation. This structure, despite redundancy, is still extant, having in turn been converted into a plunge bath and sauna for the use of the local Sikh community in about 1981. In 1903 Trippett Baths were closed and the building became the local telephone exchange. Unfortunately it was destroyed by bombing in the Second World War.

Another early example of a *mikveh* constructed in a provincial public bathhouse may be that at the Kent Street Baths in Birmingham, opened in 1851. Local historians have not yet been able to establish whether or not the *mikveh* dated back this far. In the 1870s, however, it was being used by 650–750 women. The Glasgow 'Kosher Baths', situated in the Gorbals Bathhouse, certainly did date back to its opening in 1885.[41] During the 1880s the centre of Glasgow Jewry shifted to the working-class district of the Gorbals, and it was felt by the immigrant Commerce Street *minyan* that the *mikveh* in the magnificent Garnethill Synagogue (John McLeod and N. S. Joseph, 1879), which had been functioning since the building's opening in 1879, was not accessible for the ladies of their neighbourhood. A new *mikveh* was therefore incorporated in the local bathhouse and was used until the opening in 1902 of the South Portland Street Synagogue, whose own *mikveh*, run on a profit-making basis by lessees living on the premises, survived until 1970. At the turn of the

6.8   London, Schewzik's Russian Vapour Baths, Brick Lane, E1, in 1910.
Local History Library, Tower Hamlets

century, the Glasgow Kosher Baths were used by some 200 people a week, which yielded an income of about £6.

In Leeds the decision to build a *mikveh* was taken on 27 September 1876 by the council of the Belgrave Street Synagogue, the only one in the city at the time. A 'magnificent' *mikveh* was completed six years later in Cookridge Street in the city centre, housed in a building owned by the Oriental & General Baths Company. Murray Freedman, of the Leeds Jewish Historical Society, who has kindly researched the subject on my behalf, guesses that the project must have been taken up by the Baths Company as a commercial venture without any expense to the synagogue.[42] Thus, users of the *mikveh* could also take advantage of the adjacent slipper and Turkish baths, as well as of a swimming pool. The

6.9   Leeds, Albert Grove *Mikveh* (Thomas Adamson, 1905). *Leeds Central Library*

whole splendid edifice had been opened in 1867 and was redesigned in 1882 by Cuthbert Brodrick, architect of Leeds Town Hall. In 1903 the Leeds Corporation took over the baths and, because of the shift of the Jewish population, decided to build a new facility especially for the Jewish women of the Leylands. Designed by local architect Thomas Adamson and located on the corner of Albert Grove and Leeds Terrace, the building housed two *mikvaot* and eight slipper baths (two first-class and six second-class) as well as a three-bedroomed house for the live-in caretaker, with a separate entrance on the Leeds Terrace side. The cost: £2,400, but ratepayers were assured that it would result in no extra charge to them. The official programme for the opening describes the interior layout of the bathhouse, the building materials and decor:

> The Slipper Baths are in white earthenware, glazed all round, and supplied with hot and cold water. The *Mikvah* Baths are constructed in glazed ware. The main walls round porch, vestibule, corridors and Slipper Baths are lined with cream-coloured glazed bricks, relieved by coloured bands, and the bathroom divisions with cream-coloured patent tiles. The floors are formed with best quality floor tiles.

The bathhouse was equipped with the very latest in heating and ventilation technology, and toilet facilities, euphemistically referred to as 'sanitary offices', were provided for both classes of bather and for the caretaker's house. The baths were open daily from 10 a.m. to 10 p.m.; a first-class bath cost 1s. and a second-class bath 6d., while 'non-bathers' were to be admitted at a charge of 3d. per head. According to the *Jewish World* in September 1910, there were 4,416 attendances in 1906–7, and in 1909–10 there were 9,424, that is 785 per month. Evidently, the Leeds *mikveh*, like that in Glasgow, was well used and financially profitable.[43]

A prime mover in the construction of the Albert Grove *mikveh* had been Rabbi Israel Chayim Daiches (1850–1937), *Rav* of the Beth HaMedrash HaGadol Synagogue since 1901 and 'generally regarded as the leading Eastern European rabbi in the Provinces'. In 1912 he published a *teshuva* (rabbinical responsum) entitled *Mikve Yisrael* in which he defended the presence of a water meter in the pipework of a *mikveh*, apparently

6.10   Grimsby *Mikveh*, 1916, drawn by Jeremy Gerlis. It was constructed without a water meter. *D. and L. Gerlis*, The Story of the Grimsby Jewish Community (*Hull, 1986*)

common in English *mikvaot* at the time. He argued that such a meter, used to measure the consumption of water, did not itself hold water but merely allowed water to flow through it. It did not therefore constitute a *kelei* (vessel), which would render the *mikveh* unfit. This ruling, which could conceivably have permitted the construction of *mikvaot* connected to the ordinary water supply of the city, was fiercely disputed by Rabbi Tsvi Hirsch Hurwitz, who had just arrived in Leeds from Sunderland, where he had had experience with a similar *mikveh* and had declared it not kosher. Rav Hurwitz enlisted the support of the Or Sameach, Rabbi Meir Simcha HaCohen of Dvinsk, and Daiches' opinion was finally overruled. Henceforth use of the water meter was forbidden in Britain and it seems that a number of provincial *mikvaot* were put out of use as a result, including Cleethorpes.[44]

After the First World War the Leeds *mikveh* went into decline. The Leeds Board of Shechita took on financial responsibility for it from the Corporation and, from the late 1920s onwards, operated it at a financial loss. In 1935 the Board persuaded the Corporation to shoulder the burden again, but after a couple of years when even heavier losses were sustained, the Board of Shechita was forced to resume its obligation. The Board's minute books reveal that attendances were about 110 per month in 1935. Women were charged about 5s. a dip. Mrs Frieda Schiller (*née* Peretz), who was the '*mikveh* lady' at the time, remembers:

> I was working in the swimming baths . . . and being the only Jewish girl as far as I know, they [the Baths Committee of Leeds Corporation] asked me to take over [the *mikveh*]. I had to see the Rev. Samuels [*sic*, Jacob Samuel] [minister of the Mariempoler Synagogue in 1905 and, by this time, of the United Hebrew Congregation] and he said I was caperable [*sic*] and Mrs Pinsky had to go and I took over. After a year I left to get married.

Frieda Peretz obviously did not receive much instruction in the religious aspects of her duties: 'The Rev. Samuels only asked me some questions and told me what blessing I had to say. I never saw him after that.' Indeed, it was most unusual for a young unmarried girl to be put in charge of the *mikveh*; perhaps this is an indication of the lack of suitable or willing candidates in Leeds at the time. Frieda lived on the premises with her parents and family. Her testimony supports the impression that use of the *mikveh* had fallen: 'The users were usually young brides who came with the mother or some adult person. Not many. Also only the very religious came each month. Not many . . . It was also used by men before a High Festival and only by elderly foreign men. About a dozen or so.'[45]

By 1957 attendances had dropped to about 40 per month. Clearly, the practice of *mikveh* was being abandoned by the English-born children of immigrant Jews in Leeds. In 1964 Ernest Krausz recorded the attitudes of Leeds Jews on the topic of *mikveh*:

> I don't approve of the *mikveh*. I've been only once in my life. It is a thing of the past. Now there are facilities at home.

> I think it is out of date. There may be some who are very *froom* [religious] and keep it up but they are very few.

The *mikveh* is going out. The girls are too shy. They get embarrassed and will avoid it.

It's died out. It was just a tradition. One goes just before marriage. But it is not necessary because of modern conditions.[46]

In the late 1950s the Albert Grove *mikveh* 'was in a rather bad state of repair and situated in a district which was not too salubrious so that many women preferred to go to Manchester *mikvaot* rather than use it'.[47] It finally closed on 5 January 1968 and had been due to be replaced by a new facility incorporated in a planned municipal bathhouse, which included an Olympic-sized swimming pool. However, in 1967 a strictly Orthodox community in Moortown opened a *mikveh* of its own on the site of the Shomrei Hadas Synagogue, in the centre of the Jewish part of Leeds. The Board of Shechita decided to contribute towards the upkeep of the new facility, and this situation pertains to the present day. In 1994 a brand new *mikveh* was built in the grounds of the Etz Chaim Synagogue. It remains to be seen whether the dwindling population of Jews in Leeds will be able to sustain two such facilities in the long term.

Mikvaot built by local authorities, with their running costs subsidized by the Jewish community, exist today at Cardiff (1959) and Brighton (1982). Such *mikvaot* were to be found at Bournemouth (Piers Baths, 1930s) and Birmingham (Bournville Baths, 1973) until quite recently. To take the example of Cardiff, the *mikveh* was constructed at the Empire Pool in Wood Street, with monies donated largely by Abe Sherman, a successful Merthyr businessman. The £650,000 complex contains a single *mikveh* pool, sunk to a depth of about five feet, the water level being four feet and the temperature kept at a constant 37–38° Centigrade. There is one bath *cum* shower room adjacent, with a toilet and separate

6.11   Cardiff *Mikveh*, Wales Empire Pool, 1959. *Dorene Jacobs*

changing room and hair dryer. A distinct drawback to the Cardiff *mikveh*, as with others in public bathhouses, is its limited opening hours; it is open until 10 p.m. on weekdays but only until 5.30 p.m. on Saturdays, and is shut on Sundays. There is no on-site attendant. The fact that the Cardiff *mikveh* is the only facility of its kind left in the Principality notwithstanding, there is an average of only ten to 20 *mikveh* bookings per month.[48] Situated in public bathhouses, both Cardiff and Brighton are taken advantage of by the Reform movement for conversions (see below).

SYNAGOGUE ORGANIZATIONS AND THE PROVISION OF *MIKVAOT*

The United Synagogue

Only in the twentieth century have large synagogue organizations, as opposed to local synagogues and private individuals, taken responsibility for the provision of communal *mikvaot* in Britain. Of the four main Orthodox groupings in London – the United Synagogue, the Federation of Synagogues, the Union of Orthodox Hebrew Congregations (*UOHC*) and the Spanish and Portuguese Jews' Congregation – the United is by far the largest (with about 39,000 members), the most established (created by Act of Parliament in 1870) – and the slowest to become involved in *mikveh* construction. Indeed, for the United Synagogue the *mikveh* was for a long time the Cinderella of religious institutions.[49] In contrast to Rabbinic law which, as noted in the introduction, places the *mikveh* at the head of communal priorities, for the United Synagogue it came very low down in the pecking order, after synagogues, burial grounds, *kashrut* and education. Notwithstanding exhortations from their spiritual guide the Chief Rabbi, the lay leaders of the United Synagogue, who until well after the Second World War were drawn largely from an anglicized and well-connected elite, were known for their financial largesse rather than their religious orthodoxy. They tended to call the financial tune. In 1912 Lord Rothschild, as president both of the United Synagogue and of the Conference of Delegates convened to choose a new Chief Rabbi to succeed the late Hermann Adler (Nathan's son), asserted:

> in defining what I consider to be an orthodox Jew I think there is a very large margin left for individual thought and action, and I hope I shall have the agreement of the Conference when I say that I do not consider it the part of an orthodox Jew to discuss the shape and size of a *mikvah*.[50]

In the late nineteenth century the United Synagogue embarked on a lavish building programme in London. The so-called 'cathedral synagogues' became the hallmark of United Synagogue Judaism. In not one of these edifices, as far as can be ascertained, was provision made for a *mikveh*. In 1866 the *Jewish Chronicle* carried an announcement that 'Mrs Jacobsons' Jewish Baths' were moving from 1 and 2 Mitre Square, Aldgate to 9 St Germain's Terrace, Westbourne Park Crescent, Bayswater.[51] It thus seems that the Bayswater *mikveh*, which was subsequently listed at 49 Westbourne Park Crescent, was the direct successor to the Great's. The

Bayswater Synagogue was opened in 1863 – pre-dating the establishment of the United Synagogue by seven years. The Bayswater community, which had a reputation for staunch traditionalism, joined the United upon its creation. Nevertheless, the *mikveh* remained a private enterprise and as such was the only facility of its kind attached to a large synagogue in the West End of London.

By the 1920s this *mikveh* was experiencing serious financial problems, owing to the need for urgent repairs to arrest its increasing dilapidation.[52] The *mikveh*'s finances were in the hands of two local trustees, Leopold Frank and Piza Barnett; a resident attendant, Mrs Fishman, was responsible for its day-to-day running. Chief Rabbi J. H. Hertz took an interest in the *mikveh* and informally tried to drum up donations towards its upkeep from individuals and congregations all over London. Through his good offices a grant of £25 was secured from the United Synagogue in 1923. Although this sum represented only one-quarter of the annual budget (excluding building repairs etc.), the money was not obtained without stiff resistance, the Executive Committee declaring that 'they are not inclined to depart from one principle hitherto guiding the United Synagogue, viz., that it is no part of its functions to provide or manage *Mikvahs* for the London Community, or to enter into competition with private enterprise in this respect.'[53]

Despite the fact that the contribution became annual, and 'exceptional grants' were also made from time to time,[54] it was clear that the United Synagogue did not see the provision of *mikvaot* as one of its tasks; nor was such an obligation included in its Constitution. Indeed a plea by the trustees in 1924 that 'We think that the time has now arrived for this institution to be taken over by the United Synagogue . . . it is a communal obligation' fell on deaf ears, as did the demand that the head office 'should provide a "Mikvah" centrally situated for the whole of their "constituents"'. Leopold Frank wrote to the Chief Rabbi suggesting that he, the London Beth Din, 'and as many ministers of the United Synagogue as you can influence' should make a declaration to the effect that the *mikveh* 'is a religious necessity and an hygienic requirement and long overdue'. Hertz was not prepared to go public with such a campaign.[55]

By the 1930s, then, the decline in the use of the *mikveh* by mainstream Anglo-Jewry meant that the provision of such institutions on a commercial basis was no longer profitable. In 1931, with the retirement of Frank, the Bayswater *mikveh* was in imminent danger of closure. Frank had evidently given Mrs Fishman notice (her salary was £12 10s. per year) without consulting the ladies' committee. This draws attention to the division of roles which dominated, and to a great extent still dominates, *mikveh* administration. Fund-raising and building are the responsibility of the men; running the service is the preserve of the women. Only in the post-war period have women, the chief consumers, really been consulted at the planning stage on the building of *mikvaot*. Indeed, as we shall see, in recent years it is pressure from women at the grass roots which has goaded the United Synagogue into taking an active interest in the subject.

In 1934 there was growing concern that the Bayswater *mikveh* was about to suffer from competition from a proposed new facility in a large red-brick Edwardian house in Cricklewood (at 6 Minster Road, NW2, site of the Kehillat Yisrael Synagogue of Rabbi J. L. Margulies, the Premiszlaner Rebbe) – the first in north-west London, an increasingly popular area of secondary Jewish settlement. Bayswater asked the Chief Rabbi not to sanction the opening of a new *mikveh* 'while this one was adequate . . .', as 'there is only need for one *mikveh* and certainly two could not be financially supported'. By 1939 Minster Road was in business, and Bayswater disappeared during the war.[56]

The Federation of Synagogues

In the late 1930s an Association of London Rabbis (*HaTakhrot HaRabbanim b'London*), which consisted of 24 rabbis and *dayanim* (religious court judges) representing all the Orthodox groupings in the capital, produced a memorandum which concluded that the practice of *mikveh* had 'fallen into neglect' and 'Matters are getting worse and not better'. This state of affairs was blamed on the 'poorish' facilities, which were 'not comfortably furnished', especially in the East End: 'Further, the price for their use is often prohibitive to poor people. For Brides, as much as ten shillings is charged for the use of the Mikvah.'

Class distinctions at the *mikveh*, as at the general baths, had been prevalent for many years. The son of the *mikveh* lady at the Great Synagogue in Manchester recalled that when he was a child, at the turn of the century,

> There were three classes of *mikveh*, first class, second class, and third class. It depended on how rich you were, how much you gave my mother. The first class had a tallboy . . . a chair and you would get a nice cup of tea and biscuits and things like that . . . I can remember the third class was just like our washhouse, just a plain common-or-garden bathroom and not as posh as the other ones. Mother never asked for any money, that was a sort of gratuity, you understand.

So, he was asked, how did his mother know which *mikveh* to direct the lady to, if she did not ask for her fee in advance? 'If you were well dressed, you know, she went into number one, do you follow what I mean?'[57]

An initiative by Dayan H. M. Lazarus of the London Beth Din (the ecclesiastical authority of the United Synagogue) to create a communal *mikveh* ran into the ground during the Second World War (August 1941)[58] and was not revived until the creation of the London Board of Mikvaot in 1946. This body, which existed for only four years, had one lasting achievement to its credit: the construction of the appropriately named Dunk Street *mikveh* on ground adjoining the Dzikower Federation Synagogue (32 Dunk Street, E1) at a cost of £1,000.[59] This, the last surviving *mikveh* in the East End, operative between 1949 and 1961, was used by some 80 women each month in 1950. It had an on-site caretaker, who lived in the two-storey flat above. Men were charged 1s. a dip, or 2s. per week for daily use. It appears that among its principal customers were the members of the nearby Beth HaMedrash Klal Chasodim, and that the women went in free.

During the Second World War, much of east London was destroyed by the Blitz, and this precipitated the flight of Jews to the suburbs which had been gathering pace during the 1920s and 1930s. Major synagogues, the Great and the Central, were bombed and so too were not a few of the private *mikvaot* which, as seen, had proliferated in the East End. By 1946 only two remained, at Exmouth Street and at 131 Cannon Street Road. These, too, had disappeared by the end of that decade.[60]

The London Board of Mikvaot was established on the initiative of the Federation of Synagogues, which had itself been created in 1887 as an umbrella organization for the *chevrot* in the East End. Consequently, the Federation was closer to the immigrant masses, and indeed in its heyday in the 1930s it had approaching twice as many members as the United. In 1946 a special committee set up by the Federation to investigate the state of the *mikvaot* in London came to the conclusion that facilities were 'hopelessly inadequate'.[61] Allegations were made in the *Jewish Chronicle* about 'the complete indifference' of communal leaders, 'both lay and clerical'.[62] But the task of meeting the crisis was too vast for the Federation to undertake alone. The young Kopul Rosen, who was Principal Rabbi of the Federation between 1945 and 1949, was the moving spirit behind the establishment of the London Board of Mikvaot. The Board was to consist of six representatives each from the Federation, United and UOHC, plus two from the Spanish and Portuguese. Its leading lights included the late A.B. Olivestone and Isaac Landau of the Federation and Aba Bornstein and Dr Jacob Braude of the UOHC. The Federation provided £2,000 spread over two years, representing 40 per cent of the estimated expenditure; the UOHC provided £250 per annum. Monies were promised by the Sephardim, and it was envisaged that the United Synagogue would furnish another 40 per cent. Such a pooling of funds would enable the new Board both to construct new *mikvaot* and to maintain existing ones. However, complaints were soon voiced in the councils of the Federation that

> the London Board of Mikvaot was supposed to be a Communal organisation, but at the moment the Federation was making by far the biggest contribution to its funds and in consequence ought to have proportionate representation. The Union of Orthodox Hebrew Congregations were not paying the full amount they had promised, whilst no payment whatsoever had so far been received from the United Synagogue.[63]

It seems that, despite the urgings of Dayan Abramsky, the United Synagogue did not join the Board. The London Board of Mikvaot collapsed. The Federation, through its own East London Mikvah Committee, struggled to support Dunk Street throughout the 1950s.[64] An annual grant of £300 was made over to the *mikveh* (plus a further £100–£300 per annum to the Grove Lane Beth HaMedrash's *mikveh* in Stamford Hill).[65] The time-honoured methods of approaching individual synagogues, ladies' guilds and even advertising in the Jewish press were resorted to.

In 1970 the Federation opened a new *mikveh* in a private house converted for the purpose in Gants Hill (463 Cranbrook Road, Ilford) at a cost of £20,000. Some of the funding came from the redundant Dzikower Synagogue and *mikveh* in Dunk Street, which had been compulsorily purchased by the Greater London Council in 1961 as part of its redevelopment plans.[66]

The United Synagogue 1958–95

In the late 1950s there was another abortive attempt to involve the United Synagogue in *mikveh* provision. In November 1958 the Council of the United Synagogue approved the setting up of a United Synagogue Mikveh Committee with a view to the establishment of a new *mikveh* in north-west London,[67] which was by this time the major area of Jewish settlement in the capital. Two private houses in Golders Green were to be converted for the purpose. However, the initiative had come from local women who, for the first time, were invited for consultation on the design of the projected development. The responsibility for raising the capital was, nevertheless, still in the hands of the men. The United Synagogue executive was willing to countenance the scheme – admitting that 'The lack of a mikveh was perhaps the only remaining feature of a well organised kehilla that was missing'[68] – largely because the proponents undertook to raise most of the £50,000 needed themselves, with only a minimal subsidy from Head Office. Considerable energy was expended on discussing the best strategy for raising the cash from ordinary members of the United Synagogue, many of whom, especially of 'the younger generation', it was feared, did not approve of *mikvaot* or see any point in their construction. A suggestion that a compulsory levy be added to the annual '*shool* bills' of members was, for this reason, strongly opposed.[69] Education, it was felt, was a necessary precondition for successful fund-raising in this sphere. Perhaps the fact that no more was heard of the United Synagogue Mikveh Committee is an indication of the enormous amount of work still to be done in that department in the 1950s, 1960s and 1970s.

While it is true that the United Synagogue continued to give small annual subsidies to other London *mikvaot* during those years,[70] it was not until 1978 that it undertook to build a *mikveh* of its very own. The *mikveh* in the grounds of the Kingsbury United Synagogue (1967) was finally opened in 1980 – the first United Synagogue *mikveh* established in the 110 years of that organization's existence. Although it was to be officially designated 'the United Synagogue Mikveh at Kingsbury Green', only £5,000 of the £55,000 final bill was provided by Head Office. The Kingsbury Synagogue made no direct contribution at all.[71] Pressure to build had once again come from local women and especially from the Chief Rebbetzin Amelie Jakobovits, who took a personal interest in the fund-raising, as did Rabbi Maurice Hool of Kingsbury. Indeed, the structure, which consists of two *mikvaot* plus three bathrooms and waiting area, was quickly dubbed 'Hool's Pool' by the press.[72]

By the end of the 1970s, in common with trends in Israel and the United States, the climate was changing. There is considerable sociological evidence of a limited religious revival particularly among the post-war generations of Anglo-Jews. A return to traditional values has been accompanied by a renewed interest in observances rejected by these generations' parents or grandparents as old-fashioned or irrelevant, one such being *mikveh*. A lecture on the subject held in 1980 attracted four times the expected number of women. The *Jewish Chronicle* commented: 'The presence of so many women suggests that the communal leaders have underestimated the interest in mikvaot. Are we about to see a mikva revival?'[73]

Indeed the 1980s saw an explosion of *mikveh* construction. Today there are more *mikvaot* in both London and the provinces than at any time in the history of the Anglo-Jewish community – and still others are being planned. Rabbi Meir Posen has acted as *halakhic* consultant and architect for almost all the *mikvaot* built in this country since the 1960s. The United Synagogue even became involved in the provision of *kelim mikvaot*. Besides the one built at Willesden (1948), such facilities were provided at Bushey (1984), Finchley, Hendon (1989), Kingsbury and Streatham (1991) United synagogues, although in each case the funding came from private donations.[74] Nevertheless, the United Synagogue lagged behind the strictly Orthodox communities which, as ever, set the pace (see below).

The Edgware and District Communal Mikveh, opened in 1991 in the grounds of the Edgware United Synagogue, had taken no less than 17 years to come to fruition. The idea of building a *mikveh* in a neighbourhood which boasts no fewer than four Orthodox synagogues – the most senior of which, the United (the congregation being founded in 1932), is housed in the largest synagogue building in the country – was first mooted by Dayan Gershon Lopian of the Edgware Yeshurun Federation. Local women, from Edgware, Stanmore and Mill Hill, formed themselves into the Edgware Mikveh Committee in 1980, and in 1983 they presented to United Synagogue Head Office a petition with 400 to 500 signatures endorsing the proposal. When plans to build on alternative

6.12   London, Edgware *Mikveh* (Rabbi Meir Posen and Stern Thom Fehler Architects, 1991). *Mandy Estrin*

sites at the Adath Yisrael (UOHC) and Yeshurun (Federation) synagogues ran into trouble, the United finally gave permission for the *mikveh* to be constructed on its land, leased to the Edgware Mikveh Trust, set up for that purpose, on condition that 'under no circumstances would Edgware [United] Synagogue or the United Synagogue be asked through its members to contribute to the building or maintenance of the facility'.[75]

In the end, the £300,000 needed was largely raised by the strictly Orthodox community through the good offices of the National Council for Taharat HaMishpakha and its chairman, the Sassover Rebbe, Rabbi Simcha Rubin. The two largest benefactors were private businessmen, Erwin Landau and Chaim Ellinson; the Federation contributed £10,000 and the United Synagogue £30,000, that is, 10 per cent of the cost. The magnificent structure, designed by Rabbi M. Posen jointly with architects Stern Thom Fehler, based on an unusual double-triangle motif and containing six bathrooms serving one central *mikveh* pool, was, however, not welcomed by all members of the United Synagogue, judging by correspondence in the *Jewish Chronicle*. One 39-year-old life-long member of Edgware United complained bitterly about the onset of 'radical orthodoxy' in that organization and threatened to join the Reform.[76]

The Reform Movement and Mikveh

Unexpectedly, however, even the Reform were not immune to changing times. Classical Reform Judaism, which had begun in response to the German Enlightenment in the early nineteenth century and which spread west primarily to America, had from the beginning rejected both the concept and practice of *mikveh* as outmoded. Its adherents in Britain, starting with the West London Reform Synagogue (established 1840), congregations in Bradford, Manchester and Liverpool, and the more radical Liberal Jewish Synagogue (forerunner 1902), followed suit. Nevertheless, in 1977 the Rabbinical Council of the Reform Synagogues of Great Britain (RSGB) voted to reintroduce *tevila* for Reform converts to Judaism – although this ruling was not taken up by the Liberal Synagogues, which remain a distinct entity. The issue of personal Jewish status – that is, Jewish birth, marriage, divorce and conversion – has long been the cause of the most fundamental schism between the Orthodox and Reform worlds. Thus proselytes converting under Reform auspices found themselves barred from using *mikvaot* owned and maintained by Orthodox Jews. Only two *mikvaot* were available for their use, in the public baths at Cardiff and Brighton, as already mentioned.

The necessity of making a long journey in order to perform *tevila* was resented by the Reform establishment. In March 1989, they announced plans to build a *mikveh* of their own on the ground floor of a new youth and education annex to their headquarters in the Sternberg Centre (formerly the Manor House, a convent) in Finchley, London, N3. This rainwater *mikveh* was duly completed in 1991, designed by John Millard at Hildebrand and Glicker, built to *halakhic* specifications under the direction of Rabbi Dr Louis Jacobs and supervised by the Beth Din of the RSGB. Fund-raising of the order of £30,000 was undertaken by the Reform Assembly of Rabbis and the facility is shared by the Masorti (Conservative) Jewish community.[77]

According to Jonathan Romain, minister of the Maidenhead Reform Synagogue, the new *mikveh* is intended not only for converts. He explained to the *Jewish Chronicle*:

> In the Reform movement, going to the mikvah is optional. But there is a small band of younger women who are interested in the tradition because it signifies the renewal of women's bodily rhythms and is one of the few significantly female rituals, like the Rosh Chodesh [new moon-lunar calendar] groups which are beginning to develop among younger, more Jewishly orientated women.[78]

Thus, for some elements within the Reform movement the *mikveh* has been rendered acceptable within the context of feminist ideas. On the other hand, when the woman rabbi of the Bromley Reform Synagogue tried to promote fund-raising for the new *mikveh* among her congregants, she encountered fierce hostility, not least from 'traditionally-minded' Reform Jews who had come to England from central Europe before the war, and to whom the very idea of *tevila* was anathema, a 'sexist' insult to womanhood.[79] Thus the *mikveh* 'revival' has not left the Reform untouched and the response has been mixed.

The Union of Orthodox Hebrew Congregations

As may be expected, the strictly Orthodox wing of the Anglo-Jewish community has consistently regarded the provision of *mikvaot* as an essential requirement for a fully functioning *kehilla* – and has been largely self-sufficient with respect to funding. The fiercely independent North London Beth HaMedrash, a German congregation which was founded in Tottenham in 1886, had its own small *mikveh* in Essex Road from 1892. It appears from the *Jewish Year Book* that this facility was moved from 353 to 367 Essex Road during the First World War (although it is also possible that the street was renumbered). In 1909 the congregation had appointed the Hungarian-born Rabbi Avigdor Schonfeld as its spiritual leader, and in 1911, renamed the Adath Yisrael Synagogue incorporating the North London Beth HaMedrash, it opened a purpose-built house of worship at 124–126 Green Lanes. A *kelim mikveh* was added in the grounds of the synagogue in 1913 and a second full-scale *mikveh*, at 126 Green Lanes, was operative from 1920 to 1928. In 1926 Schonfeld brought together a number of like-minded London congregations, whose numbers were to be augmented in the 1930s by strictly Orthodox central European refugees from Nazi persecution, including chasidim, under the aegis of the Union of Orthodox Hebrew Congregations. It was 'an organisation unique in Anglo-Jewry in that it is and has always been managed and dominated more by its rabbis rather than by its lay leaders'.[80]

Rabbi Dr Solomon Schonfeld, Avigdor's son and successor from 1933, was the moving spirit in the construction and extension of *mikvaot* through the UOHC's Central Mikvaot Board, which he created in 1937 and revived in 1950 after the collapse of the London Board of Mikvaot. Schonfeld purchased land in Hendon in 1943 upon which the Hendon Adath Yisrael Synagogue was subsequently built (1948). A *mikveh* came first, at 10A Shirehall Lane (1946). This *mikveh* was the direct descendant of the first pre-war *mikveh* to be built in north-west London, Minster Road. Even the attendant, Viennese-born Mrs Hedwig Strahlberg, made the move from Cricklewood to Hendon. She served for over 50 years.[81]

Originally with one communal *mikveh* served by five bathrooms and a shower room, Shirehall Lane was the most up-to-date facility of its day. It was well used, because its catchment area embraced the whole of the growing north-west London Jewish community. It was patronized by an estimated 200 women a month in 1955, 800 in 1963 – on one single day as many as 55 users – and 600 (after extension) in 1981.[82] Nevertheless, this *mikveh* was in constant financial difficulties owing to the lack of 'proper grants' and was a drain on the Adath Yisrael's resources. Rumour had it that certain ministers of the United Synagogue supported the long-mooted rebuilding of Shirehall Lane, which was completed in 1966 (with eight *mikveh* pools with bathrooms en suite, one *mikveh* being reserved for men). But only £250 was forthcoming from United Synagogue Head Office that year.[83] Funds were raised by the Adath and by local chasidic groups: Rabbi Elchanan Halpern of the Beth Shmuel congregation and one-time president of the UOHC (he had had his own private *mikveh* for men at 171 Golders Green Road since the 1950s; in 1994 the structure was demolished and replaced by a facility to serve both men and women), the North West London Sephardish (Hager's) synagogue and the Sassover Rebbe, who was later to play an important role in the National Council for Taharat HaMishpakha, which he set up. Shirehall Lane was further extended in 1980.

In 1955 a conference of the British Agudat Yisrael (a non-Zionist political/religious party closely allied with the UOHC) launched a campaign to raise half a million pounds to build a network of *mikvaot* in Britain.[84] The main focus of strictly Orthodox *mikveh* building activity was in Stamford Hill, which, with the influx of refugees both before and after the war, became the bastion of Jewish Orthodoxy in London. The first *mikveh* built in the area after the war was at Lordship Park, at Rabbi (Rebbe) Meshullam Ashkenasy's Stanislaver Beth HaMedrash (1950–51). Schonfeld purchased land adjoining this site and extended it further in 1965. He likewise purchased the lease on the Federation Grove Lane Stamford Hill Beth HaMedrash *mikveh* in Lampard Grove in 1958 (founded in 1932 as London Jewry's largest *mikveh*) and con- tributed towards the cost of rebuilding in 1965 (Margaret Street).[85] On the initiative of Harry A. Goodman, vice-president of the UOHC and a member of the Allocations Committee of the Central British Fund for World Jewish Relief, a successful application was made to the Jewish Trust Corporation for Germany, a special compensation fund for victims of Nazism, on behalf of Grove Lane, which was largely patronized by refugees; £6,000 was awarded for the purpose of 'religious Jewish rehabilitation' in 1961.[86]

A women's *mikveh* was constructed at the new Adath Yisrael complex in Queen Elizabeth's Walk, opened in 1965. Essex Road was closed in 1964, reflecting the Orthodox drift into Stamford Hill. Other women's *mikvaot* in the area, built by a variety of independent, largely chasidic, groups, include the Satmar *mikveh* at 62 Filey Avenue (1963; recon- structed internally in the early 1970s) and the Craven Walk *mikveh* at 72 Lingwood Road (1981; opened in 1987). Men's *mikvaot* proliferate,

6.13 South London *Mikveh*, Wimbledon (Rabbi Meir Posen, 1991); ground plan of facilities. *Rabbi Meir Posen*

there being at least 14 in the north London area at the present time. *Mikvaot* have been constructed in the private homes of two well-to-do Orthodox families in north and north-west London. The Lubavitch Foundation, which is based in Stamford Hill but has a philosophy of reaching out to the wider Jewish community, initiated, through its local rabbi, the building in 1991 of a tiny *mikveh* in the grounds of its Chabad House in Wimbledon, the first-ever *mikveh* south of the Thames.[87]

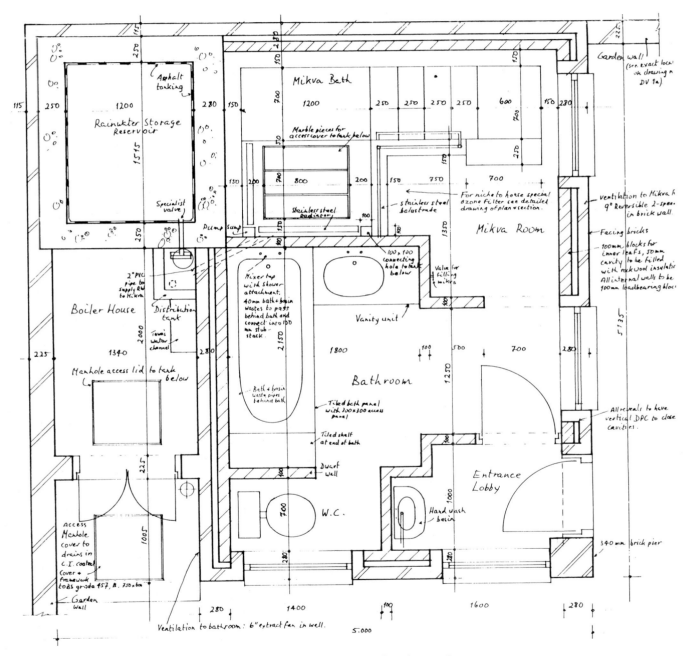

PLAN OF GROUND FLOOR

MIKVAOT IN THE PROVINCES SINCE THE END OF THE SECOND WORLD WAR

In 1972 the Beth Din of the UOHC issued a *psak* (rabbinical ruling) warning Orthodox Jews not to use *mikvaot* in provincial towns, especially holiday resorts, without consulting 'a reliable rabbinic authority', because they were likely to be *posul* (unfit for use).[88] There is certainly much evidence that *mikvaot* outside London, even where they existed, frequently fell into disrepair and were disused for long periods. I have already cited the case of the Albert Grove *mikveh* in Leeds, and indeed a rabbi from that city estimated in 1948 that the practice of *mikveh* 'had lapsed among 95 per cent of Jews in this country'.[89] 'A Provincial Jewess' agreed with other correspondents of the *Jewish Chronicle* in 1955 that 'The purpose of the mikva is not one of hygiene'. She explained:

> No one who has attended the ritual baths regularly over a number of years (as I have) would be likely to make this mistake, and from what I hear our mikva is in no way unique in this respect. Indeed, the lack of knowledge of the elementary rules of hygiene by some of those in charge of the mikva is a favourite excuse given for non-attendance . . . if [only] our respected clergy and physicians would tackle the matter from this aspect and endeavour to put cleanliness a little nearer to godliness . . .[90]

This woman may well have hailed from Liverpool, where the *mikveh* was 'situated in a squalid street marked for slum clearance' after the war. And, according to the rabbi of Prince's Road Synagogue (1874), the flagship congregation of the city, this situation had pertained 'for more than twenty years'.[91] In the north and the Midlands, in Liverpool, Leeds, Manchester and Birmingham, and in Glasgow, the Jewish community was by this time in the process of upward social mobility, from the inner-city slums to the suburbs. But in most cases the *mikveh* was left behind, responsibility for its upkeep reluctantly shouldered by the local Shechita Board, which was obliged to raise the price of kosher meat to meet the inevitable deficit. This did not make them popular even with the majority

6.14 Liverpool *Mikveh*, Childwall Synagogue (Rabbi Meir Posen, 1976).
Rabbi Meir Posen

of housewives. Attempts to build or renovate *mikvaot* often met with apathy and a reluctance to indulge what was looked upon as the 'whim' of a small minority of religious zealots, when the money could be better spent on more pressing needs.

On taking up his appointment as Chief Rabbi of Ireland in 1955, Immanuel Jakobovits (later Chief Rabbi of the United Hebrew Congregations of Great Britain and the Commonwealth) was appalled at the state of the Dublin *mikveh*, which had been built at the Adelaide Road Synagogue (1892) in 1915, and he insisted on its renovation. Nevertheless, in a numerically declining Jewish community, by 1982 this *mikveh* was again 'found to be in a very alarming state of disrepair due to fungus infestation of the structure', and the process of renovation had to be carried out afresh in 1984.[92] New *mikvaot* were constructed in the teeth of local opposition in Westcliff (1960), Glasgow (1973) and Bournemouth (1976). As in London, so too in Manchester and Leeds, 'sister' congregations of the UOHC have largely taken the initiative in building new *mikvaot* in recent years.

CONCLUSION

The discovery of the medieval *mikveh* at Bristol in 1987 is, without doubt, of international significance – even though, at the time of writing, the site still awaits rabbinical inspection to confirm its authenticity. It has, so to speak, put Britain on the *mikveh* map. This site should be officially registered on the National Monuments List as not only of outstanding importance for the history of European Jewry in the Middle Ages (of which Britain was the last outpost), but integral to the heritage of *Britain* itself: a rare trace left by one of the earliest immigrant communities to these shores.

In more recent times, we find that, even where documentation of synagogues in Britain has been undertaken (and it is still in its infancy), the presence or absence of the *mikveh* has been consistently ignored. Our findings show that, until the twentieth century, the majority of *mikvaot* in this country were built under private auspices and were not situated in communal buildings, in cellars or outhouses of synagogues, as was the practice on the Continent, especially in Germany. Almost all the rabbinically supervised ritual baths (as opposed to informal 'make-do' arrangements) have been constructed in urban centres (South Wales being a notable exception), where Jews have tended to congregate, using rainwater sources. The Chief Rabbi's Survey of 1845 revealed the religious laxity of Anglo-Jewry in the early Victorian period; half of the communities questioned did not possess a proper *mikveh*. Whilst many *mikvaot*, especially in London, were located in private houses, British Jews were exceptional in taking advantage of the provision of public bathing facilities from the middle of the nineteenth century. It appears that, as early as the 1850s, the Birmingham and Hull municipalities provided a 'kosher bath' in the local public bath houses; the corporations of Glasgow, Leeds and Plymouth (1910) and later of Bournemouth, Brighton and Cardiff followed suit. Brighton and Cardiff are still in use.

The strictly Orthodox wing of Anglo-Jewry, accounting for no more than 10 per cent of the community, has taken on a disproportionate burden of *mikveh* construction. This is not surprising, given the centrality of the practice of *mikveh* in Orthodox Judaism. By contrast, mainstream synagogue organizations in London were reluctant to shoulder responsibility for the building and maintenance of *mikvaot*. The first communal *mikveh* was built in the East End in the 1930s by the Federation of Synagogues (Dunk Street). The United Synagogue did not become involved on a significant scale until as late as the 1970s (Kingsbury). Even now their leadership is less than enthusiastic. In the past finance was clearly not the problem – *vide* the grand 'cathedral' style of synagogue favoured by the United. Arguably, this failure of the United Synagogue to build *mikvaot* may be attributed to theological indifference rather than to material considerations. Provincial congregations took their cue from the United Synagogue; a substantial building such as Singers Hill in Birmingham (Yeoville Thomason, 1856) did not include a *mikveh*; at Reading (1900) plans for a *mikveh* on the ground floor were not fully executed.[93]

Currently, something of a *mikveh* revival is underway.[94] As observed in passing, there are now more *mikvaot* in Britain than at any time in the history of Anglo-Jewry, and more are planned. Even the Reform movement, which for so long rejected the concept and practice of *tevila*, has got in on the act with the building of its own *mikveh* at the Sternberg Centre in Finchley.

Thus our researches have revealed much in the way of religious history and social attitudes, far less about architecture and building technology. While the attrition rate of historic synagogues in this country has been bad, most *mikvaot* have sunk without trace. In some cases, even the exact address of the bathhouse, even one serving a major London community (the Great Synagogue), cannot be established beyond doubt. Few interesting old *mikvaot* have survived (an exception being Canterbury), while those situated in public baths have succumbed to vandalism and decay, for example Birmingham's Bournville Baths, Leeds' Albert Grove. In the latter case, some documentation and a photograph have fortuitously been preserved. Clearly, in future, architectural surveys of synagogues ought, as a matter of course, to include details of the *mikveh*.

I hope that my research will help restore the *mikveh* to its rightful place in Jewish architectural history – not to mention in the practice of Judaism – and that it will invite comparative studies with the situation in other Jewish centres worldwide.

NOTES

1. See Rabbi Aryeh Kaplan, *Waters of Eden* (New York, 2nd edn 1982), for a general introduction to the subject in English. Rabbi David Miller, *The Secret of the Jew* (California, 1930), is useful but dated in approach; Chaim Bermant, *The Walled Garden* (London, 1974), Ch. 8. William Sanford La Sor, 'Discovering what Jewish Miqva'ot can tell us about Christian Baptism, *Biblical Archaeology Review*, Jan.–Feb. 1987, pp. 52–9 and reply by Ronnie Reich of the Israel Antiquities Department in ibid., July–Aug. 1987, pp. 59–60.

2. The following summary is based on: Kaplan, op. cit., pp. 51–9; *Encyclopedia Judaica (EJ)* on 'Mikveh'; Rabbi Meir Posen,'Mikwa – A cornerstone in Jewish Life', in *Mikwe: Geschichte und Architektur judischer Ritualbader in Deutschland* (catalogue of an exhibition held at the Frankfurt Jewish Museum, 1992; translation kindly provided by the author. I was unaware of this exhibition until the present essay was almost complete); Yosef Schonberger, *Mikvaot* (Jerusalem, 1974, in Hebrew); 'Mikveh – Arthur's Road, Sea Point' (Cape Town, South Africa: unpub. MS., Louis Karol Associates, Architects, acknowledgments to Eitan Karol).

3. Provided it flows freely, i.e. in the absence of a dam or sluice, which would render the water 'drawn' (see para. 4).

4. Ice and snow is generally regarded as valid even if manufactured from 'drawn' water.

5. A river derived mainly from rainwater may be used for *tevila* if it is partially dammed to create a '*mikveh*' containing 40 *se'ah* of water.

6. It is even permitted to sell these items in order to raise funds for a *mikveh*.

7. See *EJ*, 'Mikveh'; *Mikwe*; and Schonberger, op. cit. Richard Krautheimer, *Mittelalterliche Synagogen* (Berlin, 1927); Ronnie Reich, 'Miqwa'ot (Jewish Ritual Immersion Baths) in Eretz-Israel in the Second Temple and the Mishnah and Talmud Periods', unpub. PhD thesis, Hebrew University of Jerusalem, 1990 (Hebrew with detailed English summary). See also Danièle Iancu, 'Le Mikve et l'évolution du quartier juif médiéval à Montpellier', in Carol Iancu (ed.), *Les Juifs à Montpellier et dans le Languedoc* (Montpellier, 1988), pp. 72–92, 432–3, for a medieval *mikveh* discovered and restored as a national monument in France.

8. London, 1950, Introduction p. 14. However, at a conference on 'Jewish Life in Modern Britain' held in 1962 Roth suggested that

> there is one criterion of orthodoxy which might also serve as a method for a statistical survey of the orthodox – that is, the mikve. It should be easy to find out how many women attend the mikve. It should be possible to use this as the measure of the really orthodox element, rather than those who buy kosher meat. The number will probably be surprisingly if not regrettably small.

See the discussion on Norman Cohen's paper, 'Trends in Anglo-Jewish Religious Life', in Julius Gould and Shaul Esh (eds), *Jewish Life in Modern Britain* (London, 1964), p. 60. For a transatlantic comparison see Andrew R. Heinze, *Adapting to Abundance: Jewish Immigrants, Mass Consumption, and the Search for American Identity* (New York, 1990), pp. 57–8.

9. For example, at Sunderland in 1902 (see Arnold Levy, *History of the Sunderland Jewish Community 1755–1955* (London, 1956), pp. 171–2); at Sheffield in 1928 (see Armin Krausz, *Sheffield Jewry* (London, 1980), pp. 15, 38); at Swansea (see Ursula R. Q. Henriques, 'The conduct of a synagogue: Swansea Hebrew Congregation, 1895–1914', in Henriques, ed., *The Jews of South Wales* (Cardiff, 1993), pp. 92, 99, 100–1).

10. An exception being Rickie Burman, '"She looketh well to the ways of her household": The changing role of Jewish women in religious life c. 1880–1930', in Gail Malmgreen (ed.), *Religion in the Lives of English Women* (London, 1986), pp. 234–59, *mikveh* is referred to on pp. 245–7.

11. London, 1893 p. 236. See also Israel Abrahams, *Jewish Life in the Middle Ages* (first published 1896; New York 1985 edn, pp. 73–4). On London: Richard Serman, 'The Guildhall House – Strong Room or Ritual Bath?', *Department of Urban Archaeology Newsletter*, Museum of London (Sept. 1990), pp. 12–14; Gabriel Pepper, 'An Archaeology of the Jewry in Medieval London', *London Archaeologist*, Vol. 7, No. 1 (Winter 1992), pp. 3–6. Joe Hillaby casts doubt on this find; see his 'London: The 13th-century Jewry revisited', *Transactions of the Jewish Historical Society of England (TJHSE)*, XXXII (1990–92), pp. 89–158, esp. p. 102. Unfortunately the site has been destroyed by redevelopment, but documentary material is in the Museum of London's archives, and a photograph was featured in the Museum's 'Peopling of London' exhibition (1993–94). On Oxford: Brian Durham *et al.*, 'The Infirmary and Hall of the Medieval Hospital of St John the Baptist at Oxford', *Oxoniensia*, Vol. 56 (1991), pp. 17–73. On Bristol: Michael Ponsford *et al.*, 'Archaeology in Bristol 1986–89', *Transactions of the Bristol and Gloucester Archaeological Society*, Vol. 107 (1989), pp. 243–51, esp. pp. 249, 251. Help received from Raphi Isserlin, Michael Ponsford and John Bryant (Bristol Archaeology Unit).

12. The following paragraphs are based on an unpublished paper by Ralph Emanuel of the Council for the Preservation of Ancient Bristol, who was largely responsible for identifying the well as a *mikveh*. (Later published in R. R. Emanuel and M. W.

Ponsford, 'Jacob's Well, Bristol, Britain's only known medieval Jewish Ritual Bath (*Mikveh*)', *Transactions of the Bristol and Gloucestershire Archaeological Society*, Vol. 112 (1994), pp. 73–86.) See also *Jewish Chronicle* (*JC*), 3, 10, 17 July 1987. The Working Party on Jewish Monuments have requested English Heritage to schedule the site, but progress has been hampered by lack of access.

13. For instance in W. S. Samuel, *The First London Synagogue of the Resettlement* (London, 1924); information kindly provided by Miriam Rodrigues-Pereira, Honorary Archivist to the Spanish and Portuguese Jews' Congregation in a letter to the author, 30 March 1992; L. D. Barnett, *El Libro de Los Acuerdos* (Oxford, 1931), pp. 16, 17, 40. According to this last entry, the original site of the *mikveh* was sold off in 1670.

14. Todd M. Endelman, *The Jews of Georgian England* (Philadelphia, 1979), p. 146; Richard D. Barnett, 'The correspondence of the Mahamad of the Spanish and Portuguese Congregation of London during the Seventeenth and Eighteenth Centuries', *TJHSE*, XX (1959–61), pp. 1–50, especially p. 9.

15. Cecil Roth, *The Great Synagogue, London, 1690–1940* (London, 1950), pp. 89–93. For an example of a conversion being officially conducted under the auspices of three Ashkenazi *Dayanim* in 1806 'in the *mikva* of the widow of Abraham Nunsikh', see Tsvi Yaakov Tsimmels, '*Pesakim u'Teshuvot meBeit Dino shel Rabbi Shlomo Bar Tsvi*' (Rabbi Solomon Hirschell], in H. J. Zimmels *et al.*, *Essays Presented to Chief Rabbi Sir Israel Brodie*, Hebrew Section (London, 1966), pp. 219–42, esp. p. 222. Acknowledgments to Rabbi Dr Bernard Susser.

16. Op. cit., p. 146.

17. Chief Rabbi's Archives, Greater London Record Office (GLRO), Acc. 2712/7, Minutes of Committee Meetings of the Great Synagogue 1841–46, entry for 11 Aug. 1846 (Adler's letter dated 13 July 1846); Hambro Synagogue minute book, General Meetings 1845–63, entry for 24 Aug. 1846; New Synagogue minute book, Committee 1832–50, entry for 21 Oct. 1846. Information on Liverpool kindly provided by Joe Wolfman, Archivist to the Merseyside Jewish Representative Council, letter dated 12 Feb. 1993.

18. See *Jewish Tribune* (*JT*), 27 May 1983, p. 4; letter from Peter Barber, 17 July, 1992.

19. Rachel Daiches-Dubens, 'Eighteenth Century Anglo-Jewry in and around Richmond, Surrey', *TJHSE*, XVIII (1958), pp. 127–69, especially pp. 165–6, 168; Malcolm Brown, 'Anglo-Jewish Country Houses from the Resettlement to 1800', *TJHSE*, XXVIII (1984), pp. 20–38.

20. D. A. J. Cardozo and P. Goodman, *Think and Thank* (London, 1933), p. 10; Helen Rosenau, 'Montefiore and the visual arts', in Sonia and V. D. Lipman (eds), *The Century of Moses Montefiore* (Oxford, 1985), pp. 118–28, college p. 124; confirmation of presence of *mikveh* by George da Costa, caretaker of the Ramsgate Synagogue, via John Lipitch of Dover, letter of 22 Feb. 1993.

21. Rabbi Dr Bernard Susser, 'The Questionnaire of 1845', in Aubrey Newman (ed.), *Provincial Jewry in Victorian Britain* (London, JHSE, 1975), contains an analysis including the data on *mikveh* upon which Appendix 6.1, below, is based.

22. Malcolm Brown and Judith Samuel, 'The Jews of Bath', *Bath History*, Vol. I, No. I, pp. 150–72. Another version of this article, published in *TJHSE*, XXIX (1982–86), pp. 135–59, omits the observations about the *mikveh*.

23. Facsimile edn, Gloucester, 1981, pp. 74–5; the synagogue and school appear on p. 96.

24. Brian Torode, *The Hebrew Community of Cheltenham, Gloucester and Stroud* (Gloucester and Cheltenham, 1989), p. 46.

25. Portsmouth did have a *mikveh*. See Rabbi Eugene Newman, 'Some new facts about the Portsmouth Jewish Community', *TJHSE*, XVII (1953), pp. 251–68, at p. 257. It was situated at the 'Old' synagogue at White's Row in the eighteenth century and was accessible to members of the 'New' at Daniel's Row on payment of a fee. On Falmouth, see Rabbi Dr Bernard Susser, *The Jews of South-West England* (Exeter, 1993), p. 134; on Penzance, see Cecil Roth, *Penzance: The Decline and Fall of an Anglo-Jewish Community* (referring to *c.* 1807), reprinted from *JC*, May 1933, p. 4. The *mikveh* at the Plymouth Synagogue is extant but disused. Acknowledgments to Keith Pearce of Penzance for information on the south-west, and to Mr P. R. Aloof, President, Plymouth Hebrew Congregation (letter of 11 Aug. 1992).
    Swansea's *mikveh* dated from the 1830s; see Bernard Goldbloom, 'Swansea' in Newman (ed.), op. cit., n.p.

26. According to the opinion followed by Rabbi Posen and accepted by other rabbinical authorities in this country. See recent *teshuvot* on the validity of various water sources, e.g. sea, reservoir, for *mikveh*; Dayan Yitskhak Ya'acov Weiss (of Man-

chester), *Minkhat Yitskhak*, Vol. I (Manchester, 1969); Dayan Hanoch D. Padwa [of the UOHC], *Kheshev HaEphod*, Vol. II (London, 1977), p. 45. Acknowledgments to Anne Yardley, my *khevruta* (religious study partner).

    The Maidenhead Reform Synagogue used to use the Thames near Henley for immersing Reform converts; see *JC*, 22 Feb. 1991.

27. In AJ 168 a/2 (Anglo-Jewish Archives, Southampton University Library). Dan Cohn-Sherbok, *The Jews of Canterbury 1760–1931* (Canterbury, 1984), makes no reference to the *mikveh* but contains a delightful illustration of it by Hubert Pragnell, reproduced here.

28. Steven Singer, 'Jewish Religious Observance in early Victorian London 1840–1860', *Journal of Jewish Sociology*, Vol. 28 (1986), pp. 117–37 (pp. 126–7 on *mikvaot*); *JC*, 24 Feb. 1854, 5 May, 31 Oct. 1856; *Hebrew Observer*, 8 Dec. 1854; also announcement in *JC*, 3 Feb. 1854, for the sale of Baths 'established for upwards of Forty years and kept by the late Mrs Raphael'.

29. GLRO Acc. 2712/VIII/i, Copy Letter Book, Vol. 2 June 1851–March 1854, n.p., opposite Letter No. 7535. This version was obviously not sent, being crossed out, and a modified, less explicit version is also preserved.

30. Singer, op. cit., p. 127. The letter he cites about 'poor women' cannot now be traced in the GLRO. Australia, being part of the Empire, came within the jurisdiction of Dr Adler. The Survey also revealed a *mikveh* in Jamaica.

31. *Jewish Year Book* (*JYB*), 1897 to date; see Appendix 6.2, below. The information on London is more comprehensive than that on the provinces, where the existence and location of *mikvaot* have in many cases not been noted until very recently. The *Jewish Directory for 1874* is entirely unhelpful. See Heinze, op. cit., for a comparison with the Lower East Side of New York City.

32. Renée Kadish (*née* Shapiro) in interview, 14 May 1992; the family lived at No. 1 Langdale Street, a tiny house, and not in the Mansions.

33. Jerry White, *Rothschild Buildings* (London, 1980), p. 47.

34. Cited in George Ryley Scott, *The Story of Baths and Bathing* (London, 1939), p. 162. Such general histories, e.g. Lawrence Wright, *Clean and Decent* (London, 1960), do not refer to *mikvaot*.

35. See Scott, op. cit., pp. 157–8; Agnes Campbell, *Report on Public Baths and Wash-houses in the United Kingdom* (Edinburgh, Carnegie UK Trust, 1918); J. Weale (ed.), *London Exhibited in 1851* (London, 1851); Edward H. Gibson, 'Baths and Wash-houses in the English Public Health Agitation 1839–1848', *Journal of the History of Medicine and Allied Sciences*, Vol. 9 (Oct. 1954), pp. 391–406; Anthony S. Wohl, *Endangered Lives: Public Health in Victorian Britain* (London, 1983), pp. 74–5; *Taking the Plunge: The Architecture of Bathing* (SAVE Britain's Heritage, London, n.d. [1982]), a catalogue to accompany an exhibition at the Royal Institute of British Architects which was the first attempt to document public bathhouses in Britain; it contains a 'Checklist of Public Baths in England & Wales up to 1939' compiled by Hana Laing.

    Besides Goulston Street, there were several other public bathhouses in the East End frequented by Jews: Betts Street, St George's-in-the-East, Mile End (built 1888), and Ratcliffe Street, Limehouse (built 1900). See *JC*, 25 Sept. 1908.

36. *The Times*, 12 May 1847, p. 6. *Tower Hamlets Independent*, 10 Aug. 1878. Goulston Street was bombed in 1944. Today the now derelict Whitechapel Amenity Complex stands on the site, mostly dating from the 1960s. However the Old Castle Street facade, clearly dated 1846, does survive; see Elain Harwood, 'Whitechapel Baths, Goulston Street LB Tower Hamlets', unpub. MS., English Heritage (File No. TH 155), July 1991. Acknowledgments to Susie Barson of the London Division of EH for sending it to me. On the closure of Goulston Street, see *JC*, 3 Aug. 1990.

37. Scott, op. cit., pp. 157–8.

38. White, op. cit., p. 49 and photograph, Plate 9. Camperdown House, headquarters of the Jewish Lads' Brigade (Ernest Joseph, 1913), had shower facilities used by members. See also Richard Cork, *David Bomberg* (New Haven and London, 1987), pp. 78–80. 'Shefshick's' inspired Bomberg's painting 'The Mud Bath' (1914).

39. Pp. 1903 ix (Cmd 1742), paragraph 16298, 16 March 1903. Campbell, op. cit., p. 7. The existence of *mikvaot* is referred to only in passing in statistical tables re Leeds (p. 22) and Cardiff (p. 23).

40. See the programme, *City of Leeds, Jewish Baths, Opening by the Right Hon. The Lord Mayor, Wednesday 25th October, 1905*, in the Leeds Reference Library. Acknowledgments to Murray Freedman for researching Leeds on my behalf. See also *JC*, 3 Nov. 1905. The late Jack Lennard did extensive research on Hull: *Hull*

Advertiser, 22 April 1850, p. 5; Corporation Baths Committee Minutes 1902, 1903, April 1919; *Victoria County History, Yorkshire*; letters and telephone conversations with the author 14 Dec. 1992, 27 Jan., 8, 10 March 1993. Research in the minutes of Birmingham Hebrew Congregation by Elizabeth Lesser. Apparently there was also a *mikveh* at the Plymouth Corporation Bathhouse (1910). See Bernard Susser, *Jews of South West England*, op. cit., p. 135.

41. See Kenneth E. Collins, *Second City Jewry* (Glasgow ,1990), pp. 27, 53, 88–90. Other information provided by Harvey Kaplan.

42. Letters to the author, 9 March, 2 April 1992.

43. *JC*, 2 Sept. 1910, re plans to extend the Leeds *mikveh* discussed by the Town Council.

44. Rabbi Israel Chayim Daiches, *Mikve Yisrael* (Leeds, 1912); Rabbi Y. Shemaria, 'Rabbi Israel Chayim Daiches', *Hakshiva, Journal of the Rabbinical Council of the Provinces*, Vol. 3, No. 1 (Succot 1991), pp. 16–23, from where the 'leading Eastern European rabbi' quotation is taken; obituary, *JC*, 25 June 1937; entry in *EJ*. However, the Maharsham, Rabbi Shalom Mordechai Shvadron of Brezen, defended the water meter, and his opinion is followed by Rabbi David Miller in *The Secret of the Jew* (op. cit.). I am grateful to Rabbi Shemaria for sending me his article plus a xerox of the rare Daiches' *teshuva*. Chief Rabbi J. H. Hertz apparently stipulated that the *mikveh* at Grimsby, built in 1916 (disused by the 1930s but still standing behind the synagogue), should be constructed without a water meter; telephone conversation with Daphne Gerlis, who has researched Grimsby in the Chief Rabbi's archives, 7 Aug. 1992. The records of the London Beth Din, which may reveal more about the ban on water meters, are not yet available to researchers.

45. Letters to the author, 6 (postmarked) and 29 March 1992, in response to a call for information on my behalf by Nigel Grizzard in the *Jewish Telegraph* (Leeds edn), Feb. 1992.

46. Ernest Krausz, *Leeds Jewry: its History and Social Structure* (Cambridge, 1964), p. 110. I am informed by Rabbi M. M. Baddiel of Newcastle that the *mikveh* in that city is used by only two women; others maybe go to Gateshead (reply to my inquiry of 30 March 1992).

47. According to Murray Freedman, Albert Grove was threatened with demolition as part of a slum-clearance programme; see *JC*, 28 Aug. 1959. In 1968 it was vandalized and rendered unfit for use; see *JC*, 19 Jan. 1968. The council began work on a new *mikveh* in a planned international swimming pool *c*. 1984, but it was declared *posul* because the fibreglass bath was the wrong shape and a *kelei*; letter from Walter Rothschild, minister of Sinai Reform Synagogue, Leeds, 8 Sept. 1992; further information from Rabbi M. Posen. *JC*, 18 Nov. 1994, 15 Sept. 1995 on Etz Chaim.

48. Information supplied by Dorene Jacobs of Cardiff in a letter dated 15 March 1992; see also *JC*, 5 June 1959. (My letter in *CAJEX*, Vol. XLII, No. 3 (Sept. 1992), p. 63, requesting information on *mikvaot* elsewhere in Wales elicited no response.) There was an abortive attempt to provide a public *mikveh* in Luton during the same period. In this case the initiative came from the local rabbi and was rejected by the council; see *JC*, 7 Nov., 5 Dec. 1958, 2 Jan., 4 Dec. 1959, 1 Jan., 16, 30 June, 8 Dec. 1961, 2 Aug. 1963. The proposal was finally thrown out on grounds of expense and because 'it was likely to be used only five times a month' (*JC*, 17, 24 Jan. 1964).

   When new Bournemouth rabbi Sidney Silberg requested that the council extend the opening hours of the Piers Baths *mikveh* to enable women to use it at night, the council threatened to close down the facility owing to the staffing costs involved (*JC*, 7 June 1974). An inspection by Dayan L. Grossnas and Rabbi Posen subsequently found it to be *posul*; *JC*, 7, 14 Mar. 1975; further information from Rabbi M. Posen. Birmingham City Council is contributing one quarter of the cost of a new *mikveh* at the Central Synagogue, *JC*, 13 Aug. 1993.

49. Miller, *The Secret of the Jew* (op. cit.); introduction by C. E. Hillel Kauvar, p. 20.

50. *JC*, 19 Jan. 1912.

51. *JC*, 5 Oct. 1866; reprinted 7 Oct. 1966. The connection, if any, between Mrs Jacobson and the Mrs Jacobs whose 1854 advertisement is quoted above is not clear.

52. GLRO, Acc. 2805/37, file labelled 'Mikveh' pertaining to Bayswater 1924–34. A number of United congregations made donations.

53. GLRO, Acc. 2712/11 US Council minute book, Vol. 6, agenda, report of executive committee, 13 Nov. 1923. It seems that the United Synagogue had given the Bayswater *mikveh* an annual grant before the First World War, according to S. H. Emanuel, GLRO, Acc. 2712/54, US executive committee minute book, Vol. 4, 25 Oct. 1923.

54. In 1925, 1926 and 1930: £25 extra; in 1932: £75, see US Council minute book,

Vol. 6 (op. cit.). See also the account of the debate at the meeting in a letter from Frank to Barnett, 'Mr S. H. Emanuel KC, who was in the Chair opposed [the proposed grant of £50] strongly . . .' (Acc. 2805/37, 'Mikveh' file, 31 Dec. 1924). The evidence forces me to disagree with the conclusion of the official historian of the US, Professor Aubrey Newman, that its attitude to the funding of *mikvaot* 'could be used to prove either the orthodoxy or the lack of it in the United Synagogue'. See his *The United Synagogue 1870–1970* (London, 1975), p. 125.

55. GLRO, Acc. 2805/37, 3 March 1924, Frank and Barnett to Hertz; 4 Jan. 1925, Frank to Hertz; Hertz's reaction, marked 'private', 6 Jan. 1925; Frank to Hertz, 7 Jan. 1925. Further information provided by Mrs Rita Joseph, daughter of Mrs Matilda Fishman, the *mikveh* lady from 1928–39, letter to the author, postmarked 25 Aug. 1995.

56. Ibid. 31 Dec. 1934, Rosamund Ruben to Hertz. The Cricklewood *mikveh* is first listed in the 1940 *JYB*. The three-storey house, which is still standing, had a *mikveh* and bathroom on the ground-floor plus a hut in the big garden which served as a waiting room. Interview with Mrs H. Strahlberg (see Note 81 below).

57. AJ/F No. 5, n.d., late 1930s; Bill Williams, 'The Jewish Immigrant in Manchester: The contribution of oral history', *Oral History*, Vol. 7, No. 1 (Spring 1979), pp. 43–53, quotation on p. 49; also cited by Burman in Malmgreen (ed.), op. cit.

58. GLRO, Acc. 2712/23, US Council (Honorary Officers) minute book, Vol. 11, 18 Aug. 1941; letter from Lazarus to Sir Robert Waley Cohen dated 8 Aug. 1941.

59. See *JC*, 27 Feb. 1948, 17 June 1949.

60. Based on *JYB*; according to *JC*, 9 Aug. 1946, LBM took a 99-year lease on 131/133 Cannon Street Road to establish a *mikveh*. But it seems that one had existed at this address since at least 1929. My mother remembers using Exmouth Street after the Second World War (interview, 14 May 1992).

61. GLRO, Acc. 2893, Federation General Council minute book, 26 April 1945–30 Jan. 1963, entry for 2 June 1946.

62. *JC*, 11 April 1947, letter from Shulam Hanstater, a member of LBM.

63. Federation Council minute book (op. cit.). M. J. Turner (senior vice-president), supported by Mr Galinski, amendment, 10 March 1949. See also *JC*, 3 May, 7 June 1946, where LBM launched an appeal, the target being £25,000; 8 April 1949; at the opening of Dunk Street, reported on 17 June 1949, Dayan Abramsky contended that 'The community had as yet not given the same attention to making holy the living people as had been given to those who had passed away'.

64. Federation Council minute book (op. cit.); GLRO, Acc. 2893/271, East London Mikvah Committee minutes, May 1950–April 1953. An entry for 31 Dec. 1950 quotes the statistics on usage in that year (as already cited); *Di Tsayt* carried an advertisement for Dunk Street every Friday between March and September 1950.

65. The Grove Lane Beth HaMedrash in Stamford Hill, under Rabbi Dr E. W. Kirzner, was admitted as an affiliate of the Federation in 1928. It maintained its own *mikveh* in a house at 26 Lampard Grove, N16, entrance in Margaret Road (formerly Margaret Street). This *mikveh* received subsidies from both the Federation and the US. Even before its expansion in the late 1950s, it was the largest *mikveh* in London, and was used by *c.* 320–400 women and *c.* 200 men per month. It is still in use as the Stamford Hill District Mikveh. See *JC*, 27 May 1955, 9 May 1958, 10 July 1959, 8 Sept. 1961; see also UOHC below.

66. See Geoffrey Alderman, *The Federation of Synagogues 1887–1987* (London, 1987), pp. 80, 114. On Ilford, see also *JC*, 25 Sept. 1970; rededication after renovation *JT*, 26 March 1992, and *HaMaor*, Vol. 27, No. 2 (Rosh HaShana 1992). Information kindly supplied by Michael Goldman, the former secretary of the Federation, from the current minute books. The house was purchased by a private member of the Ilford Beth HaMedrash who donated it to the Federation, which used proceeds from the sale of the Dzikower Synagogue to pay for the conversion of the ground floor and garage areas. Today the Federation largely subsidizes the running of this *mikveh*. According to Mr Goldman, 'An unsolicited promise of £500 per annum towards maintenance, made by the Chief Rabbi's Office in 1971, never materialised'. The Ilford *mikveh* remains the only one serving the most densely populated Jewish community in London. It has an estimated attendance of only 45–50 women per month. In 1982 it was the subject of a public hearing at Ilford Town Hall over a planning dispute, see *JC*, 10 Jan. 1975, 5, 23 March 1982.

67. GLRO, Acc. 2712/126, United Synagogue Mikveh Committee minute book, Nov.–Dec. 1958.

68. Ibid., 19 Nov. 1958; US Council minute book, Vol. 15, where the US Council fought shy of committing itself financially to the project. See also Vol. 16, 19 June

1961, for the lack of progress of the Mikveh Committee. Post-war US Council minute books are still at Head Office in Woburn House, London WC1; acknowledgments to Stephen Garcia of the US for allowing me to consult them.

69. GLRO, Acc. 2712/126, 18 Dec. 1958, minutes of a meeting between Mr Asher Wingate, Chairman, and Ministers and Readers of the US. The Jewish Marriage Guidance Council, one of whose aims is to promote use of the *mikveh* by married women, was set up on the initiative of Chief Rabbi Immanuel Jakobovits, when he was still minister of the Great Synagogue, see *JC*, 23 Jan., 20 Feb., 1948, and Chaim Bermant, *Lord Jakobovits* (London, 1990), pp. 31–3. For press comment on the US's ambivalence towards the subject of *mikveh*, see *JC*, 7 June 1963, 22 Feb. 1974, 23 Sept. 1977, and *JT*, 15 Dec. 1967, 14 March 1969, the latter an attack on the US's 'paltry' grant of £250 to the North London *mikveh*.

70. That is: to the North London Mikveh at Grove Lane, N16, and the North West London Communal Mikveh at Shirehall Lane, NW4. In 1966 the annual grant to the former was doubled to £250, bringing it in line with the latter. In 1970, on the initiative of Rebbetzin Jakobovits, a US rabbi and lay leader were appointed to the North West London Mikveh Committee and a grant of £3,000, payable on an annual basis, was made to this *mikveh* in order to clear its deficit. See US Council minute book, Vol. 17, 27 Jan. 1970, and enc. EC Report, 15 Dec. 1969.

71. US Head Office did, however, subsidize the running costs and thus staved off inevitable debt. The *mikveh* is used by *c.* 200 women per month, who are charged £4 per dip. Kingsbury Synagogue paid only for a new classroom block adjacent.

72. See *JC*, 3 March, 7 April, 14 July, 29 Sept. 1978, 7 March, 13 June 1980; *JT*, 29 Sept. 1978; US Council minute book, Vol. 19, 3 April, 10 July 1978. Late in 1993 a US decision to withdraw its annual £15,000 subsidy to Kingsbury provoked an outcry in the press. See *JC*, 3, 31 Dec. 1993. The decision was reversed.

73. *JC*, 7 March 1980. In London the New West End Synagogue has ambitious plans to build a West End successor to Bayswater (see *JC*, letters, 3, 17, 31 Dec. 1993), while both Cockfosters and Elstree United Synagogues have embarked on projects of their own, *JC*, 21 Jan. 1994.

74. See *JC*, 16 April 1948 (Brondesbury), 10 Aug. 1984 (Bushey), 5 May 1989 (Hendon, plus picture), 24 May 1991 (Streatham).

75. *JC*, 3 May 1985, AGM at Edgware United Synagogue. The story of the Edgware *mikveh* may be followed in *JC* (London edn), 18 Nov., 2, 30 Dec. 1983, 6 April, 22 June, 19 Oct., 9, 23 Nov. 1984, 5, 19 April, 10, 17, 24 May 1985, 23 Jan. 1987, 19 Feb., 5 Aug. 1988, 2 Feb., 7 Aug. 1990, 1 Feb., 19 July 1991 (opening). See also *JT*, 18 July 1991; *HaMaor*, Vol. 26, No. 2 (Rosh HaShana 5752/1991), p. 3.

   The US insisted that the Edgware Mikveh Committee, in co-operation with at least three other communal organizations with an interest in the project, should set up a Repairs and Maintenance Fund and contribute to United Synagogue Trust Ltd in order to provide surplus monies to cover extraordinary building works. While incurring no financial liability thereby, the US retained the right to terminate the licence in the event of the future closure and disposal of the Edgware United Synagogue and its curtilage. If legally acceptable, such a provision for the sale of a *mikveh* must be, from the *halakhic* point of view, questionable. US Council Book, Vol. 21, 12 Jan. 1987.

76. *JC*, London Extra, 19 April 1985.

77. *JC*, 3 March 1989, 1 Feb. 1991, 4 Sept. 1992. Jonathan A. Romain, *Faith and Practice: A Guide to Reform Judaism Today* (RSGB, London, 1991), cites decisions of the Reform Assembly of Rabbis. Acknowledgments to Anne Kershen for drawing this book to my attention. Letter to author from Jonathan Black, minister of the Hertsmere Progressive Synagogue, 31 July 1992. He adds: 'I believe that one other Mikveh in the country [besides Cardiff] has been used by candidates of one particular Reform rabbi on a tacit understanding with that community.' In a follow-up reply of 4 Sept. 1992 he confirms that the *mikveh* in question was Brighton. The RSGB are charging a hefty £10 per use of their *mikveh*.

78. *JC*, 22 Feb. 1991. See also article by Sandi Mann, 'Lucky Dip' in *New Moon*, June 1992, pp. 20–3.

79. *JC*, 1 Feb., 15 Feb. 1991. A letter from Martin D. Stern of Salford drew attention to the contradictory position of the Reform movement as a whole on the question of *mikveh* for conversion. He inquired: (a) whether converts accepted under RSGB auspices *before 1977* and their female descendants should now be required to perform a retroactive *tevila*; and (b) whether the RSGB now recognizes *Liberal* converts and allows them to marry under their auspices, given that the Liberals do not require *tevila*. No reply was forthcoming from the Reform Beth Din; *JC*, 5 April 1991.

80. Quoting Julius Carlebach, 'The Impact of German Jews on Anglo-Jewry – Ortho-

doxy, 1850–1950', in Werner E. Mosse *et al.* (eds), *Second Chance: Two Centuries of German-Speaking Jews in the United Kingdom* (Tübingen, 1991), pp. 406–23, at page 418. On the early history of the Adath, see also *The Union of Orthodox Hebrew Congregations of Great Britain and the Commonwealth: Silver Jubilee Brochure 1926–1951* and *Souvenir Book published on the occasion of the consecration of the new Adath Yisroel Synagogue, 40 Queen Elizabeth's Walk, N16, 7 April 1957; The Silver Jubilee Book of the Adath Yisroel Synagogue 1911–1936.* Copies of these rare pamphlets are to be found in the Schonfeld papers, MS. 183, in Anglo-Jewish Archives at Southampton University Library, files 358/6, 491/5. Apparently there are 'no formal archives' of the UOHC, according to Cllr J. Lobenstein in a reply to my inquiry, 18 Feb. 1992.

81. See *JC*, 11 Dec. 1981 (where there is a picture of Mrs Strahlberg at the *mikveh*) and 22 Feb. 1991, 4 Sept. 1992. Tape of interview with Mrs Strahlberg (*née* Glasbruer), 28 Dec. 1992, deposited at the London Museum of Jewish Life.

82. *JC*, 27 May 1955, 10 May 1963, 11 Dec. 1981.

83. *JC*, 30 Jan. 1970: 'towards meeting the £17,000 capital indebtedness' of this *mikveh*; US Council minute book, Vol. 17, 12 June 1967, where no increase in the grant was contemplated; *JT*, 14 April 1967, on chasidic input. The Golders Green Beth HaMedrash ('Munk's') pulled out of assisting the Shirehall rebuilding on the grounds that it had its own *mikveh* (The Ridings, NW11) for the exclusive use of its own members, *JC*, 26 July 1963. The North West London Mikveh Committee has received planning permission from Barnet Council to build a new *mikveh* on land purchased near Golders Green underground station, *JC* 19 Aug., 30 Dec. 1994, 6 Jan. 1995.

84. *JC*, 3 June 1955.

85. Material on Lampard Grove and Lordship Park is to be found in AJA MS. 183 (Schonfeld,) 253/4. Other information provided by Rabbi M. Posen.

86. Correspondence between UOHC and the CBF, ibid. See also *JC* 8 Sept. 1961 and obituary of Dr J. Braude in *JT*, 20 Jan. 1978. However, a more general application on behalf of *mikvaot* was turned down, as was a similar appeal to the New York Claims Conference in 1957; see *JC*, 1 March 1957. Craven Walk and the other Stamford Hill *mikvaot* are currently experiencing financial difficulties, despite the fact that they are well frequented in a populous Orthodox neighbourhood; *JC*, 31 July 1992.

87. The US put up a substantial part of the cost in this case, see *JC*, 27 July 1990, 1 March 1991. The Sassover Rebbe is actively supporting the building of a *mikveh* at Cambridge, *JC*, 8 Dec. 1989, 31 July 1992.

88. *JC*, 22 Sept. 1972.

89. *JC*, 20 Feb. 1948 (letter to editor from Rabbi J. Gould, president of the Shomrei Torah Organisation, Leeds).

90. *JC*, 27 May 1955.

91. *JC*, 11 Oct., 1 Nov. 1946 (letter from Rabbi I. J. Unterman). The two *mikvaot* in Manchester were faced with closure as far back as 1921, despite the fact that one of them was only three years old, *JC*, 1, 15 April 1921. A *mikveh* was built at Coventry Synagogue (1870) on the express wishes of Nathan Adler, but fell into disuse on the temporary closure of the synagogue *c.* 1906. The Rabbi of Coventry, Moshe Katz, wrote to Rav Chaikin of the Federation in London complaining of the lack of interest among his more anglicized congregants in having it restored. Letter reproduced in *Seridim* (Conference of European Rabbis' Journal), No. 14, Iyar (May) 1994, pp. 26–7. Acknowledgments to Rabbi Susser.

92. See Bermant, *Lord Jakobovits*, pp. 38–9; *JC*, 30 Sept. 1955, 12 Feb., 16 April 1982 ('fungus'), 23 Nov. 1984. A similar case is that of Leicester, see *JC* 21 Sept. 1984, and letter to the author from Professor Aubrey Newman of Leicester University, 15 March 1992. The Westcliff *mikveh*, built by private initiative in 1960, had fallen into disuse by 1978 and had to be revamped in 1984, *JC*, 27 July 1984. The attempt to build at Luton in the early 1960s had been thwarted as much by local Jewish opposition as by the town council's concerns about costs, *JC*, 30 June 1961 (letter from irate Jewish Tory ratepayer). Cf. Bournemouth, where, at a stormy meeting at the synagogue, one opponent of the scheme to build a new *mikveh* to replace Piers Baths claimed that it 'had been used on an average once a week since 1960', *JC*, 29 Aug. 1975.

93. *JC*, 16 Aug. 1991, on Reading. The Chatham Memorial Synagogue (H. H. Collins, 1868) did have a *mikveh* in the cellar; letter from Mr G. Lancaster, 15 April 1993.

94. Among North African Jews in France in particular. See Patricia Hidiroglou, 'Du Hamman Maghrébin au *Miqveh* Parisien', *Journal of Mediterranean Studies*, Vol. 4, No. 2 (1994), pp. 241–62.

APPENDICES

APPENDIX 6.1
THE CHIEF RABBI'S SURVEY OF 1845: PROVISION OF *MIKVAOT*

Yes	No	Alternative arrangement
Brighton	Bath	Spa
Chatham	Birmingham	Public baths
Edinburgh	Bristol	–
Falmouth	Cardiff	–
Kingston-upon-Hull	Canterbury	Public baths
Leeds	Cheltenham	Spa
Liverpool (2):	Dover	Sea
Seel Street (Old)	Exeter	Public baths
Hardman Street (New)	Glasgow	Public baths
London:	Jersey	Sea
Great (?)	London:	
Western (private)	Hambro	–
Maiden Lane (2 private)	New (?)	–
Manchester	Lynn, Norfolk	–
Norwich	Newcastle	Public baths
Penzance	Nottingham	Public baths
Plymouth	Oxford	–
Portsmouth	Southampton	Public baths
Sheerness	Yarmouth	Sea
Sunderland		
Swansea	Dublin	Public baths
(Jamaica*)		

Totals
20 (certain)   18 (certain)

NB There are no returns for Gloucester and Ipswich, and there is some doubt about the existence of a second facility in Liverpool.

* Jamaica, as part of the British Empire, came under the jurisdiction of the Chief Rabbi, and sent in a return for the Survey.

Source: Statistical Accounts of all the Congregations in the British Empire 5606/1845 (Chief Rabbi's Archives MS. 104, now at the Greater London Record Office, Acc. 2712/viii/107. Transcribed by Rabbi Dr Bernard Susser in Aubrey Newman (ed.), *Provincial Jewry in Victorian Britain* (London, 1975).

APPENDIX 6.2
DISTRIBUTION OF *MIKVAOT* FOR WOMEN IN LONDON, 1897–1992
Computer graphics by Sydney Greenberg

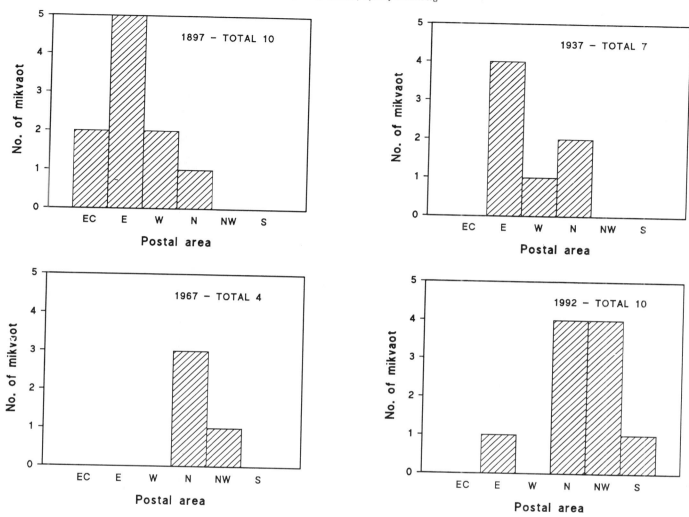

Sources: *Jewish Year Books* and Rabbi M. Posen.

APPENDIX 6.3
DIRECTORY OF *MIKVAOT* IN THE UK AND IRELAND, 1656–1995

All supplied from rainwater sources unless otherwise stated. *Mikvaot* listed in
bold type are currently in use.
Corrections and additions to this list would be welcomed by the author.

KEY
Ren. = Renovated
* = Disused but structure extant

1. LONDON

CITY

Creechurch Lane Synagogue	Extant 1664
Widow of Yehuda de Paiva's house	*c.* 1665
1 and 2 Mitre Square, Aldgate (Great Synagogue?) House	Before 1854–66
2½ Heneage Lane (Bevis Marks Synagogue) House	Extant 1853–1900
8 Sussex Place, Leadenhall Street	Extant 1854
12 Camomile Street, Bishopsgate	Extant 1856
28 Steward Street, Brushfield Street, EC	Extant 1897–1916

WEST

21 Little Newport Street, Leicester Square (one of two private *mikvaot* attached to the Maiden Lane Synagogue)	*c.* 1824–54
Western Synagogue (Private establishment)	Extant 1845
9 St Germain's Terrace, Westbourne Park Crescent, Harrow Road (Bayswater Synagogue, successor to Mitre Square in the City)	1866+
49 Westbourne Park Crescent, Bayswater (Bayswater Synagogue) Converted town house, 2 *mikvaot* on ground floor, 2 bathrooms	Extant 1897–1939
Percy Street, Tottenham Court Road	Extant 1897–1909
14 Manette Street, Charing Cross Road (West End Talmud Torah)	1920–37

EAST

19 Church Lane, Whitechapel (Simcha Baker's Beth HaMedrash) Ground floor	1879–85
Burness Street, Commercial Road	Extant 1897–1916
3 Wilkes Street, Spitalfields, E	Extant 1897–1916
17 Little Alie Street, Goodman's Fields	Extant 1897–1916
14A Osbourne Street, Whitechapel	Extant 1897–1935
26 Sidney Square, Commercial Road, E	1911–*c.* 1940

1 Teesdale Street, Bethnal Green Road, E	1904–16
9 Buckle Street, Commercial Road	Extant 1897–1920
131 Cannon Street Road, E1	Extant 1929–49
Buross Street, E1	Extant 1929–36
2 Exmouth Street, E1 ('Lacey's Baths')	Extant 1929–47
133 Oxford Street, E1	Extant 1929–*c.* 1940
133 Stepney Way, E1	1940–*c.* 1945

32 Dunk Street, E1 (Dzikower Synagogue, under London Board of Mikvaot)
    Ground floor, with 5-room maisonette
    above for attendant.
	1949–60

51 Upper Clapton Road, E5	1940–*c.* 1945
40 Knightland Road, E5 (Sander Herman's, now Schneider's Yeshiva)	Pre-1939

463 Cranbrook Road, Ilford, Essex (Federation of Synagogues)
    House, 1 pool, 2 bathrooms
    Consultant: Rabbi M. Posen
	1969+

NORTH

353 Essex Road, N (Adath Yisrael)	1892–1917
367 Essex Road, N (Adath Yisrael)	1917–64
126 Green Lanes, N (Adath Yisrael) Became Yeshiva Horomo, men only	1920–28. Rebuilt 1960 (men only); now demolished

Stamford Hill District Mikveh, 26 Lampard Grove, N16 (entrance in Margaret Street/Road). Formerly *mikveh* of Grove Lane Stamford Hill Beth HaMedrash which had 4 pools, each with 2 bathrooms, half for men and half for women
    Currently, 2 pools, 4 bathrooms, 1 shower
    Rabbi M. Posen
	1932. Rebuilt 1965 (women), 1970 (men, now demolished)

55 Lordship Park, N16 Rabbi M. Ashkenasy; originally 1 pool, 4 bathrooms. Retained pool and shell of building, and converted to men only with showers by Rabbi M. Posen	1950–67; 1967+ (men only)

62 Filey Avenue, N16 (Satmar)
    2 pools, 5 bathrooms
    Rabbi M. Posen
	1963; demolished internally, rebuilt *c.* 1972

40A Queen Elizabeth's Walk, N16 (Adath Yisrael Mikveh)
    2 pools, 6 bathrooms
    Rabbi M. Posen
	1965+

72 Lingwood Road, E5 (Craven Walk Mikveh, UOHC)
    1 pool, 6 bathrooms
    Rabbi M. Posen
	1981; opened 1987

Current men's *mikvaot* in the Stamford Hill area (N15, N16, E5):

Lieger Rebbe's, Bergholt Crescent, N16	1955+
Pinter's, Heathland Road, N16	1963+

Old Belz, 99 Bethune Road, N16	*c.* 1970
Vishnitz, 89 Stamford Hill Road, N16	*c.* 1970
Rabbi Meisel's, corner Upper Clapton Road/Filey Avenue, N16	1970s
Vishnitz Monsey, 121 Clapton Common, E5	*c.* 1975
Klausenburg, Craven Walk, N16	*c.* 1975
Bobov, Egerton Road, N16	*c.* 1975
Rabbi Leifer, Nadvorna, Portland Avenue, N16	*c.* 1980
Belz, Clapton Common, E5	1985
Satmar, 26 Clapton Common, E5	1988
Satmar, 86 Cazenove Road, N16	1988
Biala, Craven Park Road, N15	1992

NORTH-WEST

6 Minster Road, NW2 (Rabbi J. L. Margulies, the Premiszlaner Rebbe's Kehillat Yisrael Synagogue) Converted house	1940–53
North West London Communal Mikveh, 10A Shirehall Lane, NW4 8 *mikvaot* with bathrooms en suite; 1 *mikveh* served by 5 bathrooms; 1 shower	1946. Rebuilt 1966; extended 1980
171 Golders Green Road, NW11 (Rabbi E. Halpern's Beth Shmuel Synagogue) Men only, demolished and replaced by 1 pool and 3 bathrooms for women; 2 pools and showers for men Rabbi M. Posen	1950s–1988 1994+
Golders Green Beth HaMedrash, The Ridings, NW11 1 pool, 3 bathrooms, limited opening	1963+
Kingsbury Green, NW9 (US) Outhouse, 2 pools, 3 bathrooms Rabbi M. Posen	1980+
Edgware and District Communal Mikveh, Edgware United Synagogue, Edgware Way, Middlesex Outhouse, 1 pool, 6 bathrooms Rabbi M. Posen	1991+
Sternberg Centre for Judaism (RSGB), 80 East End Road, Finchley, N3 Ground floor, community centre, 1 pool, 1 bathroom Rabbi Louis Jacobs	1992+
Boreham Wood and Elstree Synagogue, Croxdale Road, Borehamwood, Herts	Under construction, 1994

SOUTH

South London Mikveh, 24 St George's Road, SW19 (Wimbledon, Chabad House) 1 pool, 1 bathroom Rabbi M. Posen	1991+

2. OTHER ENGLISH REGIONS

BIRMINGHAM

Kent Street Baths Public bathhouse. Natural spring	Extant 1850s–1973
Bournville Lane, Stirchley Public swimming pool Rabbi M. Posen	1973–87
95 Willows Road, B12 (Chabad House) Rabbi M. Posen	1982+
Central Synagogue, 133 Pershore Road, B5	Under construction 1994

BLACKBURN

Richmond Terrace Turkish Baths	1896. Ren. 1904

BOURNEMOUTH

Piers Approach Baths	*c.* 1937–74
Bournemouth Hebrew Congregation, The Synagogue, Wootton Gardens Rabbi M. Posen	1976+

BRIGHTON

Jew Street (basement)	*c.* 1789 Extant 1845
Prince Regent Complex, Church Street Swimming pool Rabbi M. Posen	1982+

BRISTOL

Rose Street Synagogue	19th century

CANTERBURY

The Synagogue	1851–1931*

CHATHAM

Old synagogue (built *c.* 1756)	Extant 1845
Chatham Memorial Synagogue, High Street, Rochester (built 1868) Cellar	1868?*

CLEETHORPES

	Disused

CLIFTONVILLE

Private house Rabbi M. Posen	Extant 1992

COVENTRY

Barras Lane	1870–*c.* 1906

EXETER

The Synagogue, Mary Arches Street	*c.* 1764–1844

FALMOUTH

Smithick Hill (formerly Parham or Parram Hill/ Fish Hill Street Synagogue)	*c.* 1808–1970*

GATESHEAD

180 Bewick Road
    Originally integral to synagogue. In 1974, original
    mikveh men only; 1 pool, 4 bathrooms for women.
    1 pool for men
    Rabbi M. Posen
	1938. Extended 1974.
	Rebuilt 1986

GRIMSBY

Fisherlads Institute, Orwell Street	*c.* 1891
The Synagogue, Holme Hill, Heneage Road	1916–1930s*

HULL

	Extant 1845
Trippett Baths, Wincolmlee Public bathhouse, 1 pool	1850–1902. Building extant till 1941
East Hull Baths, Holderness Road (1898) Public bathhouse	1919–*c.* 1970*

LEEDS

Oriental & General Baths Co. Ltd, Cookridge Street	1882–1905
Albert Grove 2 pools, 8 bathrooms, attendant's house	1905–68

Moortown Mikveh, 368 Harrowgate Road, Leeds 17
    Ground floor, converted house,
    1 pool, 2 bathrooms
    Rabbi M. Posen
	1968+
	1995+ (men only)

'Pearls', Etz Chaim Synagogue, **411 Harrogate Road, Leeds 17** Outhouse	1994+

LEICESTER

The Synagogue, Highfield Street
    Cellar
    Rabbi M. Posen
	1900. Ren. 1984

LETCHWORTH

2 Cross Street	*c.* 1940–1971

LIVERPOOL

Old Hebrew Congregation, 133 Frederick Street House converted into synagogue	Extant 1789. Rebuilt(?) 1810 or 1816–*c.* 1901

New Hebrew Congregation, Hardman Street	Extant 1845?
55 Great Newton Street, Brownlow Hill 1 pool, 8 bathrooms	*c.* 1904–*c.* 1954
3 Croxteth Grove, Sefton Park	1954–76

Childwall Synagogue, Dunbabin Road, L15
   1 pool, 2 bathrooms, outhouse
   Rabbi M. Posen
	1976+

MANCHESTER

78 Cheetham Hill Road (Great Synagogue)	Extant 1845–1939
8 Knowsley Street, Cheetham	Extant 1910–22
122 Cheetham Hill Road (New Synagogue)	Extant 1910–48
Broughton Mikveh, Teneriffe Street, Bury New Road	1926–49
Higher Crumpsall Mikveh, 99A George Street, Salford 8 (taken over by Machzikei Hadas 1958–59)	1945–59
Manchester Communal Mikveh, Tiverton Lodge, Tetlow Lane, Salford 7 (Manchester Beth Din)	1957–59
Manchester Communal Mikveh, Broome Holme, Tetlow Lane, Salford 7	1956+
Manchester & District Mikveh, Bury New Road, Prestwich (Machzikei Hadas) Rabbi M. Posen	1957–?
17 Northumberland Street, Salford 7 (Machzikei Hadas) Men only	1965+
Manchester District Mikveh, Sedgley Park Road, Prestwich, M25 (Machzikei Hadas)	1967+

Whitefields Hebrew Congregation, Park Lane, M25
   1 pool, 2 bathrooms
   Rabbi M. Posen
	1991+

South Manchester Mikveh Hale and District Hebrew Congregation, Shay Lane, Hale Barns, Cheshire Outhouse	1995+

NEWCASTLE

Temple Street	1838–1926
Leazes Park Synagogue (basement)	1880–1978

The Synagogue, Graham Park Road, Gosforth
   1 pool, 2 bathrooms
   Rabbi M. Posen
	1987+

NORWICH

	Extant 1845

PENZANCE

Hyman Woolf's private house	*c.* 1810. Extant 1845

PLYMOUTH

Vestry House, St Katherine's Lane, The Synagogue, Catherine Street	1762. Extant 1860
New 'Synagogue House' Natural spring? Ground floor of two-storey tenement attached to rear	1874–*c.* 1930s (disused 1913). Rebuilt *c.* 1935–1975*
Plymouth Corporation Bathhouse	1910–?

PORTSMOUTH

Old Hebrew Congregation, White's Row	18th century. Extant 1845

RAMSGATE

No. 1 The College, Judith Lady Montefiore College	1866–1961

READING

The Synagogue, Goldsmid Road (entrance in Clifton Street) 1 *mikveh*, bathroom, dressing room	1900*. Never used

SHEERNESS	Extant 1845

SHEFFIELD	Extant 1845
Sheffield Hebrew Congregation, North Church Street	*c.* 1873
The Synagogue, Wilson Road, Sheffield 11 Rabbi M. Posen	Ren. 1980s

SOUTHEND AND WESTCLIFF

44 Genesta Road, Westcliff Rabbi M. Posen	1960. Ren. 1984

SOUTHPORT

Arnside Road Synagogue Rabbi M. Posen	*c.* 1942. Ren. 1971

SOUTHSEA	Closed

SUNDERLAND	Extant 1845
Sunderland Hebrew Congregation, Moor Street	*c.* 1862
Sunderland Hebrew Congregation, Ryhope Road	1928
Sunderland Beth HaMedrash, Villiers Street	1899–1928

Sunderland Beth HaMedrash, Mowbray Road
    1 pool, 2 bathrooms
    Rabbi M. Posen
	1938+

WESTON-SUPER-MARE

Knightstone Baths	After 1902* (see *Jewish Chronicle*, 18 May 1956)

3. SCOTLAND

EDINBURGH

The Synagogue, Salisbury Place	1936–80*

GLASGOW

George Street Synagogue	1858–78; extended 1867
The Synagogue, 240 George Street, Garnethill	1879?–1914?
Glasgow Kosher Baths, Gorbals Bath House Public bathhouse	1885–1902
Pollokshields Mikveh (Private villa)	*c.* 1920s
Central Synagogue, South Portland Street	1902–70

**Giffnock and Newlands Synagogue, Maryville
Avenue, Giffnock, G4**
  2 pools, 4 bathrooms
  Rabbi M. Posen
	1973+. Ren. 1992

4. WALES

BRYNMWR

CARDIFF

Wales Empire Pools, Wood Street Swimming pool. 1 pool, 1 bathroom	1959+

MERTHYR

The Synagogue	1872 or 1876–1979*

NEWPORT

PONTYPRIDD

The Synagogue, Wood Road	1895

SWANSEA

Wellington Road
  Seawater
  House
	1835. Extant 1879

5. IRELAND

BELFAST

Great Victoria Street Synagogue	1892
Annesley Street Synagogue	*c.* 1904
The Synagogue, 49 Somerton Road, BT15 1 pool, 1 bathroom	1964–93

CORK

DUBLIN

Dublin Hebrew Congregation, 37 Adelaide Road,   1915. Ren. 1955, 1984
Dublin 2
   Outhouse
   Rabbi M. Posen

ACKNOWLEDGMENTS AND SOURCES

I am indebted to Rabbi Meir Posen for his expert guidance in the preparation of
this chapter. He may be contacted at 58 Queen Elizabeth's Walk, London
N16 5UX, for advice regarding the construction or renovation of *mikvaot*.

General: *JC* indexes at the newspaper's offices, Furnival Street, London EC4,
especially for post-1945 period. *JYB*, but unreliable. Mr J. R. Conrad, acting
secretary of the Central Mikvaot Board of the UOHC.

London, primary sources: Archives of the United Synagogue, Chief Rabbinate
and Federation of Synagogues, Greater London Record Office. The records
of the London Beth Din, which may yield further information, are not yet
available to researchers. There are no proper records of the UOHC accessible to
the public; Schonfeld Papers, University of Southampton, Hartley Library.

Personal assistance from the following people: Spanish and Portuguese:
Miriam Rodrigues-Pereira. Federation: Michael Goldman. UOHC: Mrs H.
Stralhberg. US: Mrs Rita Joseph. Reform: Jonathan M. Black, Anne Kershen,
Elena Rothman. East End: Renée Kadish, Sam Melnick, Aumie Shapiro.

Correspondents all over the country: Birmingham: Elizabeth Lesser, Rabbi
Shmuel Arkush. Bristol: John Bryant, Raphael Emanuel, Bob Jones, Michael
Ponsford, Judith Samuel. Chatham: Mr G. Lancaster. Coventry: Rabbi Dr
Bernard Susser. Exeter, Falmouth, Penzance: David M. Jacobs, Keith Pearce.
Gateshead: Rabbi Mordechai Orshansky. Grimsby: Daphne Gerlis. Hull: the
late Jack Lennard. Leeds: Murrey Freedman, Nigel Grizzard, Walter Rothschild,
Mrs F. Schiller, Rabbi Y. Shemaria. Leicester: Professor Aubrey Newman.
Manchester: Bill Williams. Newcastle: Rabbi M. M. Baddiel. Plymouth: Mr
P. R. Aloof. Ramsgate: John Lipitch, Miriam Rodrigues-Pereira. Sunderland:
Mr J. Schleider. Scotland: Harvey Kaplan, Dr Kenneth Collins. Wales: David
Jacobs, Dorene Jacobs, Anne Yardley. Ireland: Gail Taylor, Chief Rabbi E.
Mirvis. Anglo-Jewish country houses: Malcolm Brown, Peter Barber, Anne
Collett-White, Sarah Levitt.

7

JEWISH CEMETERIES IN THE WEST OF ENGLAND

BERNARD SUSSER

From time immemorial Jews have buried their dead. The institution of a cemetery as a common burial ground, however, is probably post-biblical. In Talmudic times the cemetery was usually located far from a town, and needed a watchman to guard against grave robbers and animals. Grave monuments in ancient times appear to have become very elaborate, as the Talmud records that 'Jewish tombstones are fairer than royal palaces' (Sanhedrin 96b).

Some Jewish cemeteries are famous; two examples that spring to mind are the ancient Jewish burial grounds in Jerusalem, the Mount of Olives, with its second-century monuments known as Absalom's Tomb, the Tomb of the Hezir family and Zechariah's Tomb, and the Prague Jewish cemetery, opened in 1254 and closed in 1787. The Jewish cemeteries of medieval England have long since vanished, and for the most part one can only guess where they were originally situated.

The first Jewish cemetery in post-Expulsion England was opened by the Sephardim at Mile End in London in 1657. This was followed by Ashkenazi burial grounds in Alderney Road in 1696/97, and at Hoxton (1707), Brady Street (1761) and Hackney (1788) in the eighteenth century. A second Sephardi ground was opened in Mile End in 1725. In the second half of the eighteenth century provincial Jewish congregations began to establish their own burial grounds. By 1800 there were some 20 Jewish cemeteries outside London, a number which had doubled by 1840.[1]

There is no strict definition of what is meant by 'the west of England'; this chapter looks at Jewish cemeteries in the counties of Cornwall, Devon, Avon and Gloucester.

The furthest point west in England is Land's End. Some medieval Jewish scholars referred to Britain as *Ketzei HaAretz* ('Land's End') although the more usual term was *Iyyei HaYam* ('Islands of the Sea').[2] Perhaps the Jews' first contact with Britain was at Land's End, and they afterwards used the name to designate Britain as a whole. Travelling east from Land's End towards London, we come to Penzance. The Jewish cemetery here is in Leskinnick Terrace. When the Penzance Hebrew

7.1 Penzance Cemetery; the tombstones of Aaron and Hannah Selig. Aaron Selig died in 1841. *Godfrey Simmons and Mrs Alberg*

Congregation built its first synagogue in 1807[3] it already had a cemetery. There are a number of beautifully incised slate gravestones, the oldest dated 1791, and they are wonderfully preserved, because they were almost entirely protected by houses built all round the cemetery and close to it. In 1965 I found 48 stones and made a transcript of the 45 which were then legible.

Still travelling east, we come to Falmouth. The Jewish cemetery is on the Penryn road. It was said that the ground was presented to the congregation by Lord de Dunstanville in the 1790s.[4] In 1913 Mr A. A. de Pass, a Jew then living in the area, learned that the land had not, in fact, been donated but was subject to a lease, which had expired. He duly bought the land, and the cemetery, like the one in Penzance, is now cared for by the Board of Deputies of British Jews.[5] B. L. Joseph had made a transcript of the tombstone inscriptions, which was in the possession of Samuel Jacob in 1910. Seven inscriptions which Joseph had read were indecipherable by me, and I found a further eight which he had not transcribed. The earliest stones appear to be dated 1791.[6] In all there is a record of 43 inscriptions.

Leaving Cornwall, we cross the Tamar Bridge into Devon and stop at Plymouth. Here there are two Jewish cemeteries. The older is on Plymouth Hoe, just below the Citadel in New Street. When I first visited it in 1961 only the tops of a half-dozen tombstones were visible; the rest were drowned in a sea of weeds, brambles and rubbish. This cemetery

7.2 Plymouth Hoe Cemetery, 1988 –
before clearance. *Bernard Susser*

7.3 Plymouth Hoe Cemetery Open
Day, 1989 – after clearance. *Bernard Susser*

started in a garden owned by Mrs Sarah Sherrenbeck in the 1740s. Contiguous additional land was bought in 1758, 1811 and 1815.[7] In one section there are more tombstones than there is space for graves. This might well indicate that a layer of earth was added and the same ground was then reused. An 1825 minute records: '. . . agreed to cover in the old cemetery some graves which will be chosen according to the letter which came from the Rav, the Gaon of the holy community of London.'[8] In all, I was able to decipher 146 inscriptions, and there were another dozen or so which might be read if one had two or three hours to spend on each stone. Around 1900 the Reverend Dr M. Berlin made a transcript of the vital information from 95 tombstones, but 50 of these had totally disappeared by the time I transcribed those still extant in the 1960s.

Continued expansion of the Plymouth Hebrew Congregation necessitated a further purchase in 1868 of land in Gifford Place adjoining the Old Plymouth Cemetery near Central Park.[9] In 1978 Dr H. Greenburgh made a computerized alphabetical list containing 506 English names and the date of death of all the persons buried in this cemetery.[10]

Some 40 miles east of Plymouth is Exeter. The Jewish cemetery is in Magdalen Street, and the story of its purchase is clearly recorded. On 28 March 1757 the Exeter City Council 'agreed with Abraham Ezekiel for a term of 99 years determinable on three lives in late Tanner's plot in the parish of Holy Trinity at the yearly rent of 10s 6d for a burial place for the Jews and the Town Clerk is directed to make the lease accordingly'.[11] The lives were Abraham Ezekiel himself, then aged 31, his daughter Rose, aged two, and Israel Henry, the son of Israel Henry, also aged two. This lease was renewed on 7 January 1803 by Moses Mordecai on three lives (Solomon Ezekiel, aged 17, Simon Levy and Jonas Jonas, both aged 12), for a consideration of five shillings and a yearly rent of one guinea. Four years later, on 23 June 1807, the lease was further renewed, together with an additional plot of land, the consideration being the surrender of the previous lease, payment of five shillings, and again a yearly rent of one guinea. In the 1920s and 1930s Sir Thomas Colyer-Ferguson, the great Gentile genealogist of Anglo-Jewry, made a note of English inscriptions of families which particularly interested him, notably the Ancona, Ezekiel and Gompertz families. The Reverend Michael Adler, DSO, made a transcript of the English inscriptions which were extant in 1940. I added names and information recorded in Hebrew in the 1960s. Down to 1958 there were 110 readable inscriptions.

From Exeter we make our way north-eastwards on the M5 motorway. We pass through Honiton, where in 1270 'Jacob of Norwich, Jew, is resident without the King's licence', and on through Glastonbury, where legend has it that Joseph of Arimathea, a wealthy Essene Jew, planted his staff as he stopped to rest. At Bristol, in the county of Avon, there are two Jewish cemeteries, a twentieth-century one in Oakdene Avenue, off Fishponds Road, and a nineteenth-century one in Barton Road, which was in use from 1840 for about 60 years. The Barton Road cemetery also contains the remains, and some of the tombstones, of Jews who were buried in Bristol's first Jewish cemetery in Rose Street, a site which now forms part of Temple Meads Station.[12] Mrs Judith Samuel deciphered some 116 English inscriptions. With my son Jacob, I was able to decipher

7.4   Bath Cemetery; the O*hel*. *Judith Samuel*

the Hebrew inscriptions of 92 of these stones, giving corresponding English names and/or dates of death, and the Hebrew inscriptions on a further 15 stones which had no English at all.

After visiting Bristol we can go east on the A4 to Bath. The Jewish cemetery here is situated in Bradford Road, Coombe Hill, and is administered by the Board of Deputies. This cemetery was acquired in 1836, and the first burial took place in that year. It was surveyed by A. Reese and helpers in 1983, at which time there were some 50 stones standing with legible inscriptions, although Dr N. de Lange's list contains only 35 inscriptions.[13]

Travelling north from Bath on the A46, we enter the county of Gloucester and make our way through Stroud, whose synagogue ceased to function in 1908,[14] and on to the city of Gloucester. According to Brian Torode, the eighteenth-century Jewish cemetery was in Organ's Passage, off Barton Street, on land bought in 1780 from the then rector of St Michael's Parish; it measured about 12 by 9 yards. Torode states that the first burial was in 1794, but one of the inscriptions published in translation in *Gloucester Notes and Queries, 1890* indicated that Uri known as Feiss, the son of Jacob Halevi, died in October 1784 and was one of the first to be buried in the Gloucester cemetery. The latest inscription of the 35 extant in 1890 was dated 1886. That cemetery was closed in 1938, and the bodies were re-interred and the tombstones re-erected at Coney Hill cemetery.[15] Dr N. de Lange reports that there are now only 17 legible inscriptions, dated between 1807 and 1887.

Some six miles from Gloucester, travelling eastward on the A40, we come to the genteel town of Cheltenham. Once again we rely on Mr Torode, who tells us that the land for the Cheltenham Jewish cemetery was purchased in Worcester Row on 30 November 1824. In 1835, 1839, 1845, 1860 and possibly 1892, further land was bought adjoining the original burial ground. The earliest legible gravestone dates from 1833,[16] though a Hebrew wall plaque commemorates a four-month-old child who died in May 1822,[17] 30 months before the cemetery was purchased. Up to 1872, Jewish burials from Stroud, Ross, Hereford and Gloucester

7.5   Cheltenham Cemetery. *Brian Torode*

7.6   Plymouth Hoe Cemetery; the tombstone of Lyon Joseph of Falmouth and Bath who died in 1825. *Bernard Susser*

were interred at Gloucester, but in July 1872 the Trustee of the Gloucester Burial Ground wrote to the Warden of the Cheltenham Synagogue confirming that the Gloucester Ground was henceforth annexed to the Cheltenham Congregation.[18] The Cheltenham ground is still in use and is a walled plot on the corner of Elm Street and Malvern Street, Cheltenham. There are some 79 legible inscriptions of the nineteenth century.

Much may be learned from tombstone inscriptions. West-country Jewish cemeteries clearly demonstrate the process of acculturation. At first only Hebrew was used on the stones. In the Plymouth cemetery English began to appear on the reverse side of stones *c.* 1825 – for example, 'In memory of Lyon Joseph Esq. (merchant of Falmouth, Cornwall), who died at Bath, June, AM 5585/VE 1825'[19] – and on the same side as the Hebrew from *c.*1840: 'Our lives are in thy hands O God. / And the length of our days / Are as nought before thee. / *Here lies David the son of Abraham* / For 50 years a member of the Congregation of this town . . .'[20] In Cheltenham, as we have seen, the earliest English inscription is dated 1833.[21] In the South-West, from 1840 the Jewish name is still in Hebrew but the secular name as well as the Jewish date appear in English. There were isolated uses of the common era year in the first six decades of the nineteenth century, but after 1870 it invariably appears. Surnames themselves may be an indication of the assimilatory process: Kennard, Palmer, Harding and Walter in the South-West; Shane in Cheltenham and Gloucester; Brooks in Bath; Campbell, Churchill, Jackson, Morse and Rousseau in Bristol. Hebrew names ending in '*the son/ daughter of our father Abraham*' indicate a convert to Judaism. Perhaps the ultimate stage in the process occurs in the Torquay Jewish cemetery

7.7   Snuff-box presented to Aaron Nathan, Constable of Plymouth, in 1837. *Jewish Museum, London*

in Paignton, which dates from 1962 and is a railed-off part of the municipal cemetery. There is a stone there which when approached from the Jewish section displays on its front a *Magen David* but when looked at from the municipal part has on its rear a cross!

Until the third quarter of the nineteenth century religious sentiments are to be found. On the tombstone of Mary Nathan (d. 1858) is inscribed '*Miriam . . . wife of Aaron Nathan. May her pains and poverty which she bore in her lifetime atone for her sins . . .*'. Her poverty was no exaggeration. In 1827 her husband had written to the 'Plymouth Congeratation [*sic*] . . . I am Drove to the last Extramity, without a farthin in the world having disposed of Everything I could make money of – so as my wife and sevon children should not starve . . .'[22]

Real belief in the doctrine of the resurrection of the dead is evidenced by inscriptions such as '*His body lies in the ground, but his soul is in Gan Eden* [the Garden of Eden]' on the stone of Woolf Emden, who died in 1867,[23] and, on the stone of Reichla, widow of Naphtali Benjamin, who died in 1817: ' . . . *A woman who fears the Lord she shall be praised. She went to her everlasting world 17 years after her husband, and there they shall delight in honour with all the righteous men and righteous women in Gan Eden, and stand at their portion* [i.e. will receive their reward] *at the end of days.*'[24]

7.8   Plymouth Hoe Cemetery; the tombstone of Abraham Emden who died in 1872. *Bernard Susser*

Pride in being native-born, whether of the city in which the cemetery was situated or elsewhere in Britain, is often expressed. On the Penzance tombstone of James Jacob Hart, for example, is inscribed: '. . . late her Majesty's consul for the kingdom of Saxony. A native of Penzance. Died London 19 February 1846'.[25] The stone of Abraham Emden, a town councillor of Plymouth who died in 1872, proclaims: '. . . *and was gathered to the place of his fathers*'.[26] The stone of Andrew George Jacob, who died in 1900, reads: '. . . born at Falmouth, Cornwall. Died at Exeter.'[27]

A former place of residence in Britain is often given. Thus Miriam Jacobs (d. 1850), born in Devon in 1771, is described in Hebrew and English as '. . . wife of Nathan Jacobs, formerly of Dartmouth'.[28] David Moses (d. 1812) was '*from Norwich*'.[29] He was born in Saarbruck in 1737, landed in Harwich in 1759, went straight to Norwich, where he stayed until 1793, and then moved to Plymouth, where he spent the last 19 years of his life. Similarly, her tombstone in the Exeter cemetery tells us that Rachel (d. 1826), wife of Gershon Levy, was 'of Guernsey'.[30] The tombstone of Moses Solomon (d. 1838) tells us that he was '*from the city of London which was the city of his birth and formerly of Scotland*'.[31] In the Cheltenham cemetery, Selena Myers, Solomon Lazarus, Abraham Myer and Sidney Myer came from Hereford; Lipman Goldsmith was from Ross and formerly Southampton; Fanny Sington, the daughter of a physician from Lissa, came from Manchester; Moses Moses was late of the City of Gloucester; Helen Amelia Joel came from Portsea and Southsea; Joseph Hart formerly resided at Exeter; and Miriam Samuel came from Cardiff.[32]

Immigrants often had their former or native town or country recorded. Thus we are told that the Reverend Moses Horwitz Levy (d. 1834), who ministered to the Exeter Hebrew Congregation for 42 years, was '*from Danzig*.[33] In the Plymouth Hoe cemetery, David Jacob Coppel (d. 1805) was '*from Bialin in Polin*';[34] in 1832 a '*Ze'ev ben Judah from Shatwinitz in the country of Polin died of the plague*';[35] Jacob Phillip Cohen (d. 1832) was '*from Lontschotz*';[36] Esther (d. 1831), wife of Lazarus Solomon, was '*from the holy congregation of Lublin in the state of Polin*'.[37] In Bristol, Adam Louis Sametband (d. 1883) was '*from Warsaw*';[38] in Bath, Henrietta Leon, who died there aged 71, was born in Hildesheim on 26 July 1823.[39] In the Cheltenham cemetery, Samuel Gurnier (d. 29 December 1863) was born in Bojanowo, Prussia, in 1825; Solomon (d. 30 May 1861) and Sarah (d. 31 December 1870) Mendes da Silva were born (in 1781 and 1783 respectively) in Jamaica, as was Moses Quixano Henriques (d. 2 July 1866), who was born on 9 July 1800.[40] It is perhaps noteworthy that foreign provenance is always recorded in the Hebrew part of the inscription, whereas British former residence or place of nativity generally appears in the English part.

Stones which recorded an east European origin are of interest insofar as they indicate an immigration from eastern Europe much earlier in the nineteenth century than has been generally recognized. The trend is corroborated by an examination of the Decennial Census returns for Devon and Cornwall from 1851 onwards.

Snippets of information can be gleaned from the inscriptions regarding individuals' characters and activities. Thus we are told that 'Samuel Cohen (died 1860) was of the stock of martyrs . . . hastening to his prayers evening, morning and noon'.[41] From the chronogram *'And you shall circumcise the foreskin of your hearts'*, Moses ben Isaac (d. 1780) must have been a *mohel*.[42] Descriptions of men as *ha-rabbani hamuflag, parnas u-manhig* or *ha-nadiv* indicate that they were respectively an outstanding scholar, a president of the congregation, or a philanthropist. *Yashish* is used to describe both bachelors and married men,[43] though in the Sephardi tradition the term is reserved for elderly bachelors of high repute. *Zaken* (an old man) was used mainly of octogenarians,[44] though once a 64-year-old is so described.[45] Abraham Alexander, who died in Clifton on 22 July 1870, 'represented Russia as Consul in the City of Bristol for forty-two years'.[46]

In the early nineteenth century the balmy South Devon air attracted a number of wealthy anglicized Jews from London. One of these, Barent Gompertz (d. 1824), a member of a well-known Anglo-Jewish family, lies in an altar tomb which was inscribed with no less than 12 lines of a poem written by his brother Isaac.[47] The inscription is now illegible, but fortunately it was copied by Sir Thomas Colyer-Ferguson.

A small but elite Sephardi settlement in Devon is evidenced by the tomb of Hannah, relict of Moses Ancona and daughter of Moses Vita Montefiore, who died in Exeter in 1839.[48] Cheltenham had a small coterie of Sephardim in the late nineteenth century; as noted above, inscriptions there record the deaths of Solomon Mendes da Silva, his widow Sarah, and Moses Quixano Henriques, all born in Jamaica.[49]

The hardships of foreign travel, even post mortem, are brought to light, as this inscription indicates: *'The bachelor Issacher Behrman the son of the President Joshua Levy the righteous Priest from the holy congregation of London, died Yom Kippur 5565* [October 1804] *in the Island of Madeira and was buried here in Plymouth on Friday, the eve of Sabbath, 6 Iyyar 5565* [May 1805]'.[50] The dead man was the son of Levy Barent Cohen, progenitor of the distinguished Cohen family of nineteenth-century London. One of Issacher's sisters, Hannah, married Nathan Mayer Rothschild; another, Judith, married Sir Moses Montefiore. The Plymouth Hebrew Congregation still owns a magnificent silver ewer and bowl for the use of the *cohanim* (priests), presented in 1807 by his brothers and his widowed mother *'for the loving kindness bestowed on the bones of her son'*. The Plymouth Congregation likewise made itself responsible for the mortal remains of another traveller, Rodolfo A. Correa, whose stone records that he 'died on board the Royal Mail Steamer *Nile*, 26 April 1875, on the passage from Savanilla to this port, Lat. 49° 0' N Long. 18° 31', aged 35 years and 20 days . . .'[51]

Communities settled in ports or by rivers are bound to have more than their share of deaths by drowning. Pathetic inscriptions in the Cheltenham and Plymouth cemeteries respectively recall Walter Emanuel Levason of Hereford, aged nine, 'accidentally drowned in the River Wye',[52] and Nathan Fredman, aged 25, who died on 8 June and was buried on 29 June 1884: *'It should not happen to you who travel on the way / Look and see my pain, for taken / From me was my son, my only son, who drowned in the sea'*.[53]

The danger of travelling the countryside is illustrated by another inscription: '*Joshua Falk the son of Isaac from Breslau. He was slain in the place of Fowey by the wicked man Wyatt and drowned in the waters 14 Kislev 5572 and buried on the 17th thereof* [30 November 1811]'.[54] Isaac Valentine, as he was called, became the *shochet* (ritual slaughterer) of the Plymouth congregation in 1811, when he was paid £25 per annum. He augmented his wages by acting as an agent for the Joseph family of Plymouth who, in turn, were agents of the London brokers Goldsmid, buying up for the government golden guineas in return for paper money during the Napoleonic Wars. Valentine was enticed to bring £260 to Fowey by an innkeeper called Wyatt who murdered him and dropped his body into the dock. Wyatt was hanged at Bodmin in the presence of a large crowd which flocked in from the surrounding countryside.

Tragedies of a different nature are recorded on war graves. In the Plymouth Hebrew Congregation's Gifford Place cemetery there is a tombstone erected to 'John Lithman, late of the Judeans 38/40 Royal Fusiliers, died 8th January 1919/5679 aged 16 years and 9 months', described in the Hebrew inscription as *mi-tzeva ha-yehudit* (from the Jewish Army).[55] I wondered how a lad who was 16½ years old when the First World War ended in November 1918 came to be in the army at all, and whether perhaps he died in the post-war flu epidemic. I made inquiries at the War Office but they had no information other than Lithman's army number and the fact that the War Graves Commission knew of the location of his grave. Inquiries at Bet HaGedudim, the museum near Netanya, Israel, devoted to the history of the Jewish Brigades in the British Army in the First and Second World Wars, were similarly fruitless. But a speculative telephone call to a person bearing the same surname elicited the unexpected response: 'I was his brother, and remember that as a young boy I attended his funeral.' Later he told me that John Lithman had falsified his age to get into the army and had died in some kind of accident.

Another Judean who was laid to rest in the Gifford Place cemetery was Myer Nyman of Swansea, who served under the name Private Michael Burns. He died on 2 February 1919, aged 18 years and four months.[56] Another First World War grave in this cemetery is that of Stoker Harry Phillips of HMS *Vivid*, who died on 2 April 1918 aged 29;[57] from the Second World War there are the graves of Sergeant Ralph Emdon of the Queen's Royal Regiment, who died in 1944 of wounds received at Dunkirk,[58] and Sergeant Morris Solomon of the Royal Australian Air Force, who died on 21 July 1942 aged 23.[59] We are reminded of those dark days when we contemplate the double stone marking the deaths on 10 July 1940 of a mother and daughter, Mary and Esther Smith, who were Plymouth's first civilians to die from Nazi bombing.[60]

Why should we take an interest in our past? Perhaps a lesson I learned from the late Rabbi Dr Louis Rabbinowitz will answer this question. He told me that once, after he had conducted a funeral and before leaving the cemetery, he had paused by the grave of a rabbi who had died a long time before and who had left no family. There he recited a psalm. As he made his way back to his car, he recalled, he happened to look back. He saw a cemetery groundsman go over to the rabbi's grave, clear away some grass and weeds which had overgrown the tombstone, and wash it down. 'Because I had taken notice of that grave the groundsman realized that it was of some special significance, and therefore took an interest in it.'

If we do not want others to vandalize and rubbish our sacred places, perhaps we should show the way and demonstrate our own respect for them.

NOTES

The writer gratefully acknowledges help generously given to him by Dr Nicholas de Lange, Mrs Judith Samuel and Mr Brian Torode, who supplied transcripts and other information about the Jewish cemeteries in Bath, Bristol, Cheltenham and Gloucester.

Tombstone inscriptions printed in italic type are translations from original Hebrew phraseology. Tombstone numbers indicate the number of the stone in transcripts in the writer's possession.

1. On a medieval ground which was probably Jewish, see J.M. Lilley *et al.*, *The Jewish Burial Ground at Jewbury*, The Archaeology of York, 12/3, The Medieval Cemeteries (York, 1994). C. Roth, *The Rise of Provincial Jewry* (London, 1950), p. 24. [Alderney Road was surveyed in 1993 as part of an ICOMOS–UK/ICOMOS–Israel student exchange project, in cooperation with the Working Party on Jewish Monuments. Rabbi Susser is currently preparing the results for publication – Ed.]
2. *Voice of Jacob*, 13 March 1845. See also *Transactions of the Jewish Historical Society of England (TJHSE)*, XVII (1952), p. 74, n.2.
3. C. Roth, 'Penzance', Jewish Chronicle Supplement, May 1933.
4. *Directory and Guide for Falmouth and Penryn, 1864*, p. 45.
5. *64th Annual Report of the Board of Deputies of British Jews* (London, 1915), p. 45.
6. Falmouth tombs 2 and 3.
7. Leases in the possession of the Plymouth Hebrew Congregation (PHC). PHC Minute Book II, pp. 64, 108.
8. PHC Min. Bk II, 195. 'The Frederick Street, Liverpool, Jewish cemetery was covered over with a thick layer of earth and graves dug anew three times' (M. Margoliouth, *History of the Jews in Great Britain* (London, 1851), Vol. III, p. 113). Six hand-breadths of earth must intervene if one coffin is buried on another (*Yoreh De'ah*, 362, 2).
9. Plymouth Synagogue Catalogue 6, 1, at the Plymouth City Library.
10. In the writer's possession.
11. Exeter City Council Act Book, XIV, p. 232A. Tanner had paid only 6s. 8d. for the plot.
12. Information from Dr N. R. M. de Lange.
13. Ibid.
14. B. Torode, *The Hebrew Community of Cheltenham, Gloucester and Stroud* (Gloucester and Cheltenham, 1989), p. 61.
15. Ibid., p. 16.
16. Chelt. tomb A10.
17. Chelt. tomb X2.
18. Torode, op. cit., pp. 54–6.
19. Ply. Hoe tomb A13. Lyon Joseph (1744–1825) made a fortune shipping goods to the ports of the Peninsula not occupied by Napoleon. He lost his fortune owing to the accidents of war and being defrauded by his captains and agents; B. Susser, *An Account of the Old Jewish Cemetery on Plymouth Hoe* (Plymouth, 1972), p. 8.
20. Ply. Hoe tomb B4.
21. Chelt. tomb A10.
22. Original letter in the writer's collection.
23. Ply. Hoe tomb B87.
24. Ply. Hoe tomb A56.
25. Penzance tomb 26. His parents seem to have been born in Penzance. He was a first cousin of Lemon Hart, the rum merchant.
26. Ply. Hoe tomb B112.
27. Exeter tomb 101.
28. Ply. Hoe tomb B48.

29. Ply. Hoe tomb S9.
30. Exeter tomb 45.
31. Ply. Hoe tomb A92.
32. Chelt. tombs A4, A6, B11, B20, A13, B1, B3, B21, C16, D14.
33. Exeter tomb 36.
34. Ply. Hoe tomb B22.
35. Ply. Hoe tomb B23.
36. Ply. Hoe tomb B26.
37. Ply. Hoe tomb Berlin O10.
38. Barton Road, Bristol tomb 28.
39. Bath tomb 19.
40. Chelt. tombs D10, D11, D12.
41. Ply. Hoe tomb B71.
42. Ply. Hoe tomb Berlin 9/10.
43. *Yashish* occurs in Job 12:12 '. . . among aged men is wisdom'. In *Moed Katan*, 25b, the phrase *geza yeshishim* (offspring of worthy men) occurs.
44. Ply. Hoe tomb Berlin O13, 13/17; Ply. Hoe tomb B27 (an 87-year-old woman).
45. Ply. Hoe tomb Berlin O18.
46. Barton Road, Bristol tomb 127.
47. The poem was printed in *Devon* (Teignmouth, 1825), p. 37.
48. Exeter tomb 6. Her daughter Sarah administered her estate, which was under £450. For a full description of Sephardi settlement in Devon and Cornwall, see B. Susser, *The Jews of South West England* (Exeter, 1993), index, under 'Sephardim'.
49. See note 40.
50. Ply. Hoe tomb Berlin R24.
51. Ply. GP tomb A8.
52. Chelt. tomb C1.
53. Ply. GP tomb Q19.
54. Ply. Hoe tomb Berlin Q24.
55. Ply. GP tomb O22.
56. Ply. GP tomb O23.
57. Ply. GP tomb O17.
58. Ply. GP tomb E17. His family was settled in Plymouth for some 250 years.
59. Ply. GP tomb D23.
60. Ply. GP tombs C18, C19.

8

'FOUR PER CENT PHILANTHROPY':
Social Architecture for East London Jewry, 1850–1914

LESLEY FRASER

The importance of Jewish philanthropic and charitable work in the second half of the nineteenth century, particularly in London, has been well recorded by social historians. In a period during which the Jewish population of London more than quadrupled, a relatively small but well-established and predominantly middle-class Anglo-Jewish community set up and ran a comprehensive range of voluntary institutions to cater for an influx of 'poor brethren' fleeing from persecution and economic distress in eastern Europe.

Although the majority of these refugees were traditional Yiddish-speaking Jews, very different from their culturally assimilated and anglicized co-religionists, the established community was able to absorb such large numbers of new members without fundamentally changing its structure or organization. Moreover, Jewish philanthropy in London is historically important beyond its influence in the Jewish community itself. The scale, scope and often the innovation of Jewish charities in London was unparalleled among any other religious or social groups not part of the State, and in many instances London Jewish charitable organizations were at the forefront of developments in Victorian welfare.

In order to put in place this wide-ranging programme, a variety of institutions to provide shelter, food, health care and education were required. Many buildings were converted or constructed from new with funds from the Jewish community and often designed by the growing number of Anglo-Jewish architects. To date, it appears that no systematic identification of these buildings has been attempted. Many that have been traced through archival sources have been demolished, leaving only a relatively few extant examples of what was a significant body of architecture.

This chapter does not provide a comprehensive survey of all Jewish philanthropic architecture in London. Instead, the cultural and historical context of this building programme and the philanthropic buildings and institutions before 1850 are briefly examined, then the impetus behind the expansion and reorganization of activity after 1850 is discussed. Next, two representative buildings are considered in greater detail, one from the general body of charitable institutions (the Soup Kitchen for the Jewish Poor, 1903, by Lewis Solomon), and the largest of the Jews' Free Schools (Bell Lane, Spitalfields, by N. S. Joseph and Pearson, 1883). Finally, the major surviving type of Jewish philanthropic building, housing, is assessed. The desirability and problems of the conservation of such social or 'secular' Jewish building types are debated by way of conclusion.

CULTURAL AND HISTORICAL CONTEXT, AND INSTITUTIONS BEFORE 1850

Philanthropy, charity and alms-giving are well-established traditions within the Jewish faith. The importance of giving to the less fortunate is highlighted in a number of Biblical texts, such as 'Deal out thy bread to the hungry' (Isaiah 58:7), and in Judaism charity is given a special term, *Tsedaka*, which has the primary meaning of 'justice'. The concept is emphasized, more strongly than in Christianity, as a definite obligation for the Jewish believer.

The first philanthropic institutions were set up therefore in association with the established synagogues, and alms-giving has generally remained a separate activity in the Ashkenazi and Sephardi communities. The earliest organizations appear to have been contributary burial societies to ensure the services, prayers, attendance of a rabbi and other

8.1   London, Jews' Hospital, Mile End, *c.* 1806. *Local History Library, Tower Hamlets*

necessary rituals during mourning. Schools were also founded during the early years of the Resettlement. The Sephardim opened the Sha'arei Tikva (Gates of Hope) school for boys in 1664 and the Villareal school for girls in 1731. In 1732 the Ashkenazim founded the Talmud Torah (religious school), which was attached to the Great Synagogue, Duke's Place.[1]

Charitable organizations grew rapidly and in a piecemeal fashion throughout the eighteenth century, broadly paralleling those in the rest of society. Specifically Jewish hospitals, schools, shelters and societies to distribute everything, from 'Bread, Meat and Coal' (from 1779) to Out Relief under the Poor Law, had been established by the middle of the nineteenth century. I have not been able to trace any eighteenth-century Jewish philanthropic building still standing in London, and unfortunately the majority of these buildings from the Georgian period are not well recorded. One exception is the Jews' Hospital at Mile End, which was built by the Sephardi community in 1806. Its architect is unknown, but illustrations show a simple stuccoed or ashlar-faced building typical of the late Georgian period. In contrast to synagogues of the time, however, it displayed prominent signs in both Hebrew and English announcing its purpose: 'Jews' Hospital for the Aged Poor and the Education and Employment of Youth'. It was founded and supported entirely by voluntary contributions.

The original building was extended and remodelled some 12 years later when a more polite neo-classical façade was provided which included a rusticated ground floor and a pedimented central section with Ionic pilasters. Its function was again spelled out in Hebrew and English on the front elevation. In 1863 the institution moved to a neo-Elizabethan building in Lower Norwood by the Christian partnership of Tillott and Chamberlain; the Mile End buildings presumably then fell out of use.[2]

8.2 London, Jews' Hospital, Mile End, *c.* 1815. *Local History Library, Tower Hamlets*

THE MASS IMMIGRATION, C. 1880–1914

The mid-nineteenth century saw attempts to organize and rationalize Jewish philanthropic institutions, as well as a rapid growth in their numbers. Many more of the buildings erected during this expansion were recorded, and some have survived to form part of the extant Anglo-Jewish heritage. The expansion and reorganization was prompted by a number of factors both from within and beyond the Jewish community itself. In the early nineteenth century a proliferation of different bodies within the Sephardi and Ashkenazi communities had resulted in over-provision and duplication of services in some cases and no provision at all in others. Assessment of need was impossible and there was generally no co-ordination of Jewish charitable relief.

Jewish charities were primarily stimulated, however, by immigration to Britain during the nineteenth century, which reached a peak in the period from 1881 to 1914. The majority of refugees were fleeing eastern Europe, especially the Russian empire, where a wave of pogroms followed the assassination of Tsar Alexander II in 1881. V. D. Lipman notes[3] that it is difficult to determine with any degree of certainty the exact number of Jewish refugees who came to settle in Britain, but estimates that in the years 1881–1905 the figure is probably in the region of 100,000. England was an attractive destination for Jewish immigrants for a variety of reasons: it had a relatively open immigration policy; there was religious toleration; it already had an established Jewish community; and it was cheap to travel to from the Continent. The fare from Hamburg to London was 15 shillings, and it cost less to travel from Europe to England and then on to the USA than to travel directly to America.[4]

Therefore the number of immigrants arriving and staying or merely passing through was considerable. The majority went to London's Jewish quarter, immediately east of the City and less than a mile from the docks, in an area centred on Spitalfields, Whitechapel and St George's. Russell and Lewis' map of 1900 shows that in a square mile around Whitechapel nearly all the streets had more than 50 per cent Jewish inhabitants, and in roughly a quarter of streets 95 per cent of the population was Jewish.

THE RESPONSE OF THE ANGLO-JEWISH COMMUNITY

The majority of refugees were fleeing with few if any possessions, and an immediate need was to find them food and shelter. Among the organizations set up for this purpose, the most prominent was the Jews' Temporary Shelter, founded in 1884, which gained financial support from the United Synagogue and the Rothschild family.[5] It provided food and accommodation for a maximum of 14 days and assisted in finding permanent work and lodgings. It appears never to have had purpose-built premises, but operated from a series of converted buildings in the Mansell and Leman Street areas.

However, apart from the problem of immediate physical need, the arrival of large numbers of eastern European immigrants presented the established Anglo-Jewish community with more long-term difficulties.

English Jews quickly perceived that the arrival of so many Yiddish-speaking, strangely dressed, impoverished and persecuted co-religionists in London and other urban centres could threaten the recently won civil liberties and social respectability of the whole community.

> We cannot stand by with our hands folded and do absolutely nothing. Events are marching rapidly. The habits of the foreign Jews in the East End, if not a menace, give rise to serious reflections on the community as a whole. Our motives are not wholly philanthropic; our own personal interests are involved, for we will have to take care of ourselves in looking after them.[6]

This pressure was intensified by the activities of 'rival' organizations such as the London Society for the Promotion of Christianity Among the Jews, which offered cheap board and lodging and free school places to immigrants in the hope of persuading them to convert. It had a substantial budget of £35,000 per annum and occupied several premises around the East End, one of which has survived on Whitechapel Road.[7]

Moreover, by the end of the nineteenth century there was considerable 'anti-alien' feeling, directed particularly against Jewish immigrants in the East End. Organizations such as the British Brothers' League whipped up vocal anti-Semitism centred on the claim that Jews were being lured to England on the promise of abundant State charity.[8]

Outside the Jewish community there was significant legislative impetus both to expand and to rationalize philanthropic efforts. In 1834 the Poor Law had been substantially remodelled in an attempt to curtail a perceived growing dependence on Out Relief (money distributed to the poor of the parish without requiring in return entry to the workhouse). As part of the 1834 Act, greater emphasis was placed on the role of voluntary charities rather than the State in providing for the poor in society.[9] This not only resulted in a general increase in the number of charities but also required of them a greater degree of organization and co-ordination than had been apparent previously. In 1902 the problems of overcrowding, poverty and 'sweated' industry in the East End persuaded the government to establish a Royal Commission on the 'Alien Question' to consider whether any new legislation was required to control the influx of refugees.[10]

The response of the Jewish community was to show that it was capable of looking after its own, and that refugees were not being attracted to Britain by the expectation of freely available State charity. Jewish charitable buildings from this period, therefore, often proclaimed that they were both Jewish and only for the 'deserving' poor.

The Jewish community appears to have been the first body to consider the problem of organizing and planning comprehensive philanthropic activity. In 1859 the Jewish Board of Guardians was established to co-ordinate Jewish charity,[11] some ten years before its Christian equivalent, the Charity Organisation Society, was set up. The Jewish Board of Guardians was to remove the responsibility for the administration of relief from individual synagogue congregations, and to create an efficient system for assessing individual claims. Lipman notes that between 1869 and 1882 the Board dealt with around 8,000 people a year, which represents between a fifth and a quarter of all Jews in London.[12]

The range of organizations established to cater for the Jewish community, particularly in the East End, was enormous. The *Jewish Directory of 1874* lists, in addition to the synagogues, one Jews' theological college, six Jewish schools, eight almshouses, 21 charitable organizations (18 in the East End) and 26 benevolent societies (25 in the East End).[13] Of course, many of these institutions did not require special premises for their activities, and most were housed in converted buildings. The Jewish Association Reading Rooms, for example, were located in part of a building in Aldgate from 1872 to 1874, when they were taken over by the Jewish Working Men's Club, which then moved to specially built premises in Alie Street in 1883. This building was extended in 1891, when the Club reached its heyday under the presidency of Sir Samuel Montagu, the first Lord Swaythling, Liberal MP for Whitechapel and a leading figure in the Ashkenazi community. The Jewish Working Men's Club, incorporating the Reading Rooms, finally closed in 1912.[14]

THE SOUP KITCHEN FOR THE JEWISH POOR

The Soup Kitchen for the Jewish Poor, whose purpose-built premises survive in Spitalfields, can in many ways be seen as an archetypal Jewish philanthropic institution. Originally founded as the London Hebrew

8.3   London, Soup Kitchen for the Jewish Poor, Brune Street, E1 (Lewis Solomon, 1902). *Lesley Fraser*

Soup Kitchen in 1854, and associated with the Jewish Bread, Meat and Coal Society, its first premises were in Leman Street.[15] Leman, Alie and Mansell Streets were on the southern edge of London's Jewish quarter, between the docks and the heart of the community, and were consequently where many charities had their offices.

The Soup Kitchen for the Jewish Poor paralleled the activities of a Christian organization, the Spitalfields Soup Society, founded in 1797 to save Spitalfields weavers from starvation, which operated from a building in Brick Lane. The Soup Kitchen for the Jewish Poor moved from Leman Street to Aldgate and then to a house at 5 Fashion Street, and in that respect is typical of many Jewish charities. It was, moreover, well supported by leading London Jews, and among its first presidents were Lionel de Rothschild, Alfred Cohen and Sir Edward Sassoon. It was funded entirely by voluntary contributions.[16] In 1902 the Soup Kitchen moved to purpose-built premises in Brune Street in the heart of the East End Jewish 'ghetto'. The architect, Lewis Solomon, provided a somewhat ostentatious building of three bays in red brick with extensive terracotta dressing. Stylistically, it is typical of contemporary commercial buildings in London, including an Arts-and-Crafts-inspired doorcase as the focal point of the elevation. However, it is interesting for its inclusion of a supposedly Jewish motif of a tureen against a scalloped ground, or the Apotheosis of Soup,[17] and it emphasizes in prominent letters on the front elevation that it is both 'Jewish' and for the 'poor', illustrating the desire of the Anglo-Jewish community to prove that it could look after its own.

This theme is further expanded in the accommodation provided. Although, as *The Builder* noted, 'the interior . . . is of a very simple character, so as to save expenditure as far as possible',[18] the principal space is a large committee room where applications were considered and the 'deserving poor' could be identified from malingerers. This room was originally panelled and included donation boards and the portraits of early benefactors. In addition, the Soup Kitchen for the Jewish Poor had several classrooms, a reading room, and a large room for recreation designed to encourage East End Jews into 'wholesome' and 'appropriate' entertainment in their spare time.

THE JEWS' FREE SCHOOL, BELL LANE

Schools were among the earliest voluntary organizations set up by the Jewish community on resettlement. Learning plays a particularly important role in Judaism, as there is great emphasis on knowledge of the Talmud. The established Anglo-Jewish community also appreciated the crucial role that schools could play in the assimilation of the East End immigrants into wider Jewish and English society.

Before 1870 schools in England were frequently established by the local church authorities, and the teaching of Christianity was a prominent part of the curriculum, making them unsuitable for the education of Jewish children. Missionary societies such as the London Society for the Promotion of Christianity Among the Jews also sought to attract Jewish

JEWS FREE SCHOOL.

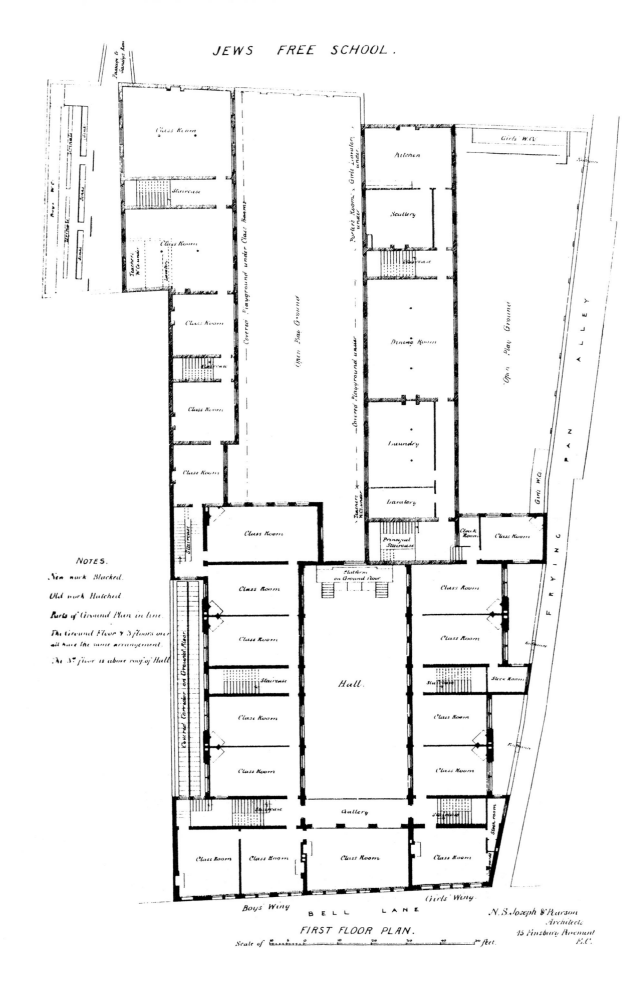

NOTES.

New work Blacked.

Old work Hatched.

Parts of Ground Plan in line.

The Ground Floor & 3 floors over all have the same arrangement.

The 3rd floor is above roof of Hall.

FIRST FLOOR PLAN.

Scale of feet.

N.S.Joseph & Pearson
Architects
45 Finsbury Pavement
E.C.

8.4 London, Jews' Free School, Bell Lane, E1 (N. S. Joseph and Pearson, 1883); the plan of the first floor. The Builder (7 July 1883)

children with the offer of free school places in a more aggressive attempt at conversion. These pressures prompted the Jewish community into the provision of a large number of free school places, predominantly in the East End but also throughout London. The Sha'arei Tikva School became a Free School in 1823 and operated until 1885. Villareal became a Free School in the same year; Westminster Jews' Free School began in 1820 and continued until 1939; Stepney Jews' Free School was founded in 1863; Bayswater in 1866; and Borough in 1867. (Schools were often established in association with synagogues.) By 1870, Levin notes[19] the combined school roll of the Free Schools was 5,687; by 1900 it had risen to 8,250. In 1894 the Jews' Free School (JFS), Bell Lane, Spitalfields, accounted for 3,600 of the available places.

Reputedly the largest school in Europe, Bell Lane was also probably the most interesting architecturally of the Free Schools. Sadly, it was demolished in the 1970s to make way for a car park, but it was well recorded in photographs and prints and in the 1957 *Survey of London* volume covering Spitalfields and Mile End New Town.[20] The school experienced several phases of building after its foundation in 1817. The site in Bell Lane was purchased in 1820, and the school was extended in 1848 and 1855 by James Tillott (of Tillott and Chamberlain, who went on to design the new Jews' Hospital in Norwood in 1863). The money for these extensions was provided by Sir Anthony de Rothschild. Bell Lane had two major phases of further rebuilding in 1883 and 1904. In

8.5 London, Jews' Free School, Bell Lane, E1; the gymnasium in 1908.
Greater London Record Office

C.F.Kell,Photo Litho,Castle St.Holborn.

Wyman & Sons,Printers,GQ Queen St.

8.6   London, Jews' Free School, Bell Lane,
E1; the Great Hall. The Builder (7 July 1883)

8.7   London, Jews' Free School, Bell Lane,
E1; the front elevation. *Greater London Record Office*

1883 the original school buildings were taken down and N. S. Joseph and Pearson were commissioned to produce modern and enlarged premises to take account of the increasing numbers of Jewish children in the area, and also to bring the school in line with the requirements of the 1870 Education Act. All the work was completed within six months, school activities being continued throughout in temporary classrooms on the site. The new internal arrangements provided an apron of 52 classrooms set around an open playground and a Great Hall. Each classroom could accommodate between 30 and 60 children to comply with the new Act, thereby doing away with the earlier large rooms where 600 could be taught at one time.[21]

The centrepiece of the interior was the Great Hall, which N. S. Joseph considered to be his major architectural achievement. Designed for school examinations and prizegivings as well as occasional use as a synagogue, it was 80 feet long, 30 feet wide and three storeys in height. As at Joseph's synagogues, the style was eclectic Romanesque or Italianate, with round-headed window arches, heavily decorated at ground-floor level, which were in turn echoed by the semicircular laminated roof-trusses. *The Builder* noted that the 'cornices, friezes, panels and other architectural features [are] carried out in glazed bricks, chiefly cream coloured, and with bands of grey, buff and brown, the enriched panels and friezes being of glazed terracotta'.[22]

The new buildings had frontages of 90 feet to Bell Lane and 116 feet to Frying Pan Alley. The *Survey of London* observed that 'the wide four storeyed front . . . is a well ordered front of early Italian Renaissance derivation carried out in red brick and terracotta, materials which impart a distinctly Bolognese flavour'.[23] It was an asymmetrical main elevation with deeply recessed windows and strongly modelled details, including continuous hoodmoulds above the windows and panels of arabesque decoration. Clearly, the aim was to create a building of some distinction which could not be mistaken for a London County Council school of the period. Nevertheless, like many contemporary synagogues, the building was not ostentatiously 'Jewish'; the only indication that it was a Jewish school was its name above the door.

N. S. Joseph's firm also designed the 1906 remodelling of the Stepney Jews' Free School, which was a much smaller and less ambitious project. Again in red brick, this building is more classical in its inspiration, with an unusual, heavily rusticated ground floor. This building has survived and is listed Grade II.

PHILANTHROPIC HOUSING – THE EAST END DWELLINGS COMPANY AND THE FOUR PER CENT INDUSTRIAL DWELLINGS COMPANY

Two Victorian Anglo-Jewish architectural practices, both better known for their synagogues, worked for the housing trusts which pioneered the provision of 'philanthropic' housing for the poor in East London: Davis and Emanuel for the East End Dwellings Company, and N. S. Joseph for the Four Per Cent Industrial Dwellings Company. The Four Per Cent was founded by Nathan Mayer, the first Lord Rothschild following a report commissioned by the United Synagogue, and was specifically, but not exclusively, aimed at Jews. The East End Dwellings Company, in contrast, was founded by the Vicar of St Jude's, the Reverend Samuel Barnett, but its clients too were mainly Jewish, because it aimed to provide accommodation for the very lowest wage-earners in the heart of the East End. The model dwelling blocks that Davis and Emanuel and N. S. Joseph built for these companies represented the largest body of Jewish philanthropic architecture, and today are the largest body of surviving Jewish architecture in London, with the exception of synagogues.

The problems of overcrowding and poor-quality housing, especially in the East End of London, were matters of national concern by the last quarter of the nineteenth century.[24] The death rate remained unacceptably high, and outbreaks of typhoid and cholera were common. Most inhabitants of areas such as Whitechapel and Spitalfields lived in slum conditions, with inadequate light and ventilation, aggravated by the lack of refuse collection and the notoriously poor water supply. A constant water supply could be guaranteed only during a cholera scare.[25]

In response, Disraeli's government passed the Artisans' and Labourers' Dwellings Improvement Act in 1875 which charged the Metropolitan Board of Works with the clearance of the worst slum areas. This was to enable commercial or philanthropic organizations to provide healthier and more sanitary accommodation in new model dwelling blocks. However, in the short term at least, the clearance of large areas of the worst – and therefore the cheapest – houses actually increased overcrowding in Whitechapel and Spitalfields, where a fall in the number of inhabited houses coincided with a rise in the population.[26]

The Metropolitan Board of Works had two main improvement schemes in the East End: the Whitechapel scheme and the Flower and Dean Street scheme. Sites from these areas were eventually sold for model dwelling blocks although in many cases it took over two years from the date of demolition. Some were sold to existing housing organizations such as the Improved Industrial Dwellings Company and the Peabody Trust. However, these established companies in effect provided housing only for the relatively better-off artisan classes. Guaranteeing a return of between seven and eight per cent per annum to investors, Peabody tenements, for example, were rented out at around 8s. a week and were therefore out of reach for those on an unskilled or casual worker's wage. Jerry White notes dryly that 'the difference between a rack-renting landlord and a "philanthropist" was perhaps 6% per annum'.[27] These units were not, therefore, designed for the vast majority who lived in the East End.

The East End Dwellings Company

The 'main endeavour' of the Reverend Samuel Barnett's East End Dwellings Company, founded in 1884, was

> to provide for the poorest class of self-supporting labourers dwelling accommodation at the very cheapest rates compatible with realising a fair rate of interest upon the capital employed. Hitherto little or nothing of this kind has been done on a large scale, the buildings of the existing

Companies and Associations being chiefly occupied by a class of industrial tenants more prosperous than those for whom this Company proposes to provide.[28]

The company's first site was purchased from the Metropolitan Board of Works' Whitechapel improvement area on the newly reconstructed Cartwright Street, behind the Royal Mint. The site was long and narrow, and, as with all Metropolitan Board of Works sites, the company was required to rehouse at least the same number of people as had been displaced by the original clearance. This dictated that the building should be a long and tall block facing the street.

The company chose Davis and Emanuel as their architects and continued to use them at least until 1906. This was Davis and Emanuel's first exercise in model housing, and it is not clear why they were chosen. Until the 1880s their practice had been confined to the design of synagogues, schools and commercial buildings. However, Barrow Emanuel is said to have had a lifelong 'warm interest in the housing of the working classes',[29] and he also appears in the minutes of the East End Dwellings Company as one of the honorary office bearers of the Jewish and East London Model Lodging House Association, as well as being a member of the Jewish Board of Guardians. It may have been, therefore, his special interest in housing, and his knowledge of and connections with the Jewish community, that recommended the firm.

Davis and Emanuel's first block for the company was Katherine Buildings, opened in March 1885. It conformed largely to the practice adopted by other model dwelling block architects, and to the ideas promoted by the housing reformer Octavia Hill. The accommodation comprised single and double room tenements accessed from long balconies which ran the length of the rear elevation. The balconies were reached from three staircases, where the communal facilities (toilets, sinks and water taps) were also situated. The company envisaged that the majority of rooms – 200 out of 280 – would be let singly to families who would rent additional space as their needs demanded and their means allowed. Rooms were to be of the simplest and most robust character, as prescribed by Octavia Hill.

> The plans were laid before the highest authorities, among those in personal touch with the poor. The prevailing ideas were that publicity should be courted, that the fittings should be of the simplest in view of the destructive habits of the tenants, the buildings airy and wholesome, and the rents low.[30]

Again as advised by Miss Hill, the block included a clubroom for the use of tenants, and rent collection was organized and carried out by ladies in an attempt to influence the manners and morals of the inhabitants. Rents varied from 1s. 6d., for a single room on the top floor, to 5s. 6d., for two rooms on the ground or first floors, and were therefore within the reach of most wage earners.

> The dwellings are inhabited by about 650 men, women and children, chiefly of the class earning a low weekly wage, for whom they were intended, the population comprising a large number of dock labourers, carmen, porters and men employed in one of the building trades, while

among the women are 20 office cleaners and charwomen, and 21 tailor-esses, needlewomen and sackmakers.[31]

The main interest of Davis and Emanuel as designers of model dwelling blocks is not in their approach to the planning and layout of the buildings, where they tended to use tried and tested methods, but in their positive contribution to the development of a more human and less grimly utilitarian dwelling block architecture. Despite the awkwardness of the site with which they had to work on Cartwright Street, Katherine Buildings was a simple and elegant solution to the problem of providing such a high density of identical accommodation behind a single elevation. In contrast to the plainer blocks of the Peabody Trustees, Davis and Emanuel's building was well articulated along the street, with advanced bays and the inclusion of chimneys rising on the front elevation which were treated as gables. The ground floor was rusticated, and the use of double stringcourses at ground- and fourth-floor level helped to disguise the scale of the building. A warm stock brick was chosen, with lighter bricks to pick out the rustication, quoins and window reveals.

The emphasis on the architecture of the block may in part be due to the influence of the Reverend Barnett, who had strong views about the effect of their surroundings on his company's tenants:

> It is, I believe, false economy, as it is false benevolence, which provides for fellow-creatures things acknowledged to be ugly. In the long run such things will be rejected, and although it is too early to form conclusions, there is evidence that repulsive looking buildings repel tenants. Benevolence had had much to do with the erection of dwellings in the neighbourhood; and in the name of benevolence, so as to encourage benevolence some argue that decoration must be given up so that such dwellings must be made to pay. Probably this is a mistake in economy; it is certainly a mistake in benevolence. To treat one's neighbour as oneself is not to decorate one's own house with the art of the world, and to leave one's neighbour's house with nothing but drainpipes to relieve the bareness of its walls. They who would be benevolent should invest money whose return would be [the] artistic pleasure of others, as they now invest money the return of which is their own artistic pleasure.[32]

Certainly the minutes of the East End Dwellings Company show that the directors took a very close interest in the construction details: 'It was resolved that stock bricks be used except in the string courses: that the walls be carried straight to the top of the windows: that the ground storey be done in rusticated work: that the chimneys be constructed with steps: that the cornice as shown on the plan be adopted.'[33]

Davis or Emanuel regularly attended the directors' meetings throughout the planning and construction of Katherine Buildings. It is nevertheless remarkable that the directors felt able to let the appearance of their blocks assume such importance; as *The Builder* noted, the East End Dwellings Company was a 'pioneer company' in attempting to 'solve the great problem of the satisfactory housing of the lower working class as a paying speculation rather than as a matter of benevolence . . . Its success or non success depends on its balance sheet . . .'[34]

It was a careful balancing act between financial and aesthetic considerations. Davis and Emanuel's Katherine Buildings appears to have gone some way towards answering the visual problems of high-density housing on a restricted budget, but there is evidence that this was at the expense of the quality of the services and the interior. Beatrice Potter (later Webb) was a social worker in the area and presents a rather different view of the building:

> Katherine Buildings was a long double-faced building on five tiers; on one side overlooking a street; on the other looking on to a narrow yard hemmed in by a high blank wall forming the back premises of the Royal Mint. Right along the whole length of the building confronting the blank wall ran four open galleries, out of which ran narrow passages, each passage to five rooms, identical in size and shape, except that the one at the end was much smaller than the others. Within these uniform cell-like apartments there were no labour saving appliances, not even a sink or water tap. Three narrow stone staircases led from the yard to the topmost gallery; on the landings between the galleries and the stairs were sinks and taps (three sinks and six taps to about sixty rooms). From a sanitary stand-point there was perhaps little to be said against the super-economical structure. But the sanitary arrangements taken as a whole had the draw-back that the sets of six closets used in common by a miscellaneous crowd of men, women and children became the obtrusively dominant feature of the several staircases, up and down which trooped, morning, noon and night, the 600 or so inhabitants of the buildings. In short, all amenity, some would say all decency, was sacrificed to requirements of relatively low rents and physically sanitary buildings.[35]

The East End Dwellings Company followed Katherine Buildings with a series of blocks throughout the East End, retaining Davis and Emanuel as company architects. Their next building, Lolesworth, was in the heart of the Jewish quarter, in the Metropolitan Board of Works' Flower and Dean Street Improvement Scheme. Its elevational treatment was similar to Katherine Buildings, but there was some improvement to the internal planning. Both Katherine and Lolesworth Buildings were demolished in the 1970s.

Further blocks followed in Bethnal Green (1888, 1890, 1892 and 1900–6), Spitalfields (1890), St Pancras (1891) and Stepney Green (1894 and 1899). Generally the company tended to provide ever more comfortable and well-serviced flats, at increasing cost, in line with developing contemporary ideas about appropriate housing for the working class. Katherine Buildings had cost around £20,000 and had provided 280 lettable rooms; in 1901 Montfort House, a small block – less than a third the size of Katherine, and of flats rather than rooms – cost over £9,000 just for its construction.[36] Of these later blocks, the last of the company's buildings at Bethnal Green and its Stepney Green development have survived relatively intact. The Stepney Green blocks deserve special mention, again for their architectural rather than their planning interest.

In 1893 the company bought a triangular site in Stepney bounded by Cressy Place, Hannibal Road and Stepney Green. The first block on the site, Cressy House, was opened in 1894. Using a plan which borrows heavily from an earlier Metropolitan Association building on Farringdon Road, Davis and Emanuel produced designs which were their most

8.8   London, Cressy House, Hannibal Road, E1; designed by Davis and Emanuel for the East End Dwellings Company in 1894. *Lesley Fraser*

elaborate and decorative to date. Cressy House is four storeys in height and is executed in red brick with a black brick plinth. The architects again use the device of strong stringcourses above the ground and second floors to reduce the scale of the building. Articulation along the street is provided by the regular staircases, which project forward of the building line, and are surmounted by curved gables. Chimneys feature prominently on the skyline, further breaking down the massiveness of the block and adding vertical punctuation. Terracotta panels, moulded bricks and decorative ironwork add to the liveliness of the elevation.

A further block, Dunstan Houses, was added along Stepney Green in 1899. Although in the same idiom, this later building has less decoration than Cressy House and omits the projecting bays of its predecessor. Instead, there are copper-covered cupolas on the hexagonal corners, and the stairs and entrances are marked by twin flanking turrets. The effect of Cressy and Dunstan Houses as a whole is to emphasize Davis and Emanuel's skill in modelling strong elevations enlivened by the restrained use of ornament, even when restricted by cost to a limited palette of materials.

Their last work for the East End Dwellings Company was in Bethnal Green along Globe Road, and represents their largest surviving development. In the years 1901–6 a total of five blocks and a small cottage development were built. The blocks follow Davis and Emanuel's by then established style with rusticated ground floors, projecting bays, turrets and ornamental gables. Their cottages are modest two-storied handed pairs in a red cold-pressed brick. They are very simple and straightforward, almost entirely without ornament except for a corbel detail marking the party walls and a rendered cornice and tympanum above the front doors giving the houses an almost Arts-and-Crafts feel.

The Globe Road cottages were the company's last East End scheme until 1935 and marked the end of their partnership with Davis and Emanuel. By that date the company had provided housing for more than 7,000 people,[37] including a large number of recent Jewish immigrants, and their blocks represent some of the best architectural solutions to the challenge of providing large-scale housing at a cheap rent and a low cost while ensuring a return of at least five per cent on the capital of investors.

The Four Per Cent Industrial Dwellings Company

The foundation of the Four Per Cent Industrial Dwellings Company in 1885 represents a specifically Jewish response to the problems of overcrowding and insanitary housing conditions in the East End, and it demonstrates all the main elements of Jewish philanthropy discussed above: a genuine desire on behalf of Anglo-Jewry to alleviate the problems of fellow Jews; a recognition that the problems of the East End were being blamed, in part at least, on Jewish immigration, and that the fate of the whole community rested on their successful resolution. Leading figures in the Jewish community, most notably Nathan, Lord Rothschild, and major Jewish institutions, the Board of Guardians and the United Synagogue, were involved in its inception; and one of the leading Anglo-Jewish architects of the day, N. S. Joseph, was employed to design all the company's buildings.

The Four Per Cent Industrial Dwellings Company was founded as a direct result of the findings of the Council of the United Synagogue's East End Enquiry Commission. The Commission, set up in 1884 with Rothschild as chairman and working in conjunction with the Board of Guardians, looked into the physical and moral well-being of the East End immigrants, who, it was feared, were in danger of remaining entirely separate from the body of Anglo-Jewry. The Commission's report made two main recommendations to alleviate the plight of the 'poorer classes of the community'. The first was anglicization: 'steps must be taken to cause the foreign poor upon arrival to imbibe notions proper to civilised life in this country.' Second: 'the physical condition of the poor and their physical surroundings must be improved'. The Commission saw these two goals as linked, noting that the provision of new homes would 'constitute the greatest of all available means for improving the conditions, physical, moral and social, of the Jewish poor'.[38] The report went on to prescribe the establishment of a model dwelling company, suggesting that 'if rentals were based on a nett return of 4%, excellent accommodation . . . could be provided at a rental not exceeding five shillings per week'.[39] Six days after the publication of the report, the Four Per Cent Industrial Dwellings Company was founded; Rothschild himself put up £10,000 of the £40,000 initial capital, the rest being raised within the Jewish community by the issue of 1,600 shares at £25 each, guaranteeing a return of four per cent per annum. The honorary architect of the United Synagogue, Nathan Solomon Joseph, brother-in-law of the Chief Rabbi, was appointed as the company's architect.

The Four Per Cent differed from the East End Dwellings Company in two major respects. First, it aimed to provide housing for the Jewish poor (although this was never specifically stated in its Memorandum of Association), and indeed the Russell and Lewis map of the Jewish East End in 1900 shows that its properties were between 95 and 100 per cent Jewish. Second, it did not have the same regard for aesthetic considerations as did the Reverend Barnett and the East End Dwellings Company. Instead, its Memorandum of Association stated that it would provide 'the maximum accommodation for the minimum rent compatible with the yielding of a nett £4 per cent per annum'.[40] N. S. Joseph's first block was consequently higher, more densely packed and more austere than those of Davis and Emanuel. At six storeys plus a semi-basement, and wrapping around three sides of the block between Flower and Dean, Lolesworth and Thrawl Streets, Charlotte de Rothschild Dwellings was the most intensive model dwelling development in the area. Especially from the courtyard, the effect must have been grim and oppressive in the extreme.

The street elevation was a little better, with a hint of decoration including red-brick courses between the windows, terracotta keystones and ornamental iron railings to the staircases and landings. The appearance of the block was undoubtedly improved by having the staircases on the front elevation, providing rhythm along the street, and by the setting back of the building behind a railed area. The main decorative elements in the scheme were the two sets of ornamental archways and gates which gave access from Thrawl and Flower and Dean Streets to the courtyard.

8.9 London, Charlotte de Rothschild
Dwellings; designed by N. S. Joseph for the
Four Per Cent Industrial Dwellings
Company in 1887. *Local History Library, Tower Hamlets*

Nevertheless, the Reverend Barnett might well have had cause to note
that Rothschild Dwellings was an example of a block with 'nothing but
drainpipes to relieve the bareness of its walls'; the *Survey of London*,
assessing Spitalfields in 1957, certainly found it the grimmest of all the
model blocks in the area.[41]

However, what was lost on the elevational treatment was to some
extent regained on the interiors. The majority of flats consisted of two
rooms plus scullery, with rents ranging from 4s. to 6s. 6d. Only 18 of the
415 rooms were to be let singly, in marked contrast to the East End
Dwellings Company's policy.[42] The Four Per Cent also provided the
majority of its flats with separate toilets and sculleries, avoiding the
criticisms levelled at the service provision in the East End Dwellings
Company's early blocks.

The Four Per Cent, like the East End Dwellings Company, went on to
build a series of model dwelling blocks over the following two decades.
Its next venture, in 1889–90, was further east, at Brady Street in Whitechapel. N. S. Joseph produced a building of similar scale and design, but,
on a bigger site, Brady Street Dwellings was not quite as oppressive as the

original block. More attention was also given to decorative detail, and curly gables, very similar to Davis and Emanuel's, were added to give vertical emphasis to the staircases and to add interest to the roofline. Diaper patterns were used to relieve the monotony of the brickwork.

This was soon followed by the construction in 1892 of Nathaniel Dwellings on a long and narrow site opposite Rothschild Buildings. However, this was the company's last inner-city slum clearance project for more than ten years, as it followed the East End Dwellings Company to the more suburban area of Stepney Green. This move, as the directors noted in their share prospectus of 1901, was to 'encourage the migration to less congested, and consequently more healthy districts than the centre of East London'.[43]

That theme is expanded in a *Jewish Chronicle* supplement relating to later developments still further from the heart of the traditional Jewish quarter:

> Still we have no wish to see the East End more thickly populated with our co-religionists than it already is. On the contrary, we desire to break up the congestion. The new issue capital of the 4% Industrial Dwellings Company is to be commended for this very reason that it marks a step in this direction. Camberwell and Stoke Newington, where the latest dwellings are being erected, are both outside the area which has become the focus of so much discussion, and the new dwellings will encourage our artisan classes to settle there. And if an additional incentive be needed, the synagogues and schools in these neighbourhoods will furnish it . . . we have no doubt that as time goes on they will find it consistent with these interests to plant their dwellings further away still from the centres of population.[44]

The move out of the city centre was accompanied by a change in the form and design of the company's buildings. The trend was away from massively scaled blocks with minimal decoration to smaller buildings with larger flats where more attention was paid to the external appearance. N. S. Joseph's first 'suburban' development for the Four Per Cent was his most decorative to date. Stepney Green Dwellings (1896) has five storeys plus a semi-basement, and is in red brick, with blue brick bands on the ground floor and at fourth-floor window-head height. The staircases have curly gables and are treated in a broadly similar fashion to those on Davis and Emanuel's Cressy House (completed two years earlier, in 1894). The Stepney Green elevation is contained by two flanking and projecting towers with hipped roofs. Joseph made great use of decorative terracotta on this building, especially around the staircase entrances, and the ornamental iron railings enclosing the basement area and on the stair landings are one of the most striking features of the development.

I conjecture that these were the last blocks that N. S. Joseph himself designed for the Four Per Cent. Although his firm continued to work for the company, the style changed dramatically after this date. Later buildings, such as the Naverino development in Stoke Newington, are in a confident and quite flamboyant Arts-and-Crafts style, unlike Joseph's earlier work.

THE CONSERVATION OF JEWISH SOCIAL
ARCHITECTURE IN LONDON

The examples of Jewish philanthropic building which survive today represent only a fraction of those originally erected. The loss of so much of the original building stock is thus significant for the conservation of the remainder. Given that many of the finest examples, both architecturally and historically speaking, have disappeared, justifying the preservation of the surviving specimens is all the more difficult. Should, for example, N. S. Joseph's rather run-of-the-mill housing block at Stepney Green be protected when his historically more important blocks in Flower and Dean Street have already been torn down? On the other hand, of course, the buildings which remain are now rare examples of a once widespread and very significant social phenomenon. Their rarity makes it all the more important that the best of those still standing should be given protection to ensure their availability for future generations to appreciate and study.

There are a number of factors which explain why so many Jewish buildings have not survived. Many buildings constructed by philanthropic institutions to house immigrants in the 1880s and 1890s were of inferior quality in the first place. Their primary function was to meet a very urgent and immediate need, to provide shelter for large numbers of people within a very confined budget: this tended to militate against the provision of grand or expensive architecture. Indeed, premises were often adapted from an existing building, or if newly constructed were utilitarian and plain in character. The vast majority of Jewish philanthropic buildings, therefore, were not of special architectural interest, and those which survive are often not of an intrinsic quality which would encourage their adaptation to alternative uses.

Probably the most obvious factor which has led to the loss of large numbers of Jewish buildings is redundancy, either because the original users have moved away or because there is no longer a call for the building's original function. It should be borne in mind that one of the principal aims of the nineteenth-century Jewish philanthropists was the dispersal of the East End community to new areas of settlement. This was successfully achieved from an early date with the effect that many buildings, such as the Jews' Temporary Shelter, had already outgrown their usefulness by the early decades of the present century. The Jewish community has been migrating from the city to the suburbs at least since the 1830s;[45] immigration from eastern Europe almost dried up after the First World War; and by the 1930s the children of the immigrants were moving to secondary areas of Jewish settlement in north-west and north-east London. The Blitz all but completed this process.

The Jews' Free School in Bell Lane was under-used by the 1930s. Legislative reform had better accommodated the needs of religious minorities in state schools where the school population warranted it, which to some extent lessened the need for separate denominational schools. The school building itself was no longer suitable for modern teaching methods.[46] As a result, when the JFS was partially destroyed by enemy action during the Second World War, the decision was taken to abandon the East End site and to rebuild in North London.

Housing was also affected by changing public policy. The Four Per Cent and East End Dwellings Companies had erected model dwelling blocks, to house the maximum number of people for the minimum cost at the end of the nineteenth century; after the Second World War, new standards of space, services and comfort were expected which these 50- and 60-year-old tenements could not meet without expensive alterations. In addition, a certain social stigma attached to the blocks because they had been provided with basic facilities for the very poor.[47] It was therefore decided to demolish rather than to refurbish. Davis and Emanuel's Katherine Buildings was pulled down in 1971, Lolesworth Buildings and Stafford House in Spitalfields in 1973, and all of their early inner-city blocks by 1980. N. S. Joseph's early blocks suffered the same fate; Rothschild Buildings was demolished in 1972, and Brady Street Dwellings in 1975.[48]

What safeguards are there for surviving buildings? Very few Jewish community buildings are given statutory protection by 'listing', largely because they tend not to be of special architectural interest. This reflects their often utilitarian design and purpose. One notable exception is the Soup Kitchen for the Jewish Poor in Spitalfields, which was listed in 1989 as a by-product of the investigation into synagogue buildings.[49] It was identified as 'perhaps the most important architectural testimony to the arrival of Jewish refugees to this country, and the process of assimilation and support which developed in response to this'.[50] This is a key listing because it is the first to recognise the crucial historic rather than architectural importance of many Jewish buildings.

Of course, listing alone will not secure the future of buildings such as the Soup Kitchen for the Jewish Poor. Buildings listed for their historic interest are notoriously more difficult to protect than those with obvious architectural merit, when owners propose, for example, demolition behind the facade or other radical alterations. Original use is often intrinsic to the interest of these buildings, and it can make finding new and sympathetic uses very difficult. The Soup Kitchen for the Jewish Poor is still partly used for its original purpose, although most of the building has now been turned over to light industrial and commercial use. The main kitchen has become an ice-cream store and has been lined with insulating materials. This could be removed in the future; the building is generally in a poor state of repair, and a more sympathetic occupant would be desirable.

None of the extant Jewish housing blocks of the Four Per Cent Industrial Dwellings Company or Davis and Emanuel's houses for the East End Dwellings Company has been listed. Of those which remain, the blocks around Stepney Green are of particular interest. Stepney Green is the largest and most comprehensive surviving Jewish development, with Davis and Emanuel's East London Synagogue (1877; Grade II), N. S. Joseph's Stepney Jews' Free School (Grade II), and housing blocks by Joseph and Davis and Emanuel. All these buildings fall within the local authority's Stepney Green Conservation Area, currently declared a priority for English Heritage grant aid.

Conservation Area status protects against demolition only,[51] and without extra 'Article 4 Directions' it cannot prevent minor but potentially visually damaging alterations. Even though blocks of flats do not have the same Permitted Development rights as individual houses,[52] alterations can be controlled by the Local Planning Authority only if they constitute a 'material alteration'. The removal of, for example, terracotta details or ornamental ironwork, or the replacement of windows or doors with plastic versions which followed the same basic pattern would be difficult to control according to such criteria. N. S. Joseph's Four Per Cent block has undergone some minor alterations, with the installation of glazed screens for additional protection in the stairwells, and the insertion of a lift. Davis and Emanuel's blocks are relatively untouched to date except for minimum alterations to modernize the interiors.

The Four Per Cent blocks remain under the control of the Four Per Cent Industrial Dwellings Company Limited, which appears to be a broadly sympathetic manager of its property. The society has a five-yearly maintenance programme to ensure the upkeep of the blocks, and has carried out repairs to its large Naverino Mansions development in Stoke Newington, where Hunt Thompson Associates were engaged to oversee the works. Timber windows have been retained and repaired, brickwork is being gently cleaned and repointed, and roofs are being repaired and reslated where necessary, using original materials throughout. Obviously keen to protect and respect its existing building stock, the Four Per Cent also held an exhibition about its housing in 1985 to celebrate its centenary.

The future of East End Dwellings Company blocks, however, appears less secure. The company has been sold at least three times in the last 20 years and by 1991 the majority of the blocks were owned by Town and Country Properties Limited.[53] Some blocks have been handed on to the local authority and some cottages sold to private owners. Although in a Conservation Area, Davis and Emanuel's Merceron House in Globe Road illustrates well the problems of protecting the character of these blocks. The local authority, Tower Hamlets, had a blanket policy of installing uPVC double-glazed window units in all its own council housing. It therefore replaced all Merceron House timber sashes with uPVC 'tip and tilt' casements, which has had a most unfortunate impact on the elevations, losing much of their original articulation and liveliness.

On the cottages opposite, the inadequacy of Conservation Area control over minor alterations is also apparent. The owners of one, clearly wishing to distinguish their newly purchased property from their neighbours', have removed the original windows, door and roof covering and have rendered the front elevation with a roughcast. Unfortunately, this cottage is centrally placed in the terrace, and the changes dramatically upset the appearance of the entire development. The application of roughcast is likely to be an irrecoverable alteration, as the original bricks will have been hacked to provide a key for the roughcast skin.

The solution to the lack of planning controls would be the declaration of an Article 4 Direction.[54] However, this would have to be done by the local authority, which, with property of its own in the area, has a vested interest in maintaining freedom of action. The answer in the first instance must be to educate building owners, including local authorities, about the particular history and value of such properties and to provide information about sensitive alternative means of repair.

CONCLUSION

Philanthropic buildings represent a large but almost entirely unrecorded element of the Jewish built heritage. Many of the original buildings have already been lost. Nevertheless, those remaining illustrate in architectural form an important historical phenomenon which had an impact not only on the Jewish community itself, but also on the history and development of Victorian charitable activity. Jewish philanthropy involved the major community institutions including the United Synagogue and the Board of Guardians, and leading Jewish families such as the Rothschilds, Cohens and Montefiores. The community increasingly used its own architects, although, as in the case of synagogues, no distinctive 'Jewish style' emerged. In many cases the buildings which survive are not of outstanding architectural merit, but they are of considerable socio-historic significance. Raising awareness, therefore, both in the community and in the planning world must be the first step towards the conservation of this little known but important part of the nation's heritage.

NOTES

1. S. S. Levin, 'The Changing Pattern of Jewish Education', in S. S. Levin (ed.), *A Century of Anglo-Jewish Life, 1870–1970* (London, 1970), p. 58. See generally, Eugene C. Black, *The Social Politics of Anglo-Jewry 1880–1920* (Oxford, 1988).
2. E. Jamilly, 'Anglo-Jewish Architects and Architecture in the 18th and 19th Centuries', *Transactions of the Jewish Historical Society of England (TJHSE)*, XVIII (1953–55), p. 141.
3. V. D. Lipman, *A History of the Jews in Britain since 1858* (London, 1990), p. 45.
4. Ibid., p. 47.
5. Ibid., p. 31.
6. Noah Davis quoted in A. Newman, 'Growth and Change', in Levin (ed.), op. cit., p. 121.
7. Levin, 'Changing Pattern', op. cit., p. 58.
8. Lipman, *History of the Jews*, p. 51.
9. Ibid., p. 34.
10. Ibid., p. 70.
11. Ibid., p. 32.
12. Ibid., p. 33.
13. A. Newman, 'Synagogues of the East End', in A. Newman (ed.), *The Jewish East End, 1840–1939* (London, 1981), p. 219.
14. H. Pollins, 'Working Men's Clubs', in Newman (ed.), op. cit., p. 177.
15. *Survey of London*, Vol. XXVII (1957), p. 244.
16. English Heritage, London Divison, Historian's Report, July 1989.
17. Ibid.
18. *The Builder*, 24 Jan. 1903.
19. Levin, 'Changing Pattern', p. 58.
20. *Survey of London*, Vol. XXVII, pp. 238–41.
21. *The Builder*, 7 Aug. 1883.
22. Ibid.
23. *Survey of London*, Vol. XXVII, p. 241.
24. 1885 Royal Commission on the Housing of the Working Classes. See Kadish on public bathhouses in this volume.
25. Lipman, *History of the Jews*, p. 54.
26. J. White, *Rothschild Buildings* (London, 1980), p. 13.

27. Ibid., p. 18.
28. Quoted in J. N. Tarn, *Five Per Cent Philanthropy* (Cambridge, 1973), p. 100.
29. *The Builder*, 20 Feb. 1904. See Jamilly, 'Anglo-Jewish Architects', op. cit.
30. Quoted in Tarn, op. cit., p. 100.
31. Minutes of the East End Dwellings Company, 1884–1900, Newham Library.
32. Quoted in J. E. Conner and B. J. Critchley, *The Red Cliffs of Stepney* (Colchester, 1980), p. 16.
33. Minutes of the East End Dwellings Company, op. cit.
34. *The Builder*, 28 March 1885.
35. Quoted in Conner and Critchley, op. cit., p. 23.
36. Ibid., p. 35.
37. L. Millar, *Charlwood Alliance Properties Ltd*, MS, Tower Hamlets Local History Library.
38. White, op. cit., p. 17.
39. Ibid., p. 18.
40. Ibid., p. 18.
41. *Survey of London*, Vol. XXVII, p. 250.
42. White, p. 23.
43. *Jewish Chronicle*, 8 Nov. 1901.
44. Ibid.
45. V. D. Lipman, 'The Development of London Jewry', in Levin (ed.), op. cit., p. 51.
46. Levin, 'Changing Pattern', p. 59.
47. White, op. cit., p. 31.
48. Conner and Critchley, op. cit., pp. 37, 50.
49. Department of the Environment, *Statutory List of Buildings of Special Architectural or Historic Interest* (Tower Hamlets), 1973, 48th Amendment, July 1989. On the listing of synagogues see Kadish, Introduction, above, and Barson and Kadish in T. Kushner (ed.), *The Jewish Heritage in British History* (London, 1992).
50. English Heritage, London Division Historian's Report to the London Advisory Committee, July 1989.
51. Planning (Listed Buildings and Conservation Areas) Act, 1990.
52. General Development Order, 1988.
53. L. M. Millar, *A History of the Tenement Dwellings Co. Ltd. and the East End Dwellings Co. Ltd*, MS, undated, Tower Hamlets Local History Library.
54. General Development Order, 1988.

9

'ALL MANNER OF WORKMANSHIP':
Interior Decoration in British Synagogues

EDWARD JAMILLY

Until the age of emancipation, the interiors of synagogues were always more important than their exteriors. Before the legality of land tenure by Jews was established, services were usually held in private houses, in a room adapted and furnished for the purpose. Sometimes converted outhouses were used, more than one elevation rarely showing behind the buildings to which they were attached. Purpose-designed places of worship for Jews, like those for Christian Nonconformists, were often hidden up alleys and behind bland façades to protect them from mobs during riots against dissenters. Little attention was paid to external appearance but the inside could be highly decorative. This essay must necessarily be selective, and concentrates on existing synagogues that exemplify the changes that have taken place in interior design.

BEVIS MARKS

The earliest synagogue extant is also the most important relic in the United Kingdom and the only Grade I listed building. Anyone who has sat in Bevis Marks Synagogue, opened in 1701, cannot but have found it powerfully evocative of 'those ancient Hebrew fathers' who came from Holland (see Figures 4.4, 5.1). Plain glass floods the square, brick-built interior with light, and, when candles are lit in the old brass candelabra donated by the parent synagogue of Amsterdam, the dark woodwork of the bench seating and wainscotting, the barley-sugar balusters and swept handrailing seem to shine as much as the marbled columns holding up the galleries and the pediment of the Ark.

The interior has been likened to a Wren city church, modified by the Puritan tradition; hence the flat ceiling and absence of rich ornamentation. How fortunate that the decorative scheme commissioned from the parish surveyor during the nineteenth century was not applied.

Bevis Marks has been extensively described by the Royal Commission on Historic Monuments[1] and needs little further comment except to emphasize the importance of its woodwork. Like its predecessor, the synagogue in Creechurch Lane,[2] the building was the creation of carpenters: Henry Ramsay, who prepared the study model, and Joseph Avis, its Quaker master-builder, who also worked on St Bride's in Fleet

Street. The joinery has the sturdiness and pleasing slight irregularities that come from good plain work honestly put together by craftsmen working with their hands and the simple tools available during the reign of Queen Anne.

GEORGIAN INTERIORS

The Georgian synagogue was built to a constant plan. However small the building, balconies were invariably provided for the separation of women. In the layout of the main floor, theological rules of orientation were always observed: entry was always at the west, even under the compulsion of a hidden approach, as at Falmouth; the Ark stayed on the east wall, with the *bima* facing it from a central position. Occasionally a lectern was introduced into the platform surrounding the Ark, more

9.1   London, the Great Synagogue; the *Aron Kodesh*. Cecil Roth, The Great Synagogue (*London, 1950*)

especially in the later years when the sermon increased in importance,[3] but there was no hint as yet of the combination of *bima* and Ark platform that came with the Reform movement and affected many Orthodox synagogues.

Of the standard equipment of the synagogue, high gallery fronts were most often a matter for comment. Lattices were made in a variety of materials – wood, brass, cast or wrought iron – and usually they were later reduced in height. Seating consisted of hard wooden straight-backed benches with scrolled arm rests; lockers were normally fitted beneath the seat, to take prayerbooks. An uncomfortable oddity in the Hambro Synagogue and at Exeter and Plymouth was the provision of tilting bookrests at the back as well as the front of a place; intended for use when standing, they lodged in the middle of a sitter's back!

In front of the *bima* a private pew was usually provided for the wardens of the synagogue and this, like the dais to the Ark, was fitted with railings and low gates of similar design to the balcony fronts.

Where classical detail was reproduced in wood, the use of the Orders varied considerably: Tuscan and a flattened Doric, almost Egyptian in character, prevailed in the smaller buildings, set against plain plastered walls; Ionic was favoured in the bigger synagogues, particularly those designed by architects.

Candelabra, massive and elaborate, are constantly mentioned in contemporary descriptions. The numbers specified must have been closely spaced for quite small interiors to accommodate them. This, one would imagine, would have given an oriental feeling to the synagogue. However, to dispel any doubts about the true aspirations of British Jews, a practical demonstration of loyalty that started about the time of the French Revolutionary Wars was the painting upon board or canvas of the prayer for the Royal Family as recited during the service; this was carefully lettered and fixed to the wall near the entrance.

The Georgian Ark

The Ark, the focal point of a synagogue, occupying the same position as the altarpiece of a church and architecturally fulfilling much the same role, deserves further comment. The synagogue Ark originated in the Biblical *Aron* 'box' or Ark of the Testament – housing the *Lukhot* (Tablets), which was carried about, slung on pole handles, by the nomad tribes of Israel and set up under the 'Tent of Meeting' in the Wilderness. The Ark in the Georgian synagogue had not yet become integrated into the structure of the building, as it now usually is, by recession into a built-in cupboard. It was still essentially a piece of furniture, an *almira* or wardrobe set against a straight east wall. Even in the earlier synagogues of Amsterdam and Bevis Marks, the Arks are quite unrelated to the building, looking rather like the reredos of a church. James Spiller's 1790 rebuilding of Dance's Great Synagogue in London[4] put the Ark into an apse with a coffered ceiling, but this was not the usual arrangement and the Decalogue is unhappily placed in the void above the Ark (see Figures 4.13, 9.1).

In smaller synagogues, this simple box, needing only to be about five feet square in elevation and deep enough to take half a dozen scrolls comfortably, was normally raised some three feet off the floor and very handsomely encased. Approached by two or three steps, surrounded by a low balustrade and gates, fitted with a pair of panelled doors (usually hinged but later converted to slide), set between columns mounted on plinths and carrying a classical entablature, surmounted by the Tablets of the Law and flanked by flambeaux or urns, a crown and orb or other heraldic device at its summit, the whole composition rose to within a few feet of the ceiling, filling and dominating the end wall.

Form and richness of detail varied according to the means available. Columns were here attached and there free-standing, single or twin, but however simple the use of Orders elsewhere in the synagogue, for the Ark it seems the choice was always the Corinthian cap, the fluted and gilded shafts. The Mosaic tablets were set upon a cartouche, or borne aloft on a scroll of leaves; the celestial crown was either painted on the tablets themselves or carved in the round and set regally at the apex.

Sometimes the woodwork was of polished mahogany with the projections gilded; in other cases this classic finish gave way to a less restrained folk-art treatment of marbling and painting in a riot of colour, using Venetian red, indigo, gamboge or raw sienna, olive green, cream and gold. Broken pediments, wreaths, swags, volutes and naturalistic leaf-carving contributed further to the elaborate, almost theatrical effect. The plainness of most provincial synagogues emphasized the care lavished upon the Ark front. More typical of Germany and the Low Countries in their Baroque effect than of Renaissance England, where the nearest equivalents are a few contemporary church monuments, the first Ark fronts were undoubtedly taken from foreign models and were thereafter copied in smaller synagogues.

It is likely that travelling joiners were responsible for several Arks in the same region; the similarity between Exeter (built 1763/64; see Figure 9.2) and Plymouth (built 1762) is strongly suggestive of that. It is interesting to note how the later example has been simplified and reduced in scale – perhaps too much, for the urns are puny – to suit a smaller synagogue and the purse of a less numerous congregation. The Portsmouth Ark is a more refined piece, carved in solid mahogany, almost certainly by a local craftsman of repute. It cost £200[5] in 1780, only £100 less than the complete chapel bought by the Jews of Dublin in 1785. The tablet bearing the Ten Commandments was taken from an earlier synagogue – a not uncommon practice which may mean that a good many movable objects such as benches, candlesticks and certainly silver are of earlier date than the buildings in which they were incorporated.

The names of those who made the Georgian Ark fronts are unknown, but they were almost certainly not Jewish. The apprenticeship system among craftsmen, the use of pattern books, the appreciation of classical detail by joiners in the eighteenth century and their inventiveness explain how these men were able to interpret alien requirements in a manner not altogether un-English and, despite obvious differences in origin, make these Ark fronts recognizable as part of the continuing tradition of wood carving exemplified by the altar fronts of such Wren City churches as St Mary Abchurch.

Whereas carved detail in other types of buildings often becomes coarser and less plentiful as surfaces recede in perspective from eye level, richness was evenly spread over the Ark front and, if anything, tended to become more elaborate towards the top. A possible explanation lies in the traditional arrangement of the synagogue: the high balcony fronts used for the screening of women cut off their view of the lower half of the synagogue and concentrated attention on the upper part of the Ark, whilst the central reading desk obstructed vision from the men's seating. Unlike the altar of a church, the Ark was consequently hardly ever seen full-height from the entrance or the majority of seats. Furthermore, as

9.2   Exeter Synagogue (1764); the interior in July 1992. *Alfred Dunitz*

Georgian synagogue interiors were generally plain and small, London synagogues excepted,[6] the detail of the Ark had to satisfy close scrutiny.

THE REGENCY AND AFTER

Architects trained in Regency manners brought a chaste Grecian simplicity[7] into the synagogues of Ramsgate (1833), Brighton, Devonshire Place (1837), both by David Mocatta, and Cheltenham (1839) by W. H. Knight. Even as late as 1847, the architect of the Egyptian revival synagogue at Canterbury, H. Marshall, resisted the lure of polychromatic temple ornamentation of the Nile Valley and designed an exceedingly plain setting of twin pylons to flank the Ark brought from an earlier synagogue.

Altogether grander were the synagogues built under Victoria.[8] The new reign was ushered in by a seminal interior, that of the New Synagogue in London (see Figure 9.3). The architect John Davies showed his drawing of the Ark at the Royal Academy in 1837, and the synagogue was completed during the following year. At the time it was one of the largest and became one of the most celebrated in London. After its opening there were, as well as extensive technical notices, a mention in *The Times* and an engraved plate to Shepherd's *London Interiors*, which achieved wide circulation. The *Illustrated London News* praised it as 'one of the most beautiful in the metropolis', this at a time when Bevis Marks, the Great, the Hambro and the Western existed – all distinguished synagogues by well-known architects or master-builders. W. H. Leeds, who could sometimes be a harsh critic, thought its interior 'quite eclipses every one of our modern churches'.

Davies's design is an important step in English synagogue development, marking the transition from reticent Georgian to more assertive Victorian architecture, and has a good deal of magnificence internally, if rather dull outside. From an architect of Nonconformist background who was a prolific chapel designer this might be thought surprising were it not for his training. Davies had spent more than three years abroad, most of the time in Italy, making careful drawings of Roman and Renaissance buildings. The New Synagogue's plan and neo-classical interior have parallels with elements of Venetian Palladianism or the basilican churches of Rome. The trabeated ceiling, the apsidal end with its coffered semi-dome, the galleries placed over the aisles, the clerestory lunettes, the ranges of Corinthian columns and their entablature, with semicircular-headed windows between, are redolent of Italy. Gone was the free-standing baroque Ark; the scrolls were now neatly recessed into the apse and curtained; stained glass appeared in the windows above and the candelabra have turned into gasoliers. Decorative cast iron was used for the balcony railings, though it was Mocatta, one of the early railway architects, whose Margaret Street Reform Synagogue (1849) was probably the first to use structural cast iron on a large scale; repetitive ornaments of *carton pierre* (*papier mâché* mounts), popularized during the Regency, are also known to have been used by Mocatta in that building.

9.3　London, the New Synagogue, Great
St Helen's, Bishopsgate (John Davies, 1838);
an engraving by H. Melville. *T. H. Shepherd,*
London Interiors (*London, 1841*)

The New Synagogue set a pattern for Italianate interiors of the next
quarter-century, among them Hull (1852), Birmingham, Singers Hill
(1856) and Manchester Great (1857; see Figure 2.4). Later still, the
Poltava Synagogue in Spital Square (1886; see Figure 5.9) was of 'heavy
Victorian classical design'.[9] By this time oriental revivals were taking
over, and synagogue design had entered its ornamental phase.

HIGH VICTORIAN

Prince's Road Synagogue in Liverpool (1874) and the New West End
Synagogue in London (1878) exemplify the oriental revival and must be
twinned for a second reason: they had the same architect. There was a
competition for Liverpool, won by the brothers George and William

9.4   London, the New West End
Synagogue, St Petersburgh Place,
Bayswater (G. Audsley and N. S. Joseph,
1878). The Builder (*17 July 1878*)

Audsley, authors of several treatises on historic ornament, illuminators of books, and architects of two Lancashire churches. They applied their researches very successfully and produced a much admired work of Moorish revival. It was perhaps significant that Owen Jones's details of the Alhambra, first published 30 years earlier, were reprinted in 1877, coinciding with this fashionable exemplar.

Within Prince's Road's red-brick Romanesque exterior (see Figures 1.7, 2.6), now more church-like than before owing to the loss of minarets deemed unsafe in 1960, the interior was splendidly refurbished during the 1970s in celebration of its centenary and after a fire had gutted the Ark. Rich in colouring, it is elaborately decorated with leaf and flower patterns, applied by stencilling both to the columns and to the Moorish arches bearing upon them. The caps and banding to the columns and leading mouldings of the Byzantine Ark are gilded. The Ark itself is elaborately ornamented, sparkling with running bands of gilded acanthus and anthemion, and crowned with a semi-dome and four smaller cupolas resting on arcaded drums.

After this success George Audsley was chosen to design the New West End Synagogue, St Petersburgh Place, Bayswater (see also Figure 5.2), in consultation with N. S. Joseph, who administered the contract and advised on liturgical aspects. In reporting to the United Synagogue on his design for rebuilding the Central Synagogue in 1867, Joseph had already dismissed neo-classical styles as pagan and Gothic as essentially Christian; he concluded that 'moresque' was the only suitable style. The coming together of the two men on a Moorish interior was obviously a meeting of minds, and the result of their architectural collaboration was even more successful than Prince's Road.

Passing through the dark red-brick and stone portal into the light hall, the visitor has little hint, other than the curious turreted clock-case on the left wall, of the exotic interior. The synagogue is a lofty treasure house of ornament, richly devised and finely executed. Once again, there are the stencilled geometric patterns and formalized foliage in tune with the ban on representational art, the polychromatic colouring and gilding, and the alabaster and marble banded Ark – here crowned with a central dome and six Assyrian turrets, made up in wood and plaster and painted. New were the carved panels of the Ark and column capitals surrounding the pulpit and *bima*, all different, the delicate arabesques in the spandrels above the arches and the inventiveness with which Hebrew characters are used as architectural ornament.

In addition to its utilitarian function, lettering has a long history of integration with buildings as an artistic element, and in that sense the synagogue design is derivative from Roman, Islamic and such Jewish sources as Toledo's El Transito synagogue. Yet there is a freshness and vitality in the way the characters curl and twist with the brass wreathing beneath the balcony front and the drama of their placing against the marble walls.

Among the craftsmen employed on the interior of St Petersburgh Place were Hart Son Peard and Co., art workers in metal, who made the gas light fittings. Decorative as well as functional, the eight polished pendants, painted and part gilded, cost £10 each; there were 24 large star

9.5   London, St Petersburgh Place; the
doorway. *Anthony Harris*

brackets, 16 smaller brackets with cut glasses and the sanctuary lamp (*ner tamid*). The polished brasswork for the pulpit was enriched with foliation. In all, their account came to just under £300. The stained-glass windows were designed and made by Westlake.[10] Charles Parnacott (successor to Harry Emanuel the silversmith) supplied a silver trowel with ornamental handle for laying the foundation stone. The pitch-pine seating cost £1,200 for the 800 places provided and was made by a Liverpool firm of joiners, Jones and Sons, doubtless on Audsley's recommendation. Teak and more exotic woods were used for doors and gallery fronts.

9.6 London, St Petersburgh Place; stained glass by Westlake. *Anthony Harris*

Save for the marbleized panels cladding its cast-iron columns, the installation of the pulpit, the extended facing of the end walls with alabaster and cipollino marble – in sympathy with the Ark – and the conversion from gas lighting to electroliers[11] during the 1890s, the New West End remains as originally conceived: a monument to High Victorian taste.

The interiors of the Byzantine-revival synagogues built to the designs of Davis and Emanuel in 1870 (Figure 9.7) and 1896 are notable more for their spatial effects than profuse ornamentation. The soaring arches of the West London Reform Synagogue, Upper Berkeley Street, and of the Spanish and Portuguese Synagogue in Lauderdale Road carry plain domes on pendentives. Upper Berkeley Street was not always plain:

9.7   London, West London Reform
Synagogue, Upper Berkeley Street
(Davis and Emanuel, 1870). Illustrated
London News (27 Jan. 1872)

before the reinstatement of fallen plaster after the Second World War,
the arched ceilings and central dome springing from the clusters of red
granite columns had been covered with geometric designs. Contemporary
stained glass based on fruit and flower designs added a grave dignity. The
cushion caps to columns, of white stone carved with incised foliage and
common to the Reform and Sephardi synagogues, derive from Ravenna;
the West London's metal grilles and gates to the Ark, its dome and use of
mosaic on the Ark platform are from an Istanbul mosque. In Maida Vale
the architects' Ark was replaced by a fretted timber Moorish pavilion
with a golden dome, a slightly discordant and theatrical note in an otherwise pure and restrained interior.

Mixing of styles was quite common. The grand Byzantine domed Ark
of Garnethill Synagogue, Glasgow, sits with its twin cupolas in a toplit
apse alongside Moorish galleries supported on Corinthian columns,
within an outwardly Romanesque stone building of 1879.[12]

THE TWENTIETH CENTURY

Although built in 1892, Hampstead Synagogue is in some ways the forerunner of those twentieth-century interiors that relied more on expression of structure than surface decoration for effect.

It was adventurous to roof a synagogue with an octagon, and the architect, Delissa Joseph, devised a vaulted roof with supporting ribs that curl like *art noveau* tendrils. When the interior was repainted in 1972 to a new colour-co-ordinated scheme designed by the present author, the colouring was changed to emphasize the vitality and beauty of the soaring forms. As in Audsley's synagogues daylight was filtered through deep tones of contemporary stained glass beneath the galleries, attributed to the architect's brother-in-law Solomon J. Solomon, RA. The strident modern glass filling upper windows is by Sochachewsky.

A series of revivals marked the inter-war years of this century, typically the timidly genteel pseudo-Georgian interiors that became vehicles for pale blue and white colouring, prevalent after the establishment of the State of Israel. Although the break with orientalism was overdue, these interiors contributed nothing to synagogue development and are best ignored.

More forward-looking were structural experiments such as Dollis Hill (1938; Figures 2.3, 10.5–7) by Sir Owen Williams, a *tour-de-force* in reinforced concrete, and, post-war, Tom Hancock's Carmel College Synagogue, largely glass-walled (1948). Their brutalism has proved too bald for some congregants to stomach, and the search for artistic content has led to the use of richer and warmer materials. Eric Lyons at Belsize Square in the 1950s and Eugene Rosenberg at Belfast in 1964 strove within limited budgets to achieve a pure but less spartan spiritual quality, while vast sums were spent elsewhere on quasi-assembly halls lined with boardroom finishes.

Although there has been little response in British synagogues to the more lyrical interiors[13] of North America – largely because synagogue bodies persist in erecting buildings with no special feeling instead of seeking for inspired architecture – a few encouraging signs can be seen in the use of modern designers for stained glass,[14] the weaving of Ark curtains and *Torah* mantles, the occasional commissioning of a sculpture and the renewed interest in Hebrew letter forms. Outstanding examples are the lovely pulpit fall[15] for High Holydays at Lauderdale Road and the richly embroidered curtain veiling the Ark at St Petersburgh Place,[16] both entirely modern in spirit, sympathetic to their Victorian settings and far removed from the trite blue velvet drapes bearing the names of their donors beneath an obligatory *Magen David*.

CEREMONIAL OBJECTS

The elaborate detailing of the Ark is the outward expression of delicate ornamentation and patient craftsmanship lavished upon the treasures of the synagogue housed within. The Scrolls of the Law, handwritten on vellum, run on to wooden rollers, wrapped in a brocade or embroidered

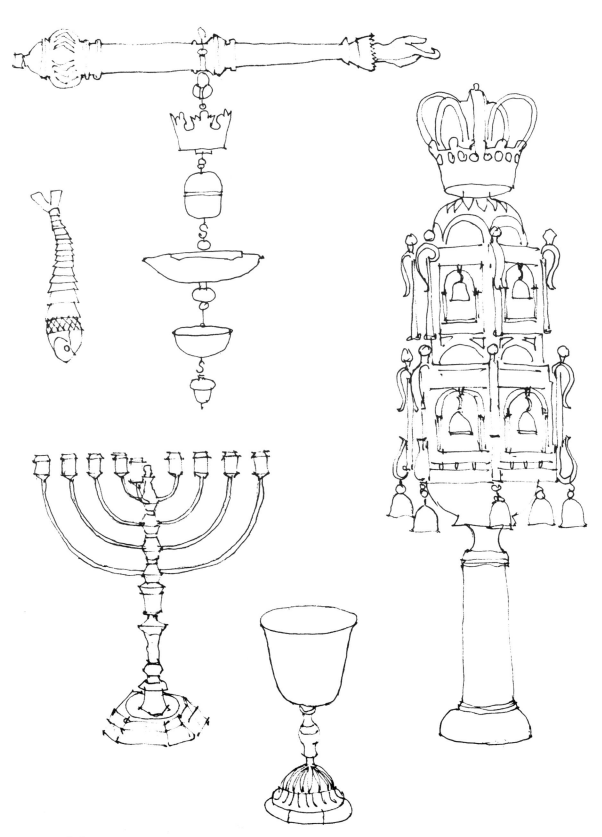

9.8   Ceremonial objects.

mantle hung with a crown and breast-plate and capped with a pair of silver finials, were always the chief possessions of a congregation. The finials, known as *rimonim* or bells, are by far the most interesting objects, because they possess forms derived from architecture.

Scrolls, being easily transportable, were often privately owned or donated to synagogues. The first *rimonim* brought to England were almost certainly Dutch, their campanile form based on the towers of baroque churches,[17] their intricate craftsmanship inherited perhaps from the Jewish silversmiths of Spain, who had excelled in filigree, enamel-inlay and *repoussé* work. The silversmith had inspired plateresque architecture; here was a case where he drew from baroque architectural sources.

From the late seventeenth century to the middle of the eighteenth the baroque turret from Holland was copied in new pairs of *rimonim* commissioned from English craftsmen, who were among the best workers of their time.[18] These miniature pagodas, hung with bells that tinkled as they were carried, were most popular, but the outline became bulbous at times; an open bowl form was also developed. The campanile form came to an end shortly after a set of finials in the 1760s for the New Synagogue was modelled on the tiered steeples of London's City churches.[19] Later pairs developed Adamesque urn-shaped bodies, obelisk forms or a series of graduated crowns.

Other ritual ornaments of the synagogue are of less direct architectural interest. The 'branches' often mentioned before the age of electricity were multi-branched candelabra set up by the Ark; they and the single candle-holders set around the *bima* – usually in the form of a classical column – were often massive.[20] Hanging sanctuary lamps (*nerot tamid*) of brass or silver – consisting of hook, crown, ball, lamp, drip pan and pendant finial – have been mistaken for church objects. That could not happen in the case of multi-lipped *chanukiot* (lamps), many examples of which are to be found in the Jewish Museum in London. Lavers and ewers, *Kiddush* cups (chalices), and almsplates were commissioned from silversmiths where they were not imported from Europe; but usually there is little to differentiate those made for the synagogue from similar items intended for the service of the church.

As synagogue silver, like church plate, was handed down from one building to the next, we are richer in ritual ornaments of the Georgian period, when silver design was at a peak, than of later periods. Few notable silver pieces seem to have been commissioned since, but among them must be counted one for the New West End Synagogue simulating its minaret and modern interpretations of traditional ornaments from living silversmiths.[21]

If the late seventeenth century was the heyday of the carpenter and the eighteenth of the plasterer and joiner, it was the great synagogue building activity of the nineteenth century that brought a wide range of materials to embellish interiors. The extended use of cast iron, wrought iron and brass, the introduction of *scagliola*, *carton pierre*, exotic woods and stained glass created the profuse ornamentation and high colouring of the Victorian era. Reacting against applied decoration, the twentieth-century interior has seen imaginative exploration of space, structure and mood but has also suffered the design poverty of revivalism.

NOTES

1. Royal Commission on Historical Monuments, *City of London*.
2. Enlarged in 1674 by William Pope, Warden and (from 1675) Master of the Carpenter's Company.
3. The first sermons in English were delivered in Seel Street Synagogue, Liverpool, after 1807.
4. See Epstein, this volume.
5. H. Slight, *A Chronicle History of Portsmouth* (1838).
6. The Adamesque interiors of Spiller's Great Synagogue (1790) and Robert Abraham's Western Synagogue (1827), both demolished, seated 750 and 400 respectively, whereas some provincial synagogues seated as few as 50.
7. Made less simple by subsequent alterations, such as marble cladding and reseating.
8. See E. Jamilly, 'Introduction to Victorian Synagogues', in *Victorian Society Annual* (1991), pp. 22–35.
9. *Survey of London*, Vol. XXVII (1957).
10. Except for the Rothschild window above the Ark, which is by the Hungarian Jewish artist Erwin Bossanyi (1935).
11. Some to the design of Sir Isidore Spielmann.
12. For which N. S. Joseph was consultant to the Scottish architect John McLeod.
13. See E. Jamilly, 'Modern Synagogue Architecture', *Jewish Chronicle*, 27 Sept. 1967, and 'The Architecture of the Contemporary Synagogue' in C. Roth (ed.), *Jewish Art* (Massada, Jerusalem, 1961), pp.756–95; 2nd edn (London, 1971), pp. 273–85.
14. Stained glass by John Clark (1992) at Queen's Park, Glasgow.
15. A subtly coloured Tree of Knowledge by Estelle Levy.
16. Designed by Alfred Cohen, this *parokhet* was embroidered by the Royal School of Needlework, see K. Salomon, *Jewish Ceremonial Embroidery* (London, 1988).
17. Cf. Hobbema's painting of the Herring-Packer Tower, Amsterdam, in the National Gallery, London. [In the Oriental and frequently too in the Sephardi tradition, the *Sifrei Torah* are housed in wooden caskets – Ed.]
18. The names of Aldridge and Co., Hester Bateman, Bolton and Humphreys, Edwards, Grundy, Sleath, Spackman and Wastell are among the marks on Georgian finials still extant. More intricate than the English silversmiths was a Jew of Dutch training, Abraham de Oliveyra; he executed an excellent series for the Hambro which was copied by others.
19. For example, Gibbs's baroque-influenced St Mary-le-Strand (1717).
20. In 1668 the Creechurch Lane Synagogue commissioned silver candelabra of 178½ ozs. each and two single holders of 534¾ ozs. To raise money for the newly-built synagogue at Bevis Marks, the same congregation sold a branched candelabra weighing 380 ozs. in 1703.
21. [Spice boxes were often wrought in architectural forms, as on the Continent. See *Migdalei Besamim* [*Towers of Spices*] (Israel Museum, Jerusalem, 1982, 2nd edn 1985) – Ed.]

10

ALTERNATIVE·USES FOR 'REDUNDANT' SYNAGOGUES

STEPHEN ROSENBERG

The oldest standing synagogue in Britain, Bevis Marks, built in 1701 on the model of the Amsterdam Synagogue of 1675, is fortunately still in use today as a synagogue, located in a back alley in the centre of the City of London, and remains the focus of an active community.[1] However, many other synagogues built in the last 300 years have been destroyed. The earliest structures usually stood near the historic centre of the town, where the first Jews lived and gathered for prayer. As the town expanded and residents moved to the suburbs, so the Jews also moved out and took their requirements for a synagogue with them. The old synagogue, now taking up a valuable city-centre site, was sold off to pay for a new one in the suburbs; the original building was demolished and the site redeveloped.

Today we are witnessing the same phenomenon in the suburbs. The second wave of synagogues, built in the inner suburbs, are losing their congregations as younger Jews are moving to the outer suburbs for cheaper and greener housing, building new synagogues as they go. This trend is leaving the inner synagogues, those of their parents, without a viable future. In many cases they struggle on with an ageing congregation, loath to give up their accustomed spiritual home. There will come a time, however, when such synagogues have to close. The stark question then arises: should one demolish the original structure and build something else or should one preserve the old building and adapt it for another use?

Where the synagogue building is listed as of architectural or historical interest, this choice may not apply, and consent to demolish will be refused by the local planning authority. 'Listed buildings' require special permission for any alteration work, and consent to demolish will be given only in the most pressing circumstances. A similar situation applies if a synagogue is sited in a Conservation Area, an area of development considered to be of especial aesthetic merit.[2] Although the individual buildings in such an area are not as strictly subject to preservation as listed buildings, special consent has to be sought before demolition is permitted. Thus a synagogue in a Conservation Area, although not of sufficient quality to be listed in itself, may be deemed essential to the character of the neighbourhood so that permission to demolish would be withheld. Even outside a Conservation Area, the synagogue may be of some merit in itself and the local non-Jewish community may want to see the building retained for some other use, rather than have it destroyed. Most purpose-built synagogues are at least distinctive in form and solidly built of good materials and workmanship. In their time, they were carefully constructed and often contain ornamental features, such as stained-glass windows and carvings, not found on other building types except churches. To members of the Jewish community, especially those whose synagogue it was, the building itself will also have a certain sentimental value.

It will often happen that a synagogue goes out of use just at a time when its style of building is going out of fashion. The layman as well as the professional may then consider it quite suitable for demolition. But we should beware of the fickle changes in architectural fashion. Whereas some 50 years ago Victorian styles were out of favour and many examples from that period were pulled down, we now regret the loss both of fine buildings and of the more modest ones which were so extensively swept away to make way for the 'new order'. It will be so again, and among the buildings of the 1950s and 1960s which we now despise, no doubt the better ones will be valued by the next generation as good examples of their style and period.

Although it is not always possible or even desirable to preserve buildings just for their own sake, with synagogues there is a case to be made for retaining examples of a building type that is rare and of religious significance. Their interest will increase with age, and a representative sample of such buildings will be of immense importance to the heritage of the host country. Can, therefore, synagogues be put to a new use? Of course, there are both desirable and undesirable uses.

The biggest physical problem with converting a conventional purpose-built Orthodox synagogue is that it will have a ladies' gallery overlooking the main body of the prayer hall, to accommodate the women seated apart from the men. New uses for a building with such a gallery are difficult to find, but there is scope. A more fundamental complication is that, in theory at least, the *Halakha* (Jewish law) proscribes the conversion of a permanent synagogue, serving a large congregation, to another use. A temporary synagogue, however, may be converted. Nowadays, therefore, when a new synagogue is planned it is constructed on the express condition, contained in the deeds, that it is being built for a limited period only. This clause enables the owners to sell the building and the site for other functions, excluding only its use for unsuitable purposes or for purposes of idolatrous worship.[3] However, its adoption by other monotheistic religions (that is, for use as a church or a mosque) is not ruled out. The main proviso is that the proceeds of the sale should be devoted to Jewish religious purposes and, ideally, that the money should be used to establish other religious or educational institutions.

When a synagogue is closed it is necessary to remove artifacts and objects of special religious significance such as the *Aron Kodesh*, the pews, and rabbinic seats and stained-glass windows, which can often be reused in other or new synagogues. There is no such procedure as the 'deconsecration' of a synagogue, but when all objects of religious significance have been removed then it automatically loses its religious status.[4] On the whole, therefore, *Halakha* does not forbid the change of use of a synagogue provided that the alternative use is a reasonable one.

Undesirable uses might include warehouses, garages and factories. I have come across all three. This kind of use is usually of a temporary nature, purely for the shelter provided by the shell of the building. Such barbarous economy is no guarantee of the preservation of the fabric of the building or of its distinctive features. In the East End of London some disused synagogues have been used as tailoring workshops, and the New Synagogue in Cheetham Hill Road, Manchester, built in an ornate brick style in 1889, is now a lampshade factory. The impressive original doorway, surmounted by a deep arch and decorative fanlight incorporating a *Magen David* window, remains in place. Attached to it, unfortunately, is the sign 'Goods at rear'.[5]

Synagogues have also been converted to more exotic uses, though the writer knows of none such in this country. In South Africa, the Old Synagogue in Pretoria, which was built in 1897, closed some 50 years later when the Jewish community had moved to the suburbs. In 1958 it was taken over and converted by the Public Works Department into a Supreme Court, and it was used for a series of treason trials, including the notorious trial of the black activist Steve Biko. A courthouse needs space for visitors and relatives to attend the trial, and the presence of the ladies' gallery in a synagogue would render it suitable for such a purpose. The original building was designed by the architects Beardwood and Ibler in a neo-Byzantine style, with polychromatic facings. Unfortunately the exterior is now – presumably since the conversion – covered in heavy cream paint.[6]

In Russia most synagogues were closed down after the Communist Revolution of 1917, but not all were demolished. In Kiev the large Brodsky Synagogue was converted to use as a puppet theatre. Again, the existence of the ladies' gallery made it suitable for accommodating an audience. It is now hoped that the building will be returned to the Jewish community and restored to its original function as a synagogue.[7]

If a synagogue cannot be preserved as such, the best alternative is to retain part of the building or site as a smaller synagogue for the benefit of the Jewish community remaining in the neighbourhood. Nevertheless, it is often difficult to reduce the size of the synagogue because of the existence of the ladies' gallery; normal practice is to close the gallery and bring the women downstairs to sit in pews behind those of the men. This reduces the quantity of seating but leaves the synagogue with as large a volume of space as before, serving a smaller congregation. The sense of intimacy is lost and there is no saving in heating and lighting costs.

A more inspired solution has been found at the synagogue in Salisbury Road, Edinburgh. The original building was opened in 1932 and was laid out on the conventional plan, with a ladies' gallery at the upper level. The synagogue itself was a simple rectangle, with the *Aron* at the east end and the *bima* in the centre. It could seat in all a congregation of 1,000 men and women. The architect was James Millar, FRIBA.[8] By the 1970s the community had declined in numbers and needed a synagogue less than half the size of the original. The solution found was to raise the whole synagogue to the level of the ladies' gallery and use the space below as the communal hall. In that way the area of seating was reduced by one-half, the volume was reduced by an equal proportion, and the synagogue committee was able to sell off the separate building that had served before as the community hall, thus releasing substantial funds.[9]

10.1   Edinburgh Synagogue; section through building before alterations. *Illustrations for this chapter supplied by Stephen Rosenberg*

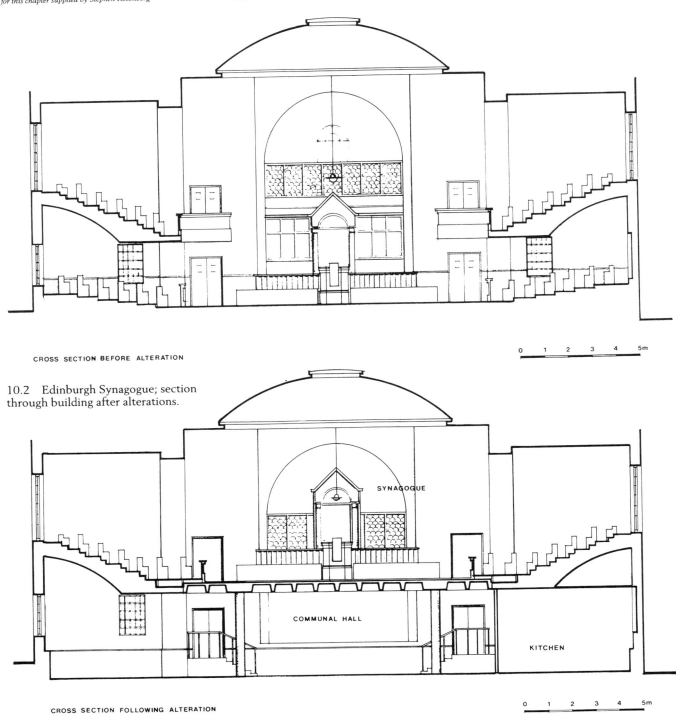

CROSS SECTION BEFORE ALTERATION

0   1   2   3   4   5m

10.2   Edinburgh Synagogue; section through building after alterations.

SYNAGOGUE

COMMUNAL HALL

KITCHEN

CROSS SECTION FOLLOWING ALTERATION

0   1   2   3   4   5m

10.3 Manchester Spanish and Portuguese Synagogue; the interior after conversion into the Manchester Jewish Museum.

A cross-section of the original building and the conversion are shown in Figures 10.1 and 10.2, which are based on the architect's drawings. The scheme was completed in 1981 and the architect was Michael Henderson of Dick Peddie and McKay.

Of desirable changes of use, the most obvious one is a museum, particularly a museum of Jewish interest. There are too many redundant synagogues for them all to be turned into viable museums, but a successful project has been carried out at the Spanish and Portuguese synagogue in Manchester (Figure 10.3). The original building was constructed in 1874 to the designs of a Jewish architect, Edward Salomons, presumably a member of the Sephardi community it was to serve. The synagogue was built in Cheetham Hill Road, north Manchester, which was the centre of a thriving community of Ashkenazi as well as Sephardi Jews for nearly 100 years. Of the many synagogues in the area, the Spanish and Portuguese was among the last to close; the final service was held in 1981. Fortunately, unlike many of its companions (especially the Manchester Great Synagogue), it was not left to become derelict and vandalized; through the energy and dedication of non-Jewish historian Bill Williams, it was purchased by a private trust and converted into the Manchester Jewish Museum in the same year.[10]

The building was restored over the following decade and clearly it is the structure itself that serves as the chief exhibit of the Museum. It has a high pitched roof with an ornate classical pillared *Aron* at the east end, surmounted by a circular stained-glass fanlight, depicting the seven-branched Temple candelabrum and the Hebrew name of God. The whole assembly is spanned by a pointed and decorated Ottoman arch springing from a pair of bracketed Ionic columns at each side. The overall effect is that of a high Victorian interior, superbly restored.

Typical of the period, and typical throughout Europe, the synagogue was neither Gothic nor classical, as either style would smack too much of a Christian or pagan origin, but was based on an eastern model, which was considered to be more neutral from a religious point of view. Here, in particular, the architect chose to introduce ogee arches and decorative ribbing typical of Moorish architecture. The exterior is in a similar but more restrained style described by the architect as 'Saracenic', presumably harking back to the close relationship between the Spanish Jews and their Moslem neighbours in medieval Iberia.

The Museum has preserved the layout of the ground floor – the men's seating, the *bima* and the *Aron* – but in the ladies' gallery the pews have been removed to provide level space for temporary exhibitions. The restoration of the building with its fine period detail amply justifies its retention as a museum and a monument to the history and vitality of Manchester Jewry.

Another desirable conversion has been the use of the Brondesbury (United) Synagogue (F. W. Marks, 1905) as a school hall. Situated in Chevening Road, NW6, the synagogue was built in the early years of this century to serve a Jewish population that was settling in this inner London suburb. It remained in use for nearly 70 years, although extensively damaged by fire in 1965. The synagogue was rebuilt after the fire, the cost being covered by insurance. But within a few years it was no longer serving a viable congregation, as most of the surviving members had moved away to the outer suburbs.[11] In 1974 the synagogue closed and the building was sold to the adjoining Kilburn and Brondesbury Comprehensive School. The school used it as a supplementary hall, which purpose it served fairly well until recently, when the school and the former synagogue were sold to the Al-Khoei Foundation Boys' School. The Foundation, part of the Islamia Trust, saw the potential of the building as a mosque and over a period of three years (1989–92) it was converted to Islamic religious practice.

The building, similar to the Manchester synagogue, had distinctive eastern features. The front elevation was dominated by a pair of copper-covered onion-shaped domes and the triple entrance doors were headed by decorative ogee arches (Figure 10.4). The synagogue was orientated due south-east which suits both its original purpose of facing the site of the Temple in Jerusalem and the Moslem requirement to face the *Kaaba* at Mecca.

In the conversion the interior has been cleared of all seating and ornament and decorated in white throughout. The pillared ladies' galleries

10.4 London, Brondesbury Synagogue after conversion into a mosque.

have been preserved for women to attend the services, and the gallery grille has been even more heavily screened than before, as required by Moslem custom. The recess of the original *Aron* has been changed to a *mihrab* (niche facing Mecca) and the centre hung with a large glittering chandelier. Externally, the Moorish features have been preserved and indeed enhanced by fitting coloured glass with Arabic lettering into the triple ogee arches over the entrance and into the large circular window in the gable above. The cost of the conversion work has been in the region of £2 million.[12]

In architectural terms, the preservation of Brondesbury Synagogue is to be welcomed, particularly as it is a rare example of its kind from the Edwardian period. The building is not on the statutory schedule of listed buildings as described above, so it is not protected by government regulations, but in 1977 it was given local listing by the London Borough of Brent as a building worthy of preservation. Clearly, the local planning authority wished to see it retained intact as far as possible. The synagogue is also situated in the Queens Park Conservation Area, so that any attempt to demolish it would have been resisted by both national and local government agencies. Unfortunately, now that the building has been converted to a mosque, there is no indication that it was originally erected as a synagogue.

Another conversion to a school hall is being effected at a later synagogue, less than two miles to the north of Brondesbury, at Dollis Hill (Parkside, NW10). The Dollis Hill (United) Synagogue (Figure 10.5) was designed in 1936 by Sir Owen Williams KBE. He was a self-made

10.5   London, Dollis Hill Synagogue – view from the south.

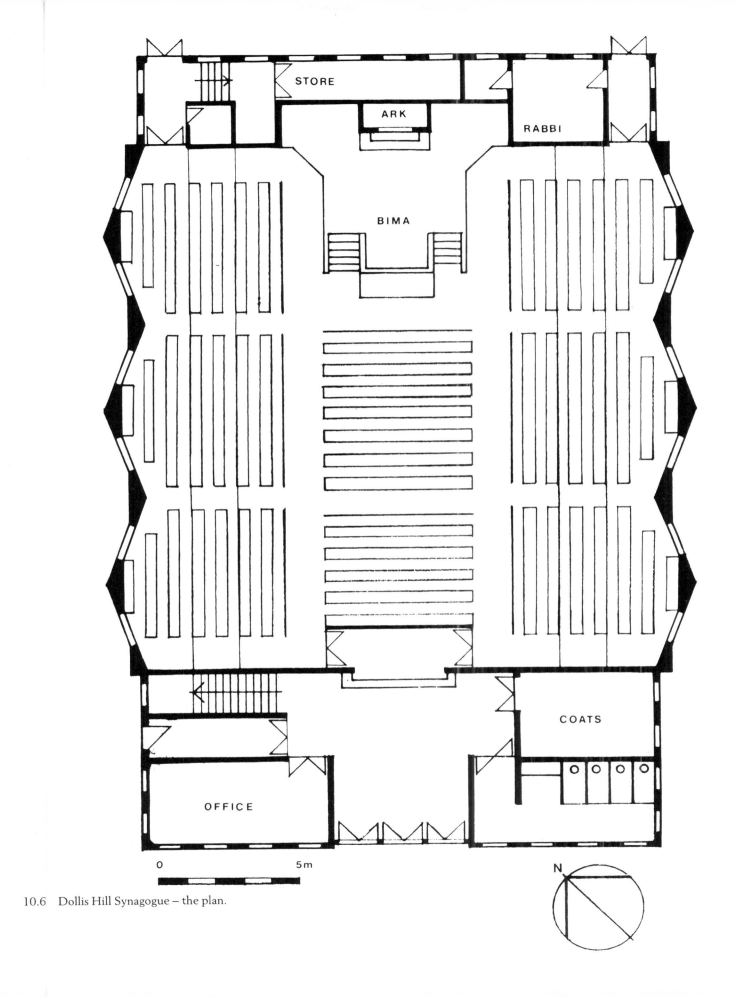

STORE

ARK

RABBI

BIMA

COATS

OFFICE

0   5m

N

10.6   Dollis Hill Synagogue – the plan.

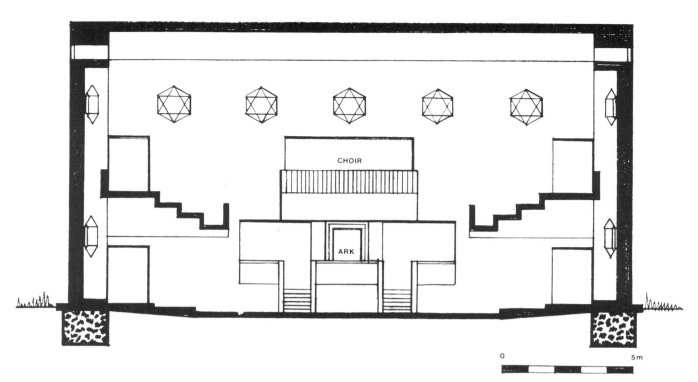

CHOIR

ARK

0   5 m

10.7   Dollis Hill Synagogue – a section.

architect who had a successful career as a civil and structural engineer, specializing in reinforced concrete work. Thanks to such ambitious projects as the Boots Factories in Nottingham and the Empire Pool, Wembley, his name was synonymous with buildings of originality in the 1930s. This relatively small synagogue at Dollis Hill was one of his more unusual commissions.[13]

However, the completed building was never to the liking of the community, as it was finished in raw concrete both internally and externally. The original intention had been to line the inside of the walls with cork insulation, but at the last minute this was omitted for the sake of economy. Nevertheless, the construction was original, ingenious and cost-effective. The main hall was covered by a saw-tooth roof of folded-plate reinforced concrete, and this shape extended down to form the walls at each side. The ladies' gallery was cantilevered from the joints or 'knuckles' of these walls (Figures 10.6 and 10.7). Window openings were integral with the structure and shaped as hexagons which could be glazed with a frame in the shape of the *Magen David*. Other subsidiary windows were U-shaped and glazed with a *menora* motif. For its unusual form and construction the synagogue was listed Grade II in March 1982 by the Department of the Environment, at the instigation of the local planning authority, the London Borough of Brent.

In recent years the Dollis Hill congregation has declined considerably, and the smaller number of worshippers can be adequately accommodated in the adjoining synagogue hall. The synagogue itself risks redundancy. The property would be hard to dispose of because it is listed, but an opportunity may arise to put it to new use in conjunction with a new school which was built on an adjoining site a few years ago. By a strange irony, that school has also become redundant, but it is possible that it will be sold by the local authority to a private Orthodox Jewish educational establishment. If this plan materializes, then the synagogue building could well be adapted as a fine school hall without too much expenditure on alteration works. The scheme depends, of course, on the same private educational establishment buying both the redundant school and the synagogue when it is offered for sale.

The synagogue, in its main length and width (20 by 20 metres) would qualify as a generous school hall, and the ladies' gallery could be maintained as additional seating for special occasions and performances. Parts of the *Aron* and *bima* (both in reinforced concrete!) would have to be removed, but the higher area of the *bima* could be adapted as a raised platform. It already has possible access from the rear, which makes it suitable as a stage, and the choir space over the *Aron* could become a useful minstrels' gallery. The building has a front wing with offices and toilets, and a rear section with a storage room, both of which can be easily adapted for use in a school hall. As the new hall could retain all the main features of the original building, the synagogue should be able to change its use without losing its original identity and without even compromising its status as a listed building. If the change occurs, it is to be hoped that a suitable commemorative tablet will record the building's first use as a synagogue.

The most radical change of use of a synagogue in Britain known to the writer is the conversion of Cricklewood (United) Synagogue to sheltered flatlets, which he himself planned in the years 1988–90. Cricklewood Synagogue was completed in 1931 to the designs of C. J. April, FRIBA, a successful commercial architect who also designed the synagogues in Raleigh Close, Hendon, and Thompson's Lane, Cambridge. Cricklewood is credited with being the first to be constructed without pillars to support the ladies' gallery. This helped to create a handsome column-free interior, which was emphasized by an ambitious vaulted ceiling. The resulting sense of grandeur was further heightened by the use of a continental brick, smaller in size than the normal English one (five courses to the foot instead of four). The front elevation in its gable window reflected the overall vault, thus making it probably the most successful element of the design. A small hall in matching style was added to the side of the synagogue, and a few years later it was completed with a first floor of classrooms above.

The synagogue was very popular in its early years but declined during the Second World War, when many families were evacuated. Membership picked up again after the war, but from the 1960s onwards numbers decreased rapidly, and by 1980 it was obvious that the reduced community of 300 members would not be able to keep the large synagogue, seating nearly 1,300 people, open for much longer.

A scheme was then proposed by the writer to convert the adjoining hall to a small synagogue and to retain the shell of the main building to house three floors of sheltered flats (Figure 10.10). Demand for such accommodation was high, and it was hoped that a Jewish housing association, with financial backing from the government's Housing Corporation, would be able to carry out and manage the project. The synagogue itself was not a listed building, but it stood in the Mapesbury

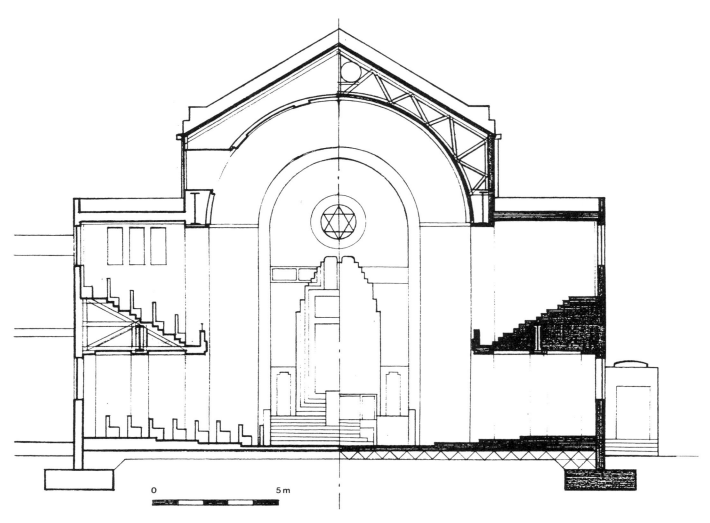

10.8 Cricklewood Synagogue; section through synagogue before alterations.

Conservation Area of the London Borough of Brent; the local residents and the Brent planning officers favoured the scheme because it would retain the shell and elevations of the original building. The project was also approved by the synagogue and its parent body, the United Synagogue Trust; but the Housing Corporation was not prepared to finance the housing side of the project. It was therefore sold to a private company which carried out the work (to its own detail design) and is running the sheltered flatlets under a Business Expansion Scheme, letting them out at a fair rent for the first five years. Proceeds from the sale of the original building went towards the conversion cost of the small synagogue (approximately £150,000), with a sum to cover the costs of running it in future years. The balance, which was substantial, accrued to the United Synagogue Trust, to become available for other community projects.

The key to the conversion of the original synagogue lay in the fact that its ample height could accommodate three floors of flatlets, with a fourth or penthouse floor in the upper section of the vaulted roof (Figures 10.8 and 10.9). In this way 32 flats could be provided within the synagogue shell. The insertion of these floors did however necessitate removal of the ladies' gallery. Being free of columns, it was on very heavy plated-steel beams, which had to be cut down into short lengths for ease of

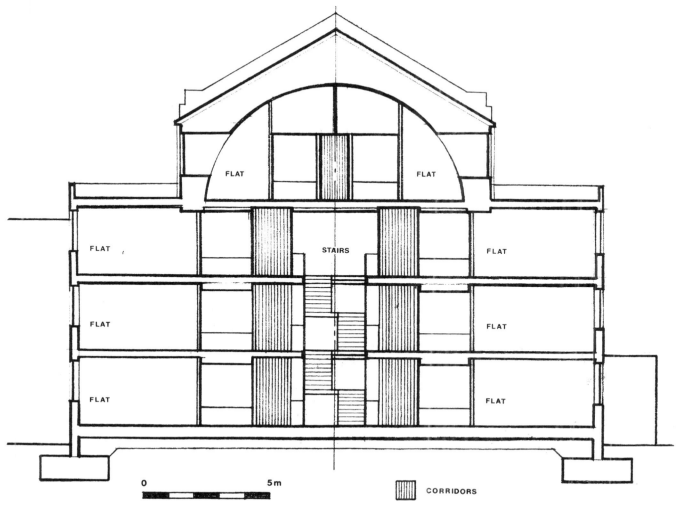

Labels within figure:
FLAT · FLAT
FLAT · STAIRS · FLAT
FLAT · FLAT
FLAT · FLAT

0   5m

▦ CORRIDORS

10.9   Cricklewood Synagogue; section after conversion to sheltered housing.

removal. In addition to the flatlets, public rooms and services were provided in the core of the building, and an additional four flats were created in the adjoining house belonging to the synagogue. The cost of the conversion work was estimated to be just over £1 million in 1989.[14]

To serve the existing community, a small synagogue was successfully created out of the original hall, providing seating for about 70 men and 50 women. Much of the furniture of the original synagogue was reused, and the fine timber-faced *Aron* was rebuilt to a smaller scale (Figure 10.11). Of the original 55 superb stained-glass windows by David Hillman, it was possible to build 28 into the fabric of the hall, whose window module matched that of the synagogue.[15] The rest of the hall and classroom complex was converted to use as a caretaker's flat, kitchen and communal offices.

One distinct advantage of the smaller synagogue in the hall was that it could be orientated directly to *Mizrakh* (south-east) to face Jerusalem. The original synagogue, which was at right-angles to the hall, faced north-east, or more towards St Petersburg than Jerusalem!

The scheme has enabled the Jewish community to continue on the site, albeit in an adjoining building. But, equally significantly, it has retained the shell and external appearance of the original synagogue and given it new life as a group of sheltered flatlets.

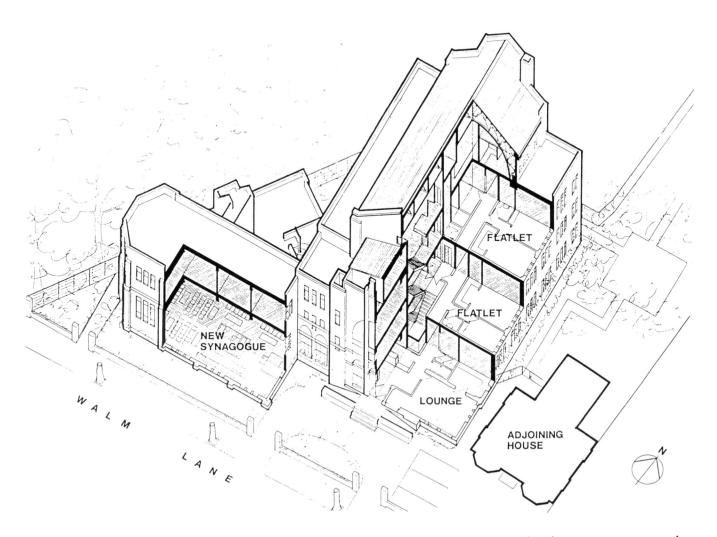

10.10 London, Cricklewood Synagogue; cut-away view of new flatlets and small synagogue.

Over the last hundred years most of the redundant synagogues in this country have been destroyed. A few have survived reduced in size or as religious buildings for other faiths. Some have been destroyed by wartime bombing, but the majority were lost through neglect and vandalism or demolished to make way for commercial and other development. Recently, a stronger policy of conservation has taken hold and synagogues are beginning to be appreciated as buildings of historical and sometimes architectural interest. It is therefore desirable to consider possible changes of function which will enable the original structure, or substantial portions of it, to remain and be put to good use. This chapter has described some successful adaptations and changes of use, supporting the opinion that there is now considerable scope for maintaining existing historic synagogue structures and finding alternative uses for them. It is an option that must be thoroughly investigated before demolition is contemplated.

10.11   Cricklewood Synagogue; view of
small synagogue.

NOTES

1. See R. D. Barnett and A. Levy, *The Bevis Marks Synagogue* (Society of Heshaim, London, 1970), and Epstein and Jamilly, this volume.
2. Listed Buildings and Conservation Areas are defined in the Planning (Listed Buildings and Conservation Areas) Act 1990 (HMSO, London, 1990). Listed buildings are classed Grade I, Grade II* or Grade II (in descending order of importance). See Susie Barson, 'English Heritage, Statutory Control and Jewish Buildings', in Tony Kushner (ed.), *The Jewish Heritage in British History* (London, 1992), pp. 166–70.
3. The actual prohibited purposes are 'a public or ritual bath, a tannery, a laundry or toilet', as quoted and discussed in the following *halakhic* sources (in Hebrew): Babylonian Talmud, *Tractate Megilla*, ff. 26A-28B; Maimonides, *Mishne Torah (Code of Law)*, Laws of Prayer Ch. 11, sections 14–20; and R. Joseph Caro, *Shulchan Aruch (Code of Law)*, Orach Chayim, Ch. 153, sections 1–9.
4. The *halakhic* sources say that a ruined synagogue still retains its holiness, but this seems to apply to one that has had to be abandoned owing to war or similar cause, and whose ownership has not been transferred to another use.
5. See Bill Williams, *Manchester Jewry, 1788–1988* (Manchester, 1988), p.53.
6. Personal communications with Linda Samuels, 18 Dec. 1992, and Human Research Council, Pretoria, 3 Feb. 1993.
7. *Jewish Chronicle*, 11 Dec. 1992.
8. *Edinburgh Hebrew Congregation*, commemorative pamphlet, 1932.
9. *Edinburgh Hebrew Congregation*, consecration of New Synagogue, commemorative pamphlet, 1981; this and the previous item were kindly lent to me by John Cosgrove, a former President of the Synagogue.
10. Bill Williams, op. cit., pp. 19–20 and 115: Tony Kushner, 'Looking Back with Nostalgia? The Jewish Museums of England', *Immigrants and Minorities*, Vol. 6, No. 2 (July 1987), pp. 200–11.
11. Personal communication, Rabbi A. Melinek, 13 Jan.1993.
12. Personal communication, Dr Mouhadi, School Principal, 17 Jan. 1993.
13. See David Cottam *et al.*, *Sir Owen Williams* (London, 1986), pp. 123–5.
14. Rosenberg and Gentle, *Feasibility Report to United Synagogue Trust* (Jan. 1986; rev. 1989).
15. [A further series of windows by Hillman have been relocated to Hendon United Synagogue, Raleigh Close, which was also designed by Epril – Ed.]

INDEX

Abraham ben Josele, 109
Abramsky, Dayan Yehezkel, 127
Acacia Charitable Trust, 10
Acculturation, 60, 64, 70, 122, 160,
    185, 189; 'English' surnames, 160
Acre, 50
Adam, Robert, 77
Adamson, Thomas, 120
Adath Yisrael, 84, 130, 131
Adler, Revd Michael, DSO, 158
Adler, Chief Rabbi Hermann, 124
Adler, Chief Rabbi Nathan, 109–11,
    114; 1845 survey, 111, 135, 144
Agudat Yisrael, British, 132
Alex, Montague, 112
Alexander II, Tsar, 170
Alexander, Abraham, 163
Alhambra, 201
Altdorfer, Andreas, 34
America, religious outlook, 24
Amsterdam, 37, 54
Ancona, Hannah and Moses, 158, 163
Androcentrism, 105
Annual Register, 70
Anti-Demolition League, Bevis Marks,
    3, 85
Anti-Semitism, 171
Archa, 45
Archaeology, 34ff., 104
Architects, 22, 24, 31, 54, 78, 191; *see
    also*, Adamson, Thomas; Audsley,
    William and George; Baly, Price
    Prichard; Bayliss, Henry J.;
    Beardwood and Ibler (South Africa);
    Bird, Thomas; Black, Misha; Brodrick,
    Cuthbert; Chambers, Sir William;
    Collins, H. H.; Davies, John; Davis
    and Emanuel; Davis, Henry; Dance,
    George, Sr and Jr; de Castro, Angelo;
    Dick Peddie and McKay; Dowton and
    Hurst; Emanuel, Barrow; Epril, C. J.;
    Hancock, Tom; Harrison and
    Abramovitz; Harrison, Peter;
    Henderson, Michael; Hildebrand and
    Glicker; Hudson, John; Hunt
    Thompson Associates; Jacobs, B. S.;
    Johnson, Philip; Joseph, Delissa;
    Joseph, Ernest; Joseph, Morris;
    Joseph, Nathan S. (and Pearson);
    Knight, W. H.; Lainson, Thomas;
    Lyons, Eric; Marks, F. W.; McLeod,
    John; Marshall, H.; Millar, James;
    Millard, John; Posen, Rabbi Meir;
    Preston Rubins Associates; Rosenberg,
    Eugene; Salomons, Edward; Schein,
    Ionel; Soane, Sir John; Solomon,
    Lewis; Spiller, James; Spiller, John;
    Stern, Robert A. M.; Stern Thom
    Fehler; Thomason, Yeoville; Thorpe,
    David; Tillott, James; Tillott and
    Chamberlain; Williams, Owen; Wren,
    Christopher; Wright, Frank Lloyd;
    Wyatt, James; Wylie, Thomas;
    Yamasaki, Minoru; Yorke Rosenberg
    Mardall
Architectural orders and styles:
    Adamesque, 72; Baroque, 196;
    Byzantine, 201, 203–4; Classical, 214;
    Corinthian, 67, 77; Doric, 195; Early
    English, 35; Egyptian Revival, 85,
    113, 195, 198; Gothic Revival, 14,
    201, 214; Graeco-Roman, 29, 197;
    Ionic, 195; Islamic, 29; Italian
    Renaissance, 178; Italianate, 178;
    Moorish, 33; neo-Classical, 14, 111,
    201; neo-Elizabethan, 169; neo-
    Gothic, 27; 'Oriental', 14, 15;
    Renaissance, 27, 29, 59; Romanesque,
    14, 27, 29, 178, 201, 204; 'Saracenic',
    214; Tuscan, 195; Victorian, 210;
    see also Columns
Architecture, as a social expression, 19,
    24, 27, 29, 167–91
Ark, Holy, 4, 5, 7, 9, 41, 43, 46, 47, 55,
    56, 58, 59, 66, 68, 76, 77, 78, 85, 93,
    198, 201, 203–5, 207, 210, 214, 216,
    221; Georgian, 195–7; Regency, 197
Art et Archeologie des Juifs en France, 35
Artisans' and Labourers' Dwellings
    Improvement Act (1875), 179
Ashkenazi, influx to England, 1
Ashkenazim, 21, 54, 59ff.
Assimilation, *see* Acculturation
Association of London Rabbis, 126
Audsley, William and George, 5, 9, 28,
    90, 200–1, 203, 205
Australia, Melbourne, 114
Avis, Joseph, 3, 19, 20, 58, 59, 87, 193
Avon, cemeteries in, 155, 158–60

Bakewell Hall, 106
Baltic Exchange, 3, 87
Baly, Price Prichard, 116
Barbados, 86

Barnett, Lionel, 86
Barnett, Piza, 125
Barnett, Richard, 86
Barnett, Revd Samuel, 117, 179, 181,
    185
Barson, Susie, 11, 223
Bath, 159
Baths, public, 116; Goulston Street, 117
Bayliss, Henry J., 2
Bayswater Jews' Free School, 175
Beardwood and Ibler (South Africa),
    211
Belisario, I. M., 21
Benas, Bertram, 96
Bendas, Revd H. M., 119
Benedict, Ellen (née Hart), 110
Benedict, Frances, 110
Benham, Mary, 47
Benjamin, Naphtali and Reichla, 161
Bensky, Mrs Levy, 108
Berlin, Revd Dr M., 158
Bet HaGedudim, Netanya, 164
Beth Din, London, 15, 84, 126
Beth HaMedrash Klal Chasodim, 126
Beth HaMedrash, London, 84, 114
Bethnal Green, 182
Bevis Marks, *see* Synagogues, London,
    Bevis Marks; Anti-Demolition League
Biala, 162
Birmingham, 109
Bird, Thomas, 8, 26, 27
Birthplace, recorded, 162
Black, Misha, 92, 203
Blake, William, 1
Blum, Barbara, 11
Board of Deputies of British Jews, 156,
    159
Board of Guardians, *see* Jewish Board of
    Guardians, London
Bobover Chasidim, 5, 88
Bodleian Bowl, 50
Bojanowo, Prussia, 162
Boot's Factories, Nottingham, 218
Bornstein, Aba, 127
Borough Jews' Free School, 175
Bossanyi, Erwin, 8, 208
Braude, Dr Jacob, 127
Bread, Meat and Coal Society, 169
Brent, London Borough of, 216, 218,
    220
Brighton, 96
Bristol, 47, 158, 163; cemeteries,

158–9; Jacob's Well, 49, 105–8; *mikveh* 42, 49; St Peter's Street, 42, 44
British Brothers' League, 171
Brodrick, Cuthbert, 121
Buckler, Samuel, 43
Builder, The, 173, 176, 178, 181, 199
Buildings, stone, 42ff.
Burial, 155
Burial Societies, 90, 168
Byzantine mosaics, 95

Camberwell, 187
Candelabra, 195, 204, 207, 208
Canterbury, 43, 44, 48
Cappidocias family, 110
Capitolum Judeorum, Colchester, 35, 46
Cardiff, 162
Carmel College, *see* Synagogues, Wallingford
Castello, Manuel, 86
Castilian friezes, 95
Cemeteries, 1, 12, 59, 88, 91, 95, 107, 155–65; Bath, Bradford Road, 159, 162; Bristol: Barton Road, 158, 162; Fishponds Road, 158; Rose Street, 158; Cheltenham, 159, 160, 162, 163; Exeter, 158, 162; Falmouth, 156; Gloucester: Organ's Passage, 159; Coney Hill, 159; Jerusalem, Mount of Olives, 155; London, Ashkenazi: Alderney Road, 155; Brady Street, 155; Bushey, 90; Edmonton, 90; Hackney, 155; Hoxton, 155; Willesden, 90; London, Sephardi: Mile End, Old and New, 87, 155; Penzance, 155–6, 162; Plymouth: Gifford Place, 158, 164; Plymouth Hoe, 156–7, 160, 162; Prague, 155; Torquay (Paignton), 160
Central British Fund (CBF), Allocations Committee, 132
Central Europe, 25, 54
Central Mikvaot Board (UOHC), 131
Centre for Metropolitan History, 10
Ceremonial objects, 5, 37, 163, 205–7; *see also Ner Tamid; Rimonim*
Chadwick, Edwin, *The Sanitary Condition of the Working Class*, 116
Chambers, Sir William, 64
Charity Commissioners, 85
Charles II, 56
Chasidim, 89, 93, 132
Chatham, 1
Chevrot, see Shtiebels
Chief Rabbinate, 15
Churches: All Hallows, London Wall, 65, 66, 76, 78; La Madeleine, Paris, 19; Penzance, 96; St Bride's, Fleet Street, London, 59, 193; St Giles, Bristol, 35; St James, Duke's Place, London, 66; St John's, Hackney, 72, 77, 78; St Mary Abchurch, 196; St Stephen's, London, 35

Churches converted to Synagogues, 92, 96, 210
Clifton, Bristol, 163
Cohen, Alfred, 173
Cohen family of London, 191
Cohen, Jacob Phillip, 162
Cohen, Levy Barent, 163
Cohen, Samuel, 163
Coin-hoards, 38, 39, 40
Colchester, 35, 36, 38, 39, 44, 46, 50; Foundry Yard, 47, 49; High Street, 40; Lion Walk, 47, 48; Pelham's Lane, 40; Stockwell Street, 50
Collins, H.H., 3, 26, 203
Cologne, medieval, 36, 38, 39, 49, 50
Columns, *see* Corinthian; Doric; Ionic; Tuscan
Colyer-Ferguson, Sir Thomas, 158, 163
Conferences: London (1991), 10, 99; New York (1990), 10, 17, 99; Southampton University (1990), 10, 99
Conservation, 12, 15, 25, 84, 90, 96; area status, 190, 209–10, 220; Article 4 Direction, 190; by alternative use, 96, 209ff.; of Jewish social architecture, 188–91; sentiment in, 30
Conservative Judaism, 92
Consuls, 162, 163
Conversion, gentiles to Judaism, 109, 160
Cookery, Jewish, 37ff.
Coppel, David Jacob, 162
Corinthian columns, 59, 66, 67, 68, 78, 196, 198, 204
Cork, 1
Cornwall, cemeteries in, 155–6; *see also* Falmouth; Penzance
Corporation of London, 61, 71
Correa, Rodolfo A., 163
Council for the Care of Churches, 10
Cracower, Mrs, 108
Cromwell, Oliver, 1, 54
Crusades, 36, 46

Da Costa family, 110
da Silva, Mendes, Sarah and Solomon, 162, 163
Daiches, Rabbi Israel Chayim, 121
Dance, George, Senior, 65ff., 76, 78, 195; Junior, 65, 66ff., 78
Danzig, 162
Dartmouth, 162
Davies, John, 6, 198
Davis and Emanuel, 4, 5, 11, 94, 178, 180–4, 187, 189–90, 203
Davis, Henry, 110
Dead Sea Scrolls, 35
de Castro, Angelo, 24
de Hooghe, Romeyne, 57
de Lange, Rabbi Dr N., 159
de Pass, A. A., 156
Decalogue, *see* 'Ten Commandments' tablets
Devon, cemeteries in, 156–8; Georgian woodwork in, 95

Dick Peddie and McKay, 213
Doric columns, 66, 68
Dowton and Hurst, 32
Duchess of Albemarle Street, *see* Levy, Judith Hart
Duke Street, 75
Dunitz, Alf, 8
'Dutch' Jews, *see* Ashkenazim
Dzikower Synagogue, 126, 127

East End Dwellings Company, 178, 179–84, 189–90
Eastern Europe, 22, 25, 115, 162
Edgware Mikveh Committee, 129
Edgware Mikveh Trust, 130
Education Act (1870) 178
Edward I, 34
Edward III, 106
Egyptian temple, 95
El Libro de Los Acuerdos, 108
Ellinson, Chaim, 130
Emanuel, Barrow, 180
Emanuel, Harry, 203
Emden, Abraham, 162
Emden, Woolf, 161
Emdon, Sergeant Ralph, 164
Endelman, Todd, *The Jews of Georgian England*, 109
English Heritage, 10, 11, 13, 87, 189
Engravers, *see* de Hooghe, Romeyne; Melville, H.; Pugin and Rowlandson; Veenhuysen, I.
Epril, C. J., 219
Exeter, 1, 158, 162
Expulsion, 35, 40
Ezekiel, Abraham, 158
Ezekiel, Rose, 158
Ezekiel, Solomon, 158

Falmouth, 1, 86, 96, 162
Federation of Synagogues, 84, 89–91, 98, 115, 126–7, 130, 136
Feminism, 105
Finsbury, London Borough of, 119
Fishman, Mrs, 125
Florence, 38
Four Per Cent Industrial Dwellings Company, 178, 184–7, 189–90
Fourth Lateran Council, 46
Fowey, Cornwall, 164
Frankfurt, Jewish Museum, 13, 15
Frank, Leopold, 125
Franks, Aaron, 64ff., 70
Franks, Abraham, 59, 63
Franks, Moses, 64
Franks, Naphtali, 64, 70
Franks, Phila, 64
Fredman, Nathan, 163
Freedman, Murray, 119

Gaon, Haham Solomon, 87
Gaster, Haham Moses, 86
George I, 60
George III, 64
Geniza, 46, 48

Gerlis, D. and L., *The Story of the Grimsby Jewish Community*, 121
Ghetto, 36, 60
Glasgow, 1, 115; Gorbals, 2, 115
Glasman, Judy, 12
Glastonbury, 158
Gloucester, 43, 155, 159–60, 162
Goldsmid, Abraham, 71, 164
Goldsmid, Benjamin, 71, 164
Goldsmith, Lipman, 162
Gompertz family, Exeter, 158
Gompertz, Barent, 163
Goodman, Harry A., 132
Gordon, Lord George, 109
Greenburgh, Dr Harry, 158
Guernsey, 162
Guidelines for Listing Synagogues, S. Barson, 11
Gurnier, Samuel, 162

Haliva, Mrs Emma, 108
Halpern, Rabbi Elchanan, 132
Hamburg, 54, 170
Hancock, Tom, 205
Harrison and Abramovitz, 24
Harrison, Peter, 63
Hart, Aaron, 60
Hart, Bilah, 64
Hart, James Jacob, 162
Hart, Joseph, 110
Hart, Joseph, 162
Hart, Moses, 60, 61, 64, 71
Hart Son Peard and Co., 201
Harwich, 162
Hebrew lettering, 201, 205
Henderson, Michael, 213
Henriques, Moses Quixano, 162, 163
Henry, Israel, 158
Hereford, 36, 43, 159, 162, 163
Heritage centres, 25, 30
Heritage Trust, 90
Herodium, 104
Hertz, Chief Rabbi J. H., 125
Hildebrand and Glicker, 130
Hildesheim, 162
Hill, J. W. F., 43
Hill, Octavia, 180
Hillman, David, 221
Historic Scotland, 8
Holland, 54, 57, 109
Holmes, Edward and Elizabeth, 65, 71
Holocaust, 16, 32
Homa, Dr Bernard, 96
Honiton, 158
Hool, Rabbi Maurice, 128
Hool's Pool, 128
Housing Corporation, 219
Hudson, John, 117
Hugo, Victor, 18, 19
Hunt Thompson Associates, 190
Hurwitz, Rabbi Tsvi Hirsch, 122
Huygens, Christian, 56
Hyamson, Albert, 86

ICOMOS, 10
Illustrated London News, 85, 198
Improved Industrial Dwellings Company, 179
Innes, Sarah, 109
Ionic columns, 56, 66, 76, 169, 214
IRA, 3, 5, 87
Ireland, 1, 10, 11; *see also* Cork; Limerick
Islamia Trust, 214
Isleworth, Surrey, 60, 64
Israel, State of, 25, 205

Jacob, Alex, 96
Jacob, Andrew George, 162
Jacob of Norwich (1270), 158
Jacob, Samuel, 156
Jacobovits, Chief Rabbi Immanuel, Lord, 135
Jacobovits, Chief Rebbetzin Amelie, Lady, 128
Jacobs, B. S., 8
Jacobs, Jacob, *Narrative of the Erection of the New Synagogue at Canterbury*, 113
Jacobs, Joseph, 105
Jacobs, Rabbi Dr Louis, 88, 130
Jacobs, Miriam and Nathan, Dartmouth, 162
Jamaica, 162, 163
Jerusalem, 1, 34
Jewish and East London Model Lodging House Association, 180
Jewish Association Reading Rooms, 172
Jewish Board of Guardians, London, 171, 180, 184, 191
Jewish Chronicle, 109, 114, 127, 128, 130, 134, 187
Jewish Directory of 1874, 172
Jewish Heritage Council, 10
Jewish Heritage in British History: Englishness and Jewishness, ed. T. Kushner, 12
Jewish Historical Society of England, 96; Leeds, 119
Jewish Memorial Council, London, 10, 85
Jewish Soup Kitchen, 11, 13
Jewish Working Men's Club, 172
Jewish World, 121
Jewish Year Book, 108, 115, 131
Jews' Free School, 84; Bell Lane, 168, 173–8, 188–9
Jews' Hospital, Mile End, London, 168, 169; Lower Norwood, 169, 175
Jew's House, 42ff.
Jews' Infant School, 84
Jews of Angevin England, J. Jacobs, 106
Jews' Temporary Shelter, 13, 170, 188
Joel, Helen Amelia, 162
Johnson, Philip, 24
Jonas, Jonas, 158

Jonas, Joseph, 109
Jones and Son, 203
Jones, Owen, 201
Joseph of Arimathea, 158
Joseph, B. L., 156
Joseph, Delissa, 5, 205
Joseph, Ernest, 7, 95
Joseph, Lyon, 160
Joseph, Morris, 8, 77, 194
Joseph, Nathan S., 5, 8, 117, 119, 184–8, 189, 201; and Pearson, 168, 174–5, 178
Judeans, 164
Judith Lady Montefiore College, Ramsgate, 110

Kaaba, Mecca, 215
Kalms Report, 5, 15, 88
Karlsruhe, 18
Kessler Foundation, 10, 15
Kilburn and Brondesbury Comprehensive School, 214
King's School, Canterbury, 85, 113
Knight, W. H., 198
Krausz, Ernest, 122
Krautheimer, Richard, 34
Kushner, Tony, 10

Lainson, Thomas, 8
La Mert, Samuel and Joseph, 113
Landau, Erwin, 130
Landau, Hermann, 117
Landau, Isaac, 127
Lazarus, Dayan H. M., 126
Lazarus, Solomon, 162
Leeds, 1, 115, 122; Leylands, 2, 115; *see also Mikveh*; Synagogues
Leeds, W. H., 198
Leon, Henrietta, 162
Leon, Jacob Judah (Templo), 56
Lesser St Augustine's, Bristol, 107
Lettering, *see* Hebrew lettering
Levason, Walter Emanuel, 163
Levy, Benjamin, 59
Levy, Elias, 71
Levy, Gershon and Rachel, 162
Levy, Judith Hart, 71
Levy, Revd Moses Horwitz, 162
Levy, Simon, 158
Liberal Judaism, 84
Limerick, 1
Lincoln Archaeological Trust, 42
Lincoln: Flaxengate, 38, 42; Jewry, 35; Jews' Court, 38, 41; Jew's House, 38, 41, 43, 97
Lipman, Vivian D., 13, 43, 96, 170, 171
Listed buildings, 11, 17, 89, 209; Grade I, 3, 88, 193; Grade II*, 5, 6; Grade II, 5, 92, 96, 178, 189, 218
Listing, 11, 86; 'Ecclesiastical exemption', 11, 12, 88
Lithman, John, 164
Liverpool, 96, 115
London Board of Mikvaot, 126–7

London Building Assize (1189), 45
London, East End of, 2, 13, 25, 30, 84, 90, 115, 126, 167, 170;
Mikvaot, 36, 37;
overcrowding, 179;
sanitation, 179;
social architecture: Brady Street Dwellings, 186, 189; Charlotte de Rothschild Buildings, 117, 185, 186, 189; Cressy House, 182, 184, 187; Dunstan Houses, 184; Katherine Buildings, 180, 189; Lolesworth Buildings, 182, 189; Merceron House, 190; Montfort House, 182; Nathaniel Dwellings, 187; Naverino Mansions, 187, 190, 191; Stafford House, 189; Stepney Green Dwellings, 187, 188;
streets: Alie, 173; Brady, 186; Brune, 173; Cartwright, 180, 181; Cressy Place, 182; Farringdon Road, 182; Fashion, 173; Flower and Dean, 179, 185, 188; Frying Pan Alley, 178; Globe Road, 184, 190; Gresham, 37, 42, 44; Hannibal Road, 182; 'Jewry', 36, 40ff.; Leadenhall Market, 37; Leman, 170, 173; Mansell, 170, 173; Milk, 37; 'Poor Jewry', 41; Stepney Green, 5; Thrawl, 185; Whitechapel Road, 171
London, North and North-West of, 90
London, Jewish Museum, 15
London, medieval, 43
London Museum of Jewish Life, 10
London Society for the Promotion of Christianity among the Jews, 171, 173
Lontschotz, 162
Lopian, Dayan Gershon, 129
Lords Cricket Ground, 92
Lowe, Edward, 112
Lubavitch Foundation, 133
Lublin, 162
Lyons, Eric, 23, 205
Lyons, Mayer, 113

Madeira, 163
Magen David, 161, 205
Mainz, 108
Manchester, 1, 10, 115, 162; Cheetham Hill, 2, 115; Red Bank, 2, 115; Jewish Museum, 8, 10, 15
Ma'on, 104
Mapesbury Conservation Area, 220
Margulies, Rabbi J. L., *see Mikveh*, London, Premiszlaner Rebbe
Marks, F. W., 214
Marriage, arranged, 64; facility for poor Jews, 75
Marshall, H., 113, 198
Masada, 104
Masorti Judaism, 84, 92, 130
Mayer, Werner, 8

McLeod, John, 8, 119
Mechitza, 46
Medieval Anglo-Jewry, 12, 34
Melville, H., 6
Menasseh ben Israel, 1, 54
Mendes da Silva, *see* da Silva, Mendes
Mérimée, Prosper, 19
Metcalfe, Richard, *The Rise . . . of Hydropathy in England . . .*, 116
Metropolitan Association, 182
Metropolitan Board of Works, 179, 180
Mezuza, 37
Mihrab, 216
Mikvaot, Directory of, 1656–1995, 146–53
Mikve Yisrael, 121
Mikveh, 1, 12, 13, 37, 38, 39, 42, 44, 46, 48, 101–35;
Mikveh, as a rite in: conjugal life (women), 101, 116, 134; conversion, 101, 109, 131; spiritual purification (men), 101
Mikveh, attendants, 108–10, 122, 124, 125, 131; salary, 108; construction of, 102; cost of attending, 110, 126; 'hidden' agenda, 105, 124; laws of, 101; location, 104; provision by municipal authority, 119, 121, 135; revival, 128–30; sea as a substitute, 112; water meters, 121
Mikveh for utensils, 101, 107: Adath Yisrael, Green Lanes, 131; Bushey, 129; Finchley, 129; Hendon, 129; Kingsbury, 129; Streatham, 129; Willesden, 129
Mikveh, medieval: Besalu, 104; Bristol (Jacob's Well), 105–8, 135; Carpentras, 104; Cologne, 104; England, 105–8; Friedberg, 104; London (Gresham Street), 105; Rouen, 104; Montpellier, 104; Oxford (St John the Baptist Hospital) 108; Prague (Pinkas Synagogue), 104; Speyer, 104; Tomar, 104; Worms, 104; York (Trinity Lane), 108
Mikveh, Nathan Adler's questionnaire, 111, 135, 144
Mikveh, towns with, or without:
Bath, 111;
Birmingham, 119, 123, 134, 135, 136;
Bournemouth, 123, 135;
Brighton, 123, 124, 130, 135;
Canterbury, 113, 136;
Cardiff, Wales Empire Pool, 123, 124, 130, 135;
Cheltenham, Montpellier Baths, 111;
Cleethorpes, 122;
Dover, 112;
Dublin, 135;
Exeter, 111;
Glasgow, 119, 134, 135;
Grimsby, 121;
Hull, 119, 135;

Jersey, 112;
Leeds: 119, 122, 135; Albert Grove, 119–23, 134, 136; Cookridge Street, 119; Etz Chaim, 123; Shomrei Hadas, 123;
Liverpool, 110, 134;
London: Adath Yisrael, Green Lanes (124–6), 131: Adath Yisrael, Queen Elizabeth's Walk, 132; Adath Yisrael, Shirehall Lane (10A), 131; Ashkenasy's (Rebbe Meshullam), Stanislaver Beth HaMedrash, Lordship Park, 132; Bayswater (St Germain's Terrace), 124; Bayswater (Westbourne Park Crescent), 115, 124, 125; Beth Shmuel, 171 Golders Green Road, 132; Camomile Street (12), 114; Cannon Street Road (131), 127; Cantor, Mrs, 9 Jewry Street, 114; Cohen, Mrs H., 114; Craven Walk, 72; Lingwood Road, 132; Cromwell House, Highgate (1638), 110; Dunk Street, 126, 127, 136; Edgware and District, 129; Exmouth Street, 115, 127; Gants Hill, 463 Cranbrook Road, 127; Great Synagogue, 136; Grove Lane (Lampard Grove) Beth HaMedrash, 127; Jacobs, Mrs, Mitre Square (1 and 2), 114, 124; Kingsbury Green, 128, 136; Lacey's, 116; Margaret Street, 132; London, East, 108, 109; London, South, 103; Manette Street (14), 115; North London Beth HaMedrash, Essex Road, 131, 132; Percy Street, 115; Premiszlaner Rebbe, 6 Minster Road, 126, 131; Raphael, Mr and Mrs, 114; Satmar, 62 Filey Avenue, 132; Sternberg Centre, 130, 136; Wimbledon, 133; Woolf, Mrs R., Sussex Place (8), 114;
Manchester: 123, 134; Great Synagogue, 126;
Newcastle, 111;
Plymouth, 135;
Reading, 136;
Westcliff, 135;
Yarmouth, 112
Millar, James, 211
Millard, John, 130
Minyan, 18, 89, 90
Mitre Court, Little Duke's Place, London, 74
Mocatta, David, 198
Mocatta, Frederic D., 117
Montagu, Sir Samuel (1st Lord Swaythling), 84, 172
Montefiore family, 191
Montefiore, Lady Judith, 110, 163
Montefiore, Sir Moses, 31, 88, 110, 163
Montefiore, Moses Vita, 163
Mordecai, Moses, 158

Morris, William, 19
Moses, David, 162
Moses, Marcus, 60
Moses, Moses, 162
Mosques, 96, 204, 215
Mudahy, Elimelech, 109
Munk, Rabbi Eli, 92
Museum of London, 42, 106
Museums, Jewish: 214; Amsterdam, 15;
    Frankfurt, 13, 15; London: Jewish
    Museum, 15, 86, 91, 98; London
    Museum of Jewish Life, 10;
    Manchester, 8, 10, 15, 27, 87, 213,
    214; New York (Orchard Street), 30;
    Prague, 15; Toledo, 15; Venice, 15
Music in the Synagogue, 70
Music Room, Great Synagogue, 69
Myer, Abraham and Sidney, 162
Myers, Selena, 162

Nathan, Aaron and Mary, 161
National Buildings Record, 85
National Council for Taharat
    HaMishpakha, 130, 132
National Heritage, Department of, 5,
    11, 12
National Monuments List, 135
National Monuments Record's Core
    Data Standard, 14
Nelson, Admiral Lord Horatio, 71
Ner Tamid, 15, 203, 207
New and Historical Survey of London, 66
New York, Lower East Side, 30
Nonconformity, 14, 27
Norfolk, 50
Norwich, 162; medieval, 36, 37, 43–5,
    50
Nyman, Myer (Private Michael Burns),
    164

Obadiah the Proselyte, 45
Odessa, 115
Olivestone, A. B., 127
Or Sameach, Rabbi Meir Simcha
    HaCohen of Dvinsk, 122
Ordnance Survey, 34
Oriental and General Baths Co., Leeds,
    119
Osterley Park, 77
Oxford, medieval, 36

Paris, Mrs Esther/Sarah, 108
Parma Academy, Italy, 66
Parnacott, Charles, 203
Parry, Hubert, 1
Peabody Trust, 179, 181
Penzance, 1, 97
Pevsner, Nikolaus, 95
Philanthropic Societies, Jewish, *see*
    Bread, Meat and Coal; Jews' Hospital,
    Mile End
Philanthropy, 30; *see also* London, East
    End of, social architecture;
    Conservation, of Jewish social
    architecture

Phillips, Stoker Harry, 164
Pinsky, Mrs, 122
Plymouth, 1, 156
Population estimates, 36
Portsea, 162
Posen, Rabbi Meir, 103, 129, 130, 133,
    134
Post Office London Directory (1853),
    108
Potter, Beatrice (Webb), 182
Pragnell, Hubert, 113
Prague, 18; Jewish Museum, 15
Preston Rubins Associates, 94
Progressive Judaism, 84
Pugin and Rowlandson, 76
Pulpit, 77, 194, 201, 204
Pulver, Revd Mr, 112

Queen of Richmond Green, *see* Levy,
    Judith Hart
Queens Park Conservation Area, 216

Rabbinowitz, Rabbi Dr Louis, 164
Ramsay, Henry, 193
Ramsgate, 87, 89; East Cliff Lodge,
    110
Rashi, 38
Rathaus, Cologne, 39
Ravenna, 204
Redundant Synagogues, 5, 6, 14, 89,
    209–22; Code of Practice, 11; other
    uses: churches/mosques, 30, 215;
    museums, 214
Reese, A., 159
Reform Judaism (RSGB), 84, 92, 124,
    130–1, 195; attitude to *Mikveh*, 130,
    136
Report on Public Baths . . ., 119
Reynolds, Joshua, 72
Rhineland, 12
Rimonim, 15, 99, 207
Rintel, Revd Moses, 114
Rise of Provincial Jewry, C. Roth, 105
Roehampton, 71
Romain, Rabbi Jonathan, 131
Rose, Julia, 110
Rosen, Rabbi Kopul, 127
Rosenau, Helen, 13, 35, 41, 77
Rosenberg, Eugene, 205
Ross, 159, 162
Roth, Cecil, 13, 34, 43, 46, 95, 99, 105,
    109
Rothschild, Sir Anthony de, 175
Rothschild family, 110, 111, 170, 191
Rothschild, Hannah and Nathan Mayer
    (1st Lord), 124, 163, 179, 184
Rothschild, Lionel de, 173
Rouen, 12; medieval, 36, 45, 50
Rowe, George, *Illustrated Cheltenham
    Guide*, 111, 112
Royal Academy, 198
Royal Commission on Alien
    Immigration, 117, 171
Royal Commission on Historial
    Monuments, 10, 25, 193

Royal Family, prayer for, 195
Rubbish-pits, 37
Ruskin, John, 19
Saarbruck, 162
Salomons, Edward, 8, 214
Sametband, Louis, 162
Samuel, Revd Jacob, 122
Samuel, Mrs Judith, 158
Samuel, Miriam, 162
Samuel, Wilfred, 86, 99
Sassoon, Sir Edward, 173
Sassover Rebbe (Rabbi Simcha Rubin),
    130, 132
Schein, Ionel, 24
Schewzick, Rabbi Benjamin, 117, 118
Schiff, Rabbi David Tevele, 70, 109
Schiller, Mrs Frieda (née Peretz), 122
Schonfeld, Rabbi Avigdor, 131
Schonfeld, Rabbi Dr Solomon, 131
Schools, Jewish, 88, 168; *see also*
    Bayswater Jews' Free School; Borough
    Jews' Free School; Jews' Free School;
    Sha'arei Tikva; Villareal; Stepney
    Jews' Free School; Westminster Jews'
    Free School
Scotland, 10, 11, 162
Scottish Jewish Archives Centre, 8
Seals, 37, 38
Selig, Aaron and Hannah, 156
Sephardi, almshouses, 87; influx to
    England, 1, 54; *Nuevo* cemetery, 87;
    preparatory school, 87
Sephardim, 19, 21, 60, 84, 86, 127, 163
Sha'arei Tikva (Gates of Hope) Sephardi
    School, 169, 175
Sheerness, 1
Shefshick's, *see* Schewzick, Rabbi
    Benjamin
Sheltered flats, 219
Shepherd's *London Interiors*, 198
Sherman, Abe, 123
Sherrenbeck, Mrs Sarah, 158
Shofar, 37
Shtiebels, 88, 91, 115
Singer, Rabbi Steven, 114
Sington, Fanny, 162
Smith, Mary and Esther, 164
Soane, Sir John, 72
Sochachewsky, 205
Solomon, Esther and Lazarus, 162
Solomon, Lewis, 168, 172, 173
Solomon, Sergeant Morris, RAAF, 164
Solomon, Moses, 162
Solomon, Solomon J., RA, 205
Soup Kitchen for the Jewish Poor, 168,
    172–3, 189
Southampton, 43, 162
Southsea, 162
Spanish and Portuguese Congregation,
    85–7; Records Committee, 86;
    Tercentenary Exhibition Committee,
    86
Spector, David, 96
Speyer, 49
Spiller, James, 21, 71, 72, 74, 78, 195

Spiller, John, 72, 74
Spitalfields, 182
Spitalfields Soup Society, 173
St Pancras, 182
Stained glass, 5, 12, 200–1, 204, 205, 208, 210, 221, 223
Stamford, 43
Starrs, 38
Stepney Green, 182; Conservation Area, 189
Stepney Jews' Free School, 11, 175, 178, 189
Stern, Robert A.M., 24
Stern Thom Fehler, 130
Stoke Newington, 187; Naverino development, 187, 190
Strahlberg, Mrs Hedwig, 131
Stroud, 159
Stroud, Dorothy, 65, 69
Sukenik, Eliezer, 35
Sunderland, 122
Survey of London, 1957, 175, 178, 186
Susser, Jacob, 158
Synagogues, 1, 12; care of, 96; construction of, 207; dedication of, 70; emotional impact, 25; interior decoration, 193–207; location of, 19, 36; materials used in the construction of, 207; orientation of, 194; redundant, *see* Redundant Synagogues; 'temporary', 210; wooden, 18
Synagogues: German, 24; Georgian, 2, 8, 84, 111, 194–8 (*see also* Synagogues, towns with, Exeter; Plymouth); Graeco-Roman, 35; Hanoverian, 84; North American, 205; Regency, 84, 198–9; Victorian, 6, 86, 198–204; Twentieth century, 205–6
Synagogues, medieval: Bristol, 45; Canterbury, 44, 45, 48; Colchester, 45; Cologne, 45–7; Hereford, 45; Lincoln, 43, 44; London, 43–5; Norwich, 44, 45; Nottingham, 45; Oxford, 37, 44, 45; Regensburg, 48; Rouen, 45; Winchester, 44; Worms, 46, 48
Synagogues, towns with, Amsterdam, 22, 195, 209; Grote Sjoel, 55, 56, 76, 78; Sephardi, 55, 57, 67; Spanish and Portuguese Great Synagogue, 3, 55, 87; Belfast, 23, 205; Berlin, 27; Birmingham: Singers Hill, 8, 10, 85, 136, 199; Bradford, 92, 130; Brighton: Devonshire Place, 198; Middle Street, 8; Bristol, 34; medieval, 35; Brno, 27; Bromley, 131; Budapest, 27; Cambridge (Thompson's Lane), 219;

Canterbury, 85, 95, 198; Cheltenham, 111, 160, 198; Colchester, medieval, 38; Cologne, 39; Dublin, 196; Adelaide Road, 135; Edinburgh (Salisbury Road), 211, 212; Exeter, 2, 8, 85, 96, 195, 196; Falmouth, 85; Glasgow: Commerce Street, 119; Garnethill, 8, 29, 119, 204; South Portland Street, 119; Hamburg, 27; Hull, 97, 199; Linnaeus Street, 8; Kiev (Brodsky), 211; Leeds: Belgrave Street, 119; Beth HaMedrash HaGadol, 121; Mariempoler, 122; United Hebrew Congregation, 122; Lincoln, 35; Liverpool, 85, 86; Hope Place, 28; Prince's Road, 8, 9, 28, 29, 199–201; Reform, 130; Livorno (Leghorn), 24; London: Adath Yisrael (Green Lanes), 131; (Hendon), 131; Barnsbury, 85; Bayswater (Harrow Road), 85, 88, 95; Bayswater (Maida Vale), 88; Belsize Square, 23, 205; Beth Shmuel (171 Golders Green Road), 132; Bevis Marks (Plough Yard and Creechurch Lane), 3, 5, 13, 19–21, 25, 57–9, 86, 87, 96, 98, 108, 193, 195, 198, 209; Borough New Synagogue (Wansey Street), 3, 85; Brondesbury (Chevening Road), 214, 215–16; Bryanston Street, 86; Burton Street, 92; Canonbury, 86; Central, 85, 88–9, 201; Coleman Street (medieval), 35; Creechurch Lane, 54, 55, 57; Cricklewood (Walm Lane), 219–23; Dollis Hill, 6, 23, 88, 205, 216–19; East London (Rectory Square), 4, 5, 6, 11, 22, 25, 85, 88, 189; Edgware Yeshurun, 129–30; Finchley (Kinloss Gardens), 32; Finchley (Masorti), 92; Golders Green, 86; Great (Duke's Place), 13, 15, 20, 54, 59ff., 84, 108, 110, 136, 194, 197; Great Garden Street (Greatorex Street), 91; Grove Lane (Lampard Grove), 132; Hambro, 60, 64, 78, 110, 114, 195, 198; Hampstead (Dennington Park Road), 5, 15, 205; Harrow, 86; Hendon (Raleigh Close), 219; Holland Park, 86; Kehillat Yaakov (Congregation of Jacob) (Commercial Road), 90; Lauderdale Road, 86, 87, 203, 204, 205; Liberal (St John's Wood Road), 92–4, 130; Machzike Hadath (Brick Lane/Fournier Street), 96–7; Maiden Lane, 85, 114; Marble

Arch, 88; Margaret Street, 92, 198; New (Egerton Road), 5–7, 10, 27, 88; New (Great St Helen's), 5, 6, 64, 78, 110, 114, 198–9, 207; New London, 92, 203, 204; New West End (St Petersburgh Place), 5, 15, 88–9, 199, 200–3, 205, 207; North West London Sephardish (Hager's), 132; North London Progressive (Amhurst Park), 92, 94; Old Montagu Street, 16; Philpot Street, 90; Princelet Street, 25, 90; St John's Wood (Abbey Road), 26, 88, 92; Spital Square, Poltava, 98, 199; Spitalfields Great, *see* Machzike Hadath; Stamford Hill, 86; Stanislaver Beth HaMedrash (Rebbe Meshullam Ashkenasy's), Lordship Park, 132; Sternberg Centre, 93; Wembley, 86; West Central (Hill Street), 94; West Central (Whitfield Street), 94; West London Reform (Upper Berkeley Street), 11, 92, 130, 203–4; Western (Crawford Street), 88, 114, 198; Wigmore Street, 86; Maidenhead, 131; Manchester, 85, 88; Great Synagogue, 8, 26, 27, 28, 88, 199, 214; Park Place, 92, 130; Spanish and Portuguese, 8, 15, 27, 29, 213, 214; redundant, uses of, 211, 214, *see also* Redundant Synagogues; Mannheim, 27; Newport, Rhode Island, 63; New York, Eldridge Street, 30; Oxford, medieval, 37; Paris, 27; rue Gaston de Caillavet, 24; Penzance, 97; Plymouth, 2, 63, 96, 195, 196; Portsmouth, 85, 196; Pretoria (South Africa), 211; Ramsgate, 31, 98, 197; Ravenna, 204; Regensburg, 34; Stroud, 159; Swansea (Goat Street), 2; Toledo (El Transito), 201; *see also* Toledo, Jewish Museum; Venice, 18; Wallingford (Carmel College), 205; Wolpa, 31; Worms, medieval, 36
Synagogues of Europe, C. H. Krinsky, 12
Syon House, 77

Tallies, 38
Talmud Torah, Great Synagogue, 169
Temple, Jerusalem, 14, 18, 22, 56, 101, 215
'Ten Commandments' tablets, 68, 78, 195
Tercentenary Exhibition Committee, 88
Thomason, Yeoville, 8, 136
Thorpe, David, 119

Tillott and Chamberlain, 169, 175
Tillott, James, 175
Times, The, 198
Toledo, Jewish Museum, 15
Torode, Brian, 159
Touro, Rabbi Isaac, 63
Tovey, D'Blossiers, 61
Tower Hamlets, London Borough of, 190
Town and Country Properties Ltd, 190
Tuscan columns, 59

Union of Orthodox Hebrew Congregations (UOHC), 84, 89–92, 127, 131–5; Central Mikvaot Board, 131
United Synagogue, 5, 6, 15, 84, 87–9, 94, 98, 115, 124, 127, 130, 135, 170, 179, 184, 191, 201, 220; attitude to *Mikveh*, 124–6, 128–30, 132, 136; Mikveh Committee, 128
University of Kent, 85
Unleavened bread, 72

Valentine, Isaac, 164
Veenhuysen, I., 55
Venice, 36; Doge's Palace, 19; Jewish Museum, 15
Victorian Society, 10
Villalpandus the Jesuit, 57
Villareal School for Girls, 169, 175

Wales, 1, 10, 11; Welsh valleys, 2
Walpole, Horace, 64
War graves, 164
Wardens' pew, 195
Warsaw, 115, 162
Wembley, Empire Pool, 218
West, Benjamin, 72
Westlake and Co., 203
Westminster City Council, 10
Westminster Jews' Free School, 175
Weston, John, 74
White, Jerry, 179
William I, 34
William of Orange, 57
Williams, Bill, 8, 33, 87, 214

Williams, Sir Owen, 6, 23, 205, 216–18
Woburn House, 15
Wolf, Lucien, 86
Wolpa, 18, 31
Women's gallery, 55, 56, 59, 63, 66, 75, 76, 194, 210, 214, 215, 218, 220
Wood, Margaret, 35, 41
Working Party on Jewish Archives, 10
Working Party on Jewish Monuments in the UK and Ireland, 10–13, 95
World Monuments Fund, 10
Worms, 18, 36, 46, 48
Wren, Sir Christopher, 3, 35, 56, 59, 196
Wright, Frank Lloyd, 24
Wyatt, James, 72
Wylie, Thomas, 28

Yadin, Yigael, 35, 104
Yakar Educational Foundation, 10
Yamasaki, Minoru, 24
Yehudah de Paiva, his widow, 108
Yeshiva, 45, 46, 50
York, 43, 46
Yorke Rosenberg Mardall, 23